THE CONSUMERIST
MANIFESTO

Ad   sing is no longer on the defensive. It has survived the
sn   y of the 50s, the conspiracy theories of the 60s and the
ser   gy of the 70s – to be embraced and apotheosised by the
triu.   alist 80s.

The   nsumerist Manifesto shows why this was so; it is the first
book   explain the advertising process both from within the
agency and from the perspective of contemporary cultural
the ry. Martin Davidson explains how advertising works, and
ho   as come to set the tone for ever wider aspects of our
m   and personal lives.

Ad ising became the key idiom of Thatcherite Britain,
re,   ; traditional notions of political and cultural value
ob   The book explores the implications of advertising's
c   al and cultural dominance for business, cultural
th   t, anthropology and language. The author concludes
by   g the possibilities – and the limits – of advertising's
ne   l cultural credibility.

Mar   vidson has worked in advertising and publishing, and
is cur   y a producer on *The Late Show* at the BBC.

COMEDIA
Series editor: David Morley

THE CONSUMERIST MANIFESTO

Advertising in postmodern times

Martin P. Davidson

A Comedia book
published by Routledge
London and New York

edia book

lished 1992
by Routledge
11 New Fetter Lane, London EC4P 4EE

Simultaneously published in the USA and Canada
by Routledge
29 West 35th Street, New York, NY 10001

Reprinted 1994

© 1992 Martin P. Davidson

Set in 10/12pt Baskerville by Florencetype Ltd
Printed and bound in Great Britain by
T J Press (Padstow) Ltd, Padstow, Cornwall

British Library Cataloguing in Publication Data
Davidson, Martin P.
The consumerist manifesto: advertising in
postmodern times. – (Comedia)
I. Title   II. Series
659.1

Library of Congress Cataloging in Publication Data
Davidson, Martin P. (Martin Peter)
The consumerist manifesto: advertising in postmodern times /
Martin P. Davidson.
p.   cm. – (Comedia)
1. Advertising.   I. Title.   II. Series.
HF5823.D315 1992
659.1 – dc20

ISBN 0–415–04619–X
0–415–04620–3 (pbk)

CONTENTS

ACKNOWLEDGEMENTS

This book got off the ground thanks to two people, Joanna Hill at J. Walter Thompson, and Helena Reckitt at Routledge. It got finished thanks to my sister, Vanessa, and my parents, whose enthusiasm for the thing survived years of incredulity that anything could take *that* long. And to Kaytea Billson, who let me use the kitchen table. To Colin Troup (sorry, Dr Colin Troup) and (about to become Dr) Nick Paske, all I can say is, sorry it's not about something more important. Next time, eh?

The author and publishers would like to thank Oxford University Press for permission to reproduce extracts from Craig Raine 'A martian sends a postcard home', from *A Martian Sends a Postcard Home*, OUP, 1979, and Bloodaxe for permission to reproduce extracts from 'The castaways or vote for Caliban', from *The Apeman Cometh*.

LIST OF ILLUSTRATIONS AND FIGURES

ILLUSTRATIONS

FIGURES

INTRODUCTION

ADVERTISING BOOKS

There is nothing rare about books on advertising. There are dozens and dozens of them, all written from two sides of an unscalable wall. On the one side there are books like James Webb Young's *How to Become an Advertising Man*, full of hints and professional advice, hectoring, unselfconscious, anecdotal, telling us 'like how it is':

> Advertising, rightly seen, is all about people. And about how to use words and pictures to persuade people to do things, feel things, and believe things. Wonderful, mad, rational and irrational people. . . . About their wants, their hopes, their tastes, their fancies, their secret yearnings, their customs and taboos. Or in academic language, about such things as philosophy, anthropology, sociology, psychology and economics.[1]

This takes its place amid a score and more of professional books, ranging from self-adulatory memoirs (like David Ogilvy's *Confessions of an Advertising Man*[2]) to case-study collections, which describe the individual triumphs of the business – the invention of the Ploughmans Lunch as a way of boosting pub food; the marketing of off-white paints (Lavender White; Apple White, etc.); or children's ready-to-eat breakfast cereals.[3]

And on the other side are the great brow-beaters. The lecturers in communication studies pummelling, dismembering and pouring polysyllabic scorn on this louche opiate of our times. The seminal book in this tradition was that psychological thriller of the 50s, Vance Packard's *The Hidden Persuaders* (*Adver-*

1

tising Age meets *The Manchurian Candidate*), with its clever paranoia catching the manipulators with their hands in the subliminal till.

> Large-scale efforts are being made, often with impressive success, to channel our unthinking habits, our purchasing decision, and our thought processes by the use of insights gleaned from psychiatry and the social sciences. Typically these efforts take place beneath our level of awareness; so that the appeals which move us are often, in a sense, 'hidden'. . . . Professional persuaders have seized upon it in their groping for more effective ways to sell us their wares – whether products, ideas, attitudes, candidates, goals or states of mind.[4]

What I want to draw out from these two quotations (which are very nearly contemporary) is how similar in content they are, but how very different in tone and purpose. One, busily pragmatic, the other laden with litigious insight; both catering for the non-fiction reading thrills of their time. The answer to any question of what role advertising plays in our world is therefore inevitably a mixture of culture and conmanship, of shared rituals and vested interests. Of 'icons' and 'I con's.

There is nothing rare then, about books on advertising. But what I hope is unusual about this one is its structure because no other book that I am aware of does both – that is, looks at how advertising is put together and at what light it sheds on how society works. The relationship between advertising as a commercial tool, and as a window onto our consumer culture is a vital one, but generally ignored or oversimplified by academic and marketer alike. Advertisers tend to assume that the connection is an easy one; for them advertising works by reflecting the world as (a) commercial. The social commentators who analyse advertising get carried away with their portentous conspiracy theories, and endow the industry with menace and cunning, but allow no sense of proportion to what it is the advertisers themselves think they are about.

Furthermore, advertising is interesting on *both* counts, and it amazes me that most studies restrict themselves to only half the story. As a commercial practice, it has a history, a culture and a methodology all its own. And as a key-hole on our world, it offers a fabulous and voyeuristic view on our cultural values, both good and bad. It is morally ambiguous, an expression of an impulse as deep as any in us – the love of trading, hustling, selling and persuading; but at the same time, it is shameless, exploitative and garish. But it is only when armed with a sense of this ambivalence that I think we can get much of a handle on it, by being prepared to explore both aspects of its divided cultural posture. The feckless adman with his 'way we live now' platitudes appals me as much as does social scientists' terminal self-righteousness – just as there are both ads which dazzle me with their problem-solving brilliance, and critical insights that chasten me with their sense of advertising's more crass and questionable assumptions.

The book's basic premise, then, is that advertising is not a static entity, but a series of quite different things, all of which have a bearing on the story I am trying to tell. It is a commercial tool, a social language, a genre of spectator/reader experience, a technique of persuasion; in fact, it is almost a world in its own right, with its own languages, customs and history, and one that sets the tone and pace for large parts of our lives.

THE COMMERCIAL TOOL

But, first and foremost, of course, it is a commercial activity, the *business* of creative selling, of products, services, corporate images and even, these days, of social policies. As a service industry it now dwarfs all but the largest of its clients. Individual ads may occasionally have enough creative panache to be able to stand on their own with all those pub debates, and word-by-word re-enactments of favourite commercials, paying tribute to how endearing and enduring a good ad can be. But for all that the purpose of advertising is to sell:

There are about 40 posters in *Happy Holidays – The Golden Age of Railway Posters*, most of them of great strength and beauty. . . . There are timeless lessons in poster design to be pleasurably re-learned just by leafing through them . . . to start with the most important question to ask about all advertising: what were these posters *for*? They were not for pinning up in classrooms, or for providing deserving illustrators with work, or for collection into a book 60 years

later. They were for selling. They were there to persuade
as many people as possible to spend as much money as
possible as often as possible on buying tickets for trains . . .
in almost every instance, the decision has been taken to sell
not the means, but the end; not the train but the
destination.[5]

Advertising is by nature corporate, has to be credible, and
would like to be creative. The most successful is all three. And
at its base lies the truism that some types of selling are more
effective than others, that, in selling, success is hard to find and
even harder to sustain. Profit needs consistency and growth,
and advertising is one way commercial operations have of trying to secure them. Advertising sells itself on the premise that
its brand of creativity is a sure route to profit. It's not the only
way, of course (Marks and Spencer don't do much, to no obvious detriment) but more and more it looks set to become the
primary one. It used to be the monopoly of two basic types of
market; grocery packaged goods (aimed at women) and glamorous consumer durables (aimed at men); washing powder
and cars. Now everybody is at it, from Friends of the Earth to
the agencies themselves; from deodorants to Sellafield Nuclear
power station; from the Methodist Church to huge privatisations. Budgets have swollen, media inflation soared, agencies
proliferated, services diversified, techniques sharpened – it is
the success story of our times, representing us in a huge number of ways.

So great, then, has this success been that the last people one
would expect to be dumb on the matter are the agencies
themselves. It is no surprise that their never-ending search for
self-respect and commercial accountability has thrown up
some revealing notions of what advertising is and how it
works at a theoretical and social level. Claims abound for
advertising as an art-form, as a friend for the consumer in
alienating times, and even, more darkly, as a new source for
social authority:

'The importance of brands in people's lives will increase',
says Tyrell (the managing director of the Henley Centre
for Forecasting). 'The need for authority is increasing. The

need for personal friends, and the scope for brands to be those authorities is rising.'[6]

It is buzzing with new-found confidence, alive with the very real jargon of our contemporary commercial sacred cows; strategies, planning, image, focus, mission, *relevance*. This is consumerism wearing its corporate sophistication on its sleeve.

A WORLD WELL GLOSSED

And from the consumer's end of the ratings' war advertising is less a precisely fashioned commercial tool than, literally, part of our environment.

Ads are everywhere, and they work to dominate our sensory worlds, to get inside our heads and with mephistophelean sureness of touch, make our decisions for us. They are created out of our 'opinions', so earnestly sought out by the market researchers, and turned into the 'ideas' that only a small elite of self-styled, switched-on maverick creatives are capable of having (the terror of the blank piece of paper, the all night brainstorming session, the inspiration in the bath at the eleventh hour – all part of the mythology of advertising). Advertising structures the relationship we have with our products, what they are to us and what we are to them. Because through such a relationship is established the basis for consumer preference, from which emerges, finally, profit.

So great has the momentum become, so familiar the tricks, that advertising's recasting of social values after its own image has made it a mass-medium culture all of its own. Ask anyone what is unique about Austin Allegros, or Carling Black Label, or Tesco, and you'll not get much of an answer; get them to draw you a picture of 'Mrs Persil' (as opposed to 'Mrs Radion') or 'Mr Guinness' (as opposed to 'Ms Cointreau'), and in front of your eyes will appear a living gallery of what are, in one sense, real people.

But those stereotypes become real, and throng their way into our lives through the creative techniques of advertising production and the insight of its planning and research. Advertising is not only a contemporary language, it is also a complete repertoire of imaginative pyrotechnics. Things are meant to happen to us when we 'turn to page 126' to finish our article in Cosmo and wade through reams of 'page-traffic', or when we lift our eyes perilously over our steering wheels to marvel at the latest sixty-four-sheet Cromwell Road super-site, or every time we sit down to watch the *News at Ten* and absorb yet another sequence set in a quarry, filmed through a fish-eye lens, set to low rumbling music, of an executive saloon hurling its high-tech machismo across our screens. And with an understanding of how these effects work comes the old, old debate about values, honesty and method. How do we get inside the ads we see, and how do we legislate for them?

-OLOGIES AND -ISTICS

But just to concentrate on these visible aspects of contemporary advertising industry is, as I have tried to suggest, to miss half the story. The great joy – and dilemma – facing the study of advertising is limits: ads are loaded with ulterior significance and it is hard to know where to stop. Because their use of language and image, of social values and cultural archetypes, goes far beyond the boundaries of the product itself, it's not long before we get embroiled in issues that seem quite foreign to the mundane business of moving boxes off shelves and cramming corn flakes down unsuspecting throats – into anthropology, sociology, psychology – even politics.

In fact, studying advertising quickly and inevitably means studying how we read language, images and myths – and how it is we build out of them our sense of (socially at least) who we are.

Similarly, to chart the way that products are transformed into brands is to get involved in the question not of what objects are (their function), but what they mean (their social value). That means putting consumerism on the line. And to look at how we consume advertising, in its turn, means pondering the nature of communication, culture, language and desire.

There is no shortage, then, of intellectual *gravitas* with which to sink the project; Marx, Freud and Weber are only whistling distance away, and even Hegel and Aristotle are not beyond the long arm of pretentious relevance. Swarming centre-stage, we have the more up-to-the-minute *cognoscenti* of our cultural mythologies: Barthes, Jean Baudrillard, Mary Douglas – as well as their populist underlings, Peter York, Gilbert Adair, Julie Burchill, Paul Morley, etc. etc. A potent and unmanageable group who have all had powerful things to say not just about advertising, but about the cultural context in which it works, about fashion, fads, styles, cultural groups, mores and the flittish *Zeitgeist* of our day.

Of all the media, perhaps advertising is the best place to quarry for a sense of how we work as a society. Not everyone knows what semiology is, but everyone knows that there is a beer that refreshes the parts that the others don't. With this ocean of half-remembered jingles, campaigns and phrases swilling around in our heads, we are ideally placed to judge how astute these commentators actually are.

That is why this book is structured as it is – tracing a thread from the particular to the general, linking advertising methods, described in their own terms, with the more sophisticated and ambitious pronouncements some advertisers now feel inspired to make on their trade's behalf – through finally to a stringent look at what the limits are both to the case so fulsomely made for advertising, and to the criticism so fashionably levelled against it.

THE DESIGNS ADMEN HAVE ON US: PERSIL

To give as vivid a sense as I can of how I think ads work, and of the terms that form the basis of this book, consider the following examples, from which can be flushed my main themes. I have chosen two campaigns, from 1984 and 1985 respectively, one for washing powder and the other for cars.

The first example is a four-sheet poster that first appeared in bus shelters and outside supermarkets (strategically positioned) in 1984 and which was the first of a series still running today. It is an advertisement which offers us a universe in a grain of sand, a perfect microcosm of that state of the art which it is the advertisers' aspiration to achieve. But on first inspection, it might appear a rather unusual choice as a paragon of creative selling. It doesn't say anything! Does it even tell me what Persil is, assuming I did not know? And even if I did, would I be able to see in this sleeping child something positive about washing powder? So, here is an ad I am making great claims for, and yet one that wilfully refuses to tell the consumer (i) what Persil is, (ii) what is so good about it, or even (iii) that I should buy it. At least, not explicitly. In most blatant terms then, it might seem a bit of a dud.

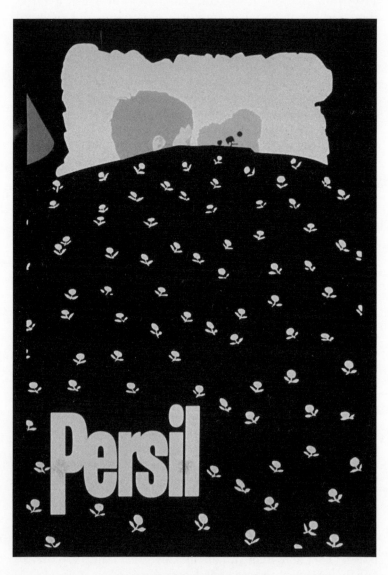

1 Persil advertisement, 1984

But on closer inspection, I think that it brilliantly exemplifies the general principles of all successful advertising. For a start, it serves to remind us that it is impossible to talk about advertising out of context. Ads are necessarily saturated with references to both what we know about the world and what we know about advertising.

Persil, for instance, has always traded on images of domestic fulfilment. Buying Persil has long reassured the mums of Britain that they were not 'short-changing' their families, delivering to them resonant overtones of being hard-working, caring and all-embracing, as well as being seen to be all these things by their charges and peers. But it is a campaign that has, in one form or another, been running for decades, most of that time as market leader. The element of time, so indispensable for the accumulation in the consumer folk memory of this larger-than-lifeness can become a liability. It must stay fresh, while also remaining true to its heritage. Quite a marketing dilemma, because the evolutionary development this requires is much easier to conceptualise than to put into practice.

The Persil poster makes a virtue out of this necessity. The creative selling is expressed 'by design' in the image, and not merely by what is depicted. Alongside traditional associations of a child's bedroom (security, warmth, tranquillity) lie a series of parallels between the design and the branding. The poster's strongest impact is its colour – blues, yellows and browns. The cold blue protects the warm, sunny colours of the sleeping child, and his inscrutably benevolent bear. The loudness of those colours harmonises with the quiet posture of the sleeping child. There is a bold unity of effects which puts us in touch with prime domestic values. The child sleeps with the tranquil depth of nightly renewal. He is being looked at around the corner of his bedroom door in a moment of quiet familial reflection. The link between the idioms of renewal (sleep, a young family and the cleaning powers of the product) are made to appear unstrained, guileless and replete in not needing words (or 'body copy').

The logo in the corner is more than a product name. It has become synonomous with all these unified effects, which mime the powder's claim to work in a bold but unobtrusive way, ministering to family needs without shouting about it. Public and intimate at the same time. The name evokes through the design that combination of renewing strength and unobtrusive action which effaces the *actual* chain of household chores by which they would normally be achieved. Cleanness and freshness are caught up in a domestic metaphor of Persil the brand which oversees a way of life, and which cherishes its consumers' lifestyle without stamping its mark all over it. It is an image of oblique insistence yet full of forbearance. Because we know that it is an ad, we search for the selling point, even when it is hidden in this soft sell.

So successfully has this been achieved here that there is a fourth element to that sequence of images of renewal – the ad itself. For its vivid originality rejuvenates an otherwise tired and jaded campaign. The stylistic panache does to our perception of a long-serving idea exactly what the image does to its subject-matter and what by implication the product does to dirty clothes. A chain of consonant images unfurls in the consumer's mind, replenishing the mythology of domesticity to which she 'brands' her allegiance every time she buys Persil. Apart from the intriguing relationship between *style* and *effacement* (which I will come back to), this appears a *tour de force*.

This must of course, seem rather over-the-top, a case of indulgent special pleading. It is extremely unlikely that the art director and copywriter had intentions anywhere near as specific as is suggested here. But they did undeniably have a general intention to use a new visual idiom to intervene into a perception the consumer had of the brand, and do something both to it, and through it. I merely make a lavish case for their having succeeded. But the point I really want to make is that implicit to it are the following general principles that I will be looking at in much more detail.

At the heart of this ad is an image:

1 an image not just of washing powder, but of Persil (*brand, not product*);
2 an image, furthermore, of domestic balm, not washing *per se* (*lifestyle end-benefit, not product specification*);
3 an image which works by inference (*lateral take-out, not literal in-put*).

And the only reason these make any sense either to the advertiser or to the consumer is because they each implicitly subscribe to the following truths, which are, namely:

1 the consumer buys washing-powder, and there are many different types to choose from (*the market*);
2 ads take a lot of specialist thought and money to think up, produce and place (*advertising is a service industry with specialised and diverse departments*);
3 campaigns go on for years, moving with the times, but consolidating common themes (*brand strategies*).

From the consumer's point of view, the ad only works when the following things are true:

1 'I know that this is an ad, and that ads have selling-points';
2 'I know what Persil is, and what place washing has in my home';
3 'I know it's only natural I should want to do the best for my family, especially as a mum with a house to run' (*and who can afford a washing-machine*).

TEXT, IMAGE, PRODUCT: BMW

The other example that I have chosen really comprises two ads, but both for the same client, BMW, which appeared in the same month (December 1985). One appeared in a British colour supplement while the other graced the pages of the American magazine *Fortune*. The differences are very telling and show what advertising is all about. A BMW car is a paragon example of a product whose prestige is as much performance-led as perception-led. In other words, the advertising has the job of enhancing something that is already functionally at the top of its class with a commensurate image for style and status. The problem is therefore one of degree, while the danger is that it might all get lost in a blur of meaningless superlatives.

> There's no question that virtually every international, top-class car has an impressive aura about it.
> The question is why? And for whom?
> The fact is that people who not only expect the best but also have very personal and individual requirements are seldom happy with the conventional concept of status.
> They want to know what lies behind it all. Naturally, a BMW offers you the level of quality, safety and value

that you've a right to expect from a car of this class. But, above and beyond that, it has a unique sense of style that sets it apart form the rest.

It combines pragmatism with vitality, the confident under-statement with a sporting personality.

And it possesses a sum of progressive and advanced auto-motive technologies that would make it exclusive, even if it weren't a BMW.

But what actually attracts you to a top-class car?

Traditional, conventional technologies?

Hardly.

Because in the end it's innovation that shapes our today and, even more, our tomorrow.

A BMW offers you forward-looking exclusivity.

If this must also inevitably mean that it carries a similar price to yesterday's interpretation of status – then at least it represents a completely different set of values.

BMW cars.

The BMW range of fine automobiles: the ultimate in per-formance, comfort and safety.[7]

The American ad suffers no such reticence, and boldly embarks in pursuit of its concept of 'status', inspired by the need to gain the credibility of rigid definition. Its brazen explicitness soon ties itself up in knots of prosaic question-begging. A jar-ring, crabbed sequence of abstractions produces not an orches-trated pattern of selling points, but mental nullity. Copywriters traditionally answer their own rhetorical questions with the sparse, verb-free syntax that we are so familiar with. Tight, specific. And relevant.

But in this ad, the technique has no bite at all, full of sprawling prolixity. Its tone of throwaway worldliness, of mute truths drawn from truisms, is affected and self-satisfied. With the normal accoutrements of a car of this class comes a 'unique sense of style' which 'sets it apart from the rest' (putting the 'taut' back into tautology). Its 'uniqueness' is based on a marriage of per-formance and perceptual 'added values', together producing a brand personality of 'forward-looking exclusivity', in a merciful climax to half a page of ugly and vacuous attudinising. This, in short, is 'copy' that is the worst of its sort.

But compared to this the other ad is a master stroke of bold, steel-edged complacency, succeeding because enough *has* been said (a stage that represents the zenith of the branding process). The US ad fails in a trick common to a lot of high-quality product advertising, that of self-consciously entertaining the facts of status and their symbolic workings; the Rolex ads have been doing this for years with their deadpan testimonial linkages of watches and various worlds of human achievement. Hard sell explicitness looks terrible, in other words!

The great feat of the second ad is to make the car 'speak for itself' and therefore command the fullest reader contribution. Language has been eclipsed by the (more than sufficient) 'articulacy' of the product, unaided by explanation. How do we *know* that enough has been said, and that this is a state of affairs BMW profits from?

Roland Barthes tells us that all ads may say different things but only in order to make the same universal point – 'Product X is excellent'. The gap between saying and telling could not be narrower than it is here, fused as it is into one minimalist piece of advertising *noblesse oblige*. The language of the ad merges with the 'language' of the product; BMW series 3 cars become a 'text', the car a 'narrative' of status and product excellence.

That is why this ad works so much better than the US one, because it is precisely this sort of story (status, excellence, power) that has to be told by objects and not by words. Language cannot be (unless you are a copywriter paid to do our talking for us) a material reflection of its owner/consumer. BMW cars tell their story of conspicuous consumption, not in explicit words, but in the context and image of advertising. Its success depends on how advertising creates its meaning and not on what that meaning is. The adman has here dispensed with the details of what we are trusted to know already, and has delivered instead the product-story with all the bravura of the *fait accompli*. How BMW has come to mean what it does is not the consumer's problem; *that* it does, is.

The ad's story comprises four elements. '3.25', the BMW logo, the image of the car's near-side rear wing and the strap line, 'Enough said'. Enough is said, because this is a spectacle of a world in which it is *natural* to know this story of car status, in which such knowledge naturally exists just the other side of words, where the prosaic slips its moorings into rhetoric. The

2 BMW advertisement, 1986

effect is one of totemic recognition, the wordless *rapprochement* with excellence (power and speed). Silent upon a peak in London, W1.

But above all it exhibits and exploits what I think has become the great consumer vested interest. Ours is a world in which it is our products that tell our stories for us. Advertising turns our products into adjectives and metamorphosises those adjectives into stories. This allows us to interact with the world in two ways; tangibly, with our tools and products and intangibly, with their connotations. And this extends to the ads themselves, which are also, in their own way, expensive consumer objects, which engage with the world in a two-fold fashion – they tell us stories and they exist to spur economic demand. In doing so, they sell themselves as much as they do their sponsoring clients, just as Renaissance poets celebrated poetry as well as Elizabeth I. The 'Enough said' strapline creates for us not just the sense that BMW cars are excellent, but proclaims its own excellence as an ad. The end-point of all ads is ideally the 'enough said' of their own technical prowess – something woefully absent from the American example.

Skewered through the heart of this brilliant economy of effort, of ellision and compression, is a chain of different cultures all resolved into the 'enough said' of adland slickness; the strapline (and advertising culture); the logo (and corporate culture); the BMW 'brand' (and consumer culture); and the product/car (capitalist culture). All of which resonate together, taking the associations of this ad to the very limits of our social worlds.

READING CULTURE AND COMMERCE, HISTORY AND MYTH

These then are the themes of this book; the methods of commercial branding and their place in our cultural values. But there are other ways of reading these sorts of public image which don't place their origin so specifically in the methods of modern advertising, and they too have their place in this book, particularly in the second half. These ways of reading help us to understand the larger values and patterns of significance at work in society, how vested interest groups communicate their search for profit and power to the rest of us and how implicated what we mean by 'culture' is in this process. Again, a couple of examples will help explain what I mean.

The most obvious example is the one, literally, closest to hand – this book itself. It is both a consumer object and a cultural object, and therefore deeply implicated in its own subject-matter. It has been transformed from a pile of typed pages into a *book*, packaged, priced and promoted to people it was hoped would find it relevant enough to buy. Publishing is not just about printing and distributing bound typescripts, but about the marketing of books, and the added values associated with reading. As a process it involves considerable commercial vetting; who will read the book? How much will they pay for it? Will the demand justify a high print-run, in turn ensuring a lower unit cost (the more you print, the less each copy costs to manufacture), which, in its turn, means the chance of a more competitive price or healthier margins (i.e. more profit)? How have other books on advertising fared?

And once published, there are all manner of other 'strategic' decisions that will have had to have been taken; hardback or paperback? Full-colour cover? Dust-jacket endorsements? Catalogue copy?

As cultural objects, books have unique kudos. They are authoritative, because they disseminate our sense of 'how things are' through the institutions of publishing, 'the academy', reviews, the 'author'. A book inevitably works on a different level of *gravitas* from a mere typescript. Before even a word is read, we have typeset indelibly in our heads assumptions about what a book stands for. We are *primed* for significance. This is precisely how culture at large works, infiltrating our minds with these sorts of expectations, formalised in the discursive institutions which feed off them. In your hands then, lies a powerful example of the web of mutual ties between commerce and culture, the culture of commerce, and the commercial packaging of culture. It is a nexus that also hosts advertising's divided nature. To buy any book and to read it, then, are related acts of profoundly commercial and cultural significance, a double intervention into the world about us. In fact, in no other market are the two so intertwined.

But beyond this sort of self-referential arabesque, there remain other ways in which culture 'recasts' history in its own image, and how we in turn read out of those images values and ideology. An example of what I mean is the statue of Boadicea found outside the Houses of Parliament, described by Michael Wood in his book *In Search of the Dark Ages*: 'Thomas Thornycroft's statue of Boadicea on the Embankment. The "regions Caesar never knew" were of course the British Empire, which Victorians saw as a historic fulfilment of the Roman Empire.'[8]

How do we make sense of this statue? Clearly it is not just an attempted representation of a long-dead but revered national figure. Why *this* woman? Why is she portrayed in this posture? And most importantly, why did those who sponsored the statue build it right outside the Houses of Parliament? Lurking behind this statue, considered in its entirety, is the (crude) sense that it expresses someone's commitment to something for someone else's edification:

> it was under that other great queen, Victoria, that she really became enshrined in popular myth, a myth symbolised by the famous colossal group on the Thames embankment next to Big Ben and the Houses of Parliament. In fact it was Prince Albert himself who sponsored the statue. It was created at the height of the British empire, a period of romantic obsession with myths of free democratic peoples.[9]

The one word not mentioned is 'sculpted', the most obvious way of describing *how* this statue was executed; in its place we have 'enshrined', 'myth', 'famous', 'sponsored', 'created', 'romantic obsession' and 'myths of' – all much bigger activities than the mere application of chisel to stone. Boadicea (or rather, 'Boadicea') is a figure of cultural significance, based on historical fact, but changed out of all recognition into a national(ist) stereotype. More than a historical figure, she triumphantly brings together a cluster of associations, making them potently available for a vast range of uses; she has been 'constructed' into a powerful source of metaphors and similes;

> the virago on the scythed chariot is so ingrained in the popular imagination that cartoonists could portray the British Prime Minister, Margaret Thatcher, as Boadicea immediately after her election victory, knowing that everyone would get the point.[10]

But in another sense it *is* specifically historical.

> To the Victorian, Boadicea was a patriotic queen, a free-
> dom fighter who died defending the liberty of her country
> against a ruthless and alien power . . . the statue encapsu-
> lates a nineteenth-century myth, not first-century reality.[11]

It takes hold of history and recasts it as a slogan (literally, a war-
cry). The statue's function is to embody a story, because it is
through stories that cultures reproduce themselves, even when
at variance with the facts (perhaps especially when at variance
with the facts):

> However, the evidence that archaeologists are finding
> suggests a far more strange and complex story than Prince
> Albert could have imagined. It is the story of the bitterest
> war ever fought in Britain; a desperate colonial war be-
> tween a backward, underdeveloped 'Third World' people
> and a remorseless, highly organised and 'civilised' imperial
> power; a war of terrible atrocities. . . . None of these things
> was new to the Roman conquerors; what made this war
> exceptional was that they had to fight it against a woman.[12]

It is inaccurate, but more important than the question of what
she did look like, or of what her chariots really were made of –
and even more important than whether the Third World resistance analogy is right (it is not, in fact could not be less so) – is
that other sense of who is using it for whom. Here, the myth
embodies the historical vision held by the Victorians – and tells
us so much more about them than it does about first-century
England. Michael Wood is content to use the discrepancy between myth and actuality as an arresting introduction to a book
on that actuality. But the matter needs taking a step further, to
give a more critical look at the mechanisms of myth and its
relationship to history.

What the 'statue' (and Wood's description of it) overlooks (or
represses, or distorts – whereby hangs another great tale) is that
nineteenth-century England, with the largest Empire the world
has ever known, can hardly in any real sincerity have based this
idealised view of itself on an image of colonial underdogs win-
ning a moral victory over their imperialist overlords! 'Boadicea'
is made to symbolise both resistance against the Romans, *and* the

notion that the British Empire was a historical consummation of the Roman one! This isn't just folklore, or even archaeological ignorance, but rampant political hypocrisy – but by their myths shall ye know them.

Social power groups express themselves through these sorts of myth, and in doing so conceal as well as celebrate certain (not necessarily consistent) views of themselves. As a 'message' then, a statue like this is important not just for what it 'says' but for what it does – and to understand this fully, we have to take all sorts of ulterior questions into account; who is behind it; for what purpose and for whom was it intended; and, in the context in which it operates, is it credible, hypocritical, harmless or in some way deeply suspicious? Myths, culture and power, then, are all embedded to greater or lesser degrees in our images, through which they work on us, and in which contradictions like this get resolved into stirring and single-minded affirmations of principle and value. But most of our critical instincts are reserved for words only, and this is a mistake.

Any image or piece of public rhetoric not only contains elements that can be seen to harbour ulterior values, but makes sense only in a larger context itself ideologically structured. The statue described, does, for instance, beg two questions; why did nineteenth-century England use a woman to symbolise military and national ideals? And why were those ideals so inevitably imperialistic ones?

Advertising also harbours ulterior purposes and 'agendas'. The external context of advertising is capitalism, which exerts its own brand of pressure on the shape of our lives; while on the *inside* of ads can be found categories of image (class, gender and race, for example) that may well prove 'problematic'. For instance, there is the rape sequence of the hand dryer rising tumescently and blowing a girl's skirt up above her flustered thighs in the Vivas body-spray ad. There is the use of a very thick-lipped black porter in the Canon commercial, with his even thicker-lipped pronunciation of the word 'brains'. And the minority of conspicuous yuppy 'haves' flaunting their insatiable wants with lobotomised brashness in the Halifax cash-card commercial.

There is also an area that lies between these two, namely the ad's immediate media-environment. Clashes here can also produce telling misreadings. At the end of a harrowing and poig-

19

nant 1986 documentary on the scarred survivors of the Falklands War, a NatWest ad for business loans appeared, stirring up its desired emotional response with buttons being pressed and a formation of armed Harriers taking off, hovering and bowing to cheering actors dressed up as grateful small businessmen. Painful and bathetic, when juxtaposed against the preceding programme.

THE LANGUAGE OF ADVERTISING AS COMMUNICATION

But the best way to understand the relationship between questions of advertising method and questions of cultural value is to look at it as a type of communication, as a sort of language.

We do, most of us, already know this, and perform this sort of 'reading' quite effortlessly. In late 1984, a poster appeared all over South London. It proclaimed 'The truth about the Belgrano' and bore the logo of the Socialist Workers' Party. Anyone seeing it would instantly and effortlessly have made the connection – 'truth–controversial issue–extremist political party'. The word 'truth' would be translated into *their* truth – propaganda, in short. But of course, this is merely an extreme example of what we should do every time that we read anything. It is merely a particularly 'opaque' example, at one end of the linguistic spectrum on which all utterances lie. Would a report of the incident in *The Times* have been any 'truer', or do questions about the relationship between the editorial policies of the newspaper, its proprietor and his well-known political feeling have to be similarly taken into account? Of course they do.

The move from opaque ('biased') to transparent ('unbiased') statements provides a useful background to this look at advertising. At one end, as it were, lies the most blatantly exploitative type of language, that of propaganda. In its ugliest forms it expresses brutal and offensive untruths (Nazi anti-semitism, for example, or some of the more inflammatory leaders in the *Sun*). Further in, comes personal assertion, the expression of beliefs or principles that are obviously not the whole answer, but which are put forward for debate ('As a Christian/Marxist/Tory, I believe . . .').

Next comes subjective declarations (I am happy/She is haunted by ghostly intimations of mortality). Not much room for dissent here, but nor can they really be shared between those expressing them and those hearing them. Getting more transparent is what one might call the received idea, a general view held by most of us (Politeness is a good thing/Throwing stones at cats is not/Children need to know road safety). More transparent still comes the scientific fact, which, when it has emerged from years of trial and error, assumes the status of unmovable reality (Water boils at 100 degrees/Men have different hormones from women). But perhaps most mysteriously transparent of all is the poetic truth, the most disinterested example of language, expressing insights of beauty and moment, on a plane beyond the indignities of negotiation or rebuttal (Thou still unravished bride of quietness and slow time).

Oddly, though, somewhere along this spectrum the critical machinery tends to get turned off. To go around questioning the motives of those who teach us that water is made of hydrogen and oxygen, or that beauty is truth and truth beauty seems not just redundant but a little perverse. Which is perhaps why the history of advertising is the history of its practioners moving their trade along this spectrum, pulling it away from its appallingly mendacious beginnings, by-passing negotiable assertions (ads are not up for debate!), through subjective declaration (all those crass testimonials) and aspiring to the condition of (at the very least) the received idea (9 out of 10 . . ./As they say in Germany . . .), daring even to become scientific fact (Vorsprung durch Technik) and ultimately, beyond censure, beyond contradiction, in the magic of language alchemised by global saturation (it's the real thing).

How then do we get to grips with it all, haul it back down the linguistic ladder, look at its myths, methods and contexts? In fact there already exist many individual responses to advertising at each of these levels. Advertising is seen as propaganda by, say, the feminists who vandalise what they see as offensive or exploitative ads; as political assertion it is often enough to highlight that a programme or an event has an interested sponsor for its credibility to be put into question. The use of subjective declarations has been the butt of many jokes, not least the spoof of the cringe-making use of 'people in the street' by the *Guardian* which ended in Rowan Atkinson's parodic voice-over telling us that six out-of-work actors could hardly be wrong. The last two examples of linguistic usage are harder to parody, of course, but spurious white coats and vapid verbal effects have long been the stuff of easy satire.

So, what *do* the methods of advertising look like when put against more rigorous and testing ways of reading? Do the theories behind them wash? And if so, just how white?

1

OBJECTS OF DESIRE
How advertising works

Start work in an ad agency and the first thing they teach you is the difference between a *product* and a *brand*. This is because it is advertising's job to change one into the other. Brands are products with something extra. All brands are products, but not all products are brands, and the difference is advertising. That extra is called *added value*. Not just mints, but the elegance and sophistication of *After Eights*; not just a hamburger bar, but the fun and optimism of *McDonalds*; not just a cube of artificial flavourings, but the quintessence of *Oxo* family life. These added values were the object of 50s conspiracy theory, 60s satire and 70s semiology. In the 80s they became all-powerful, an esperanto of desire and relevance, the language of the tribe.

The job of advertising is to ensure we actually notice a particular product within the welter of competing publicity and the ever-increasing mass of new products and services, all laying claim to those values with which we colour and shape our apprehension of the world. This is why 'identity' is so important.

It is basically what distinguishes branded from unbranded products. . . . If we have a clear picture of a brand in our minds to refer to, we can handle it easily in decision making, even at lower levels of consciousness. The identity of a brand endures over time. . . . We can bring to bear a kind of distillation of previous experience and information on the choice problem. We have the reassurance that comes with familiarity and with the sense of pattern and order this gives us.[1]

What all successful companies enjoy, then, is brand status.

Either as company names, or as manufacturers of brands, they have a relationship with the consumer:

> IBM, Kodak, Levi Strauss, Bacardi Rums, and the TSB are all examples where consumers choose their products not only because they are excellent products, which they are, but because they value the brand values which are often intangible. These companies have developed their corporate reputations through their brands, and both brand and corporate reputation reinforce each other.[2]

The commercial dividends of successful branding are enormous. Chris Wilkins, creative director of Davis Wilkins, applauded the success enjoyed by Persil:

> I have seen research for a rival brand which showed that Persil users would go on using Persil even if they were convinced that another product worked better. Why? Because they liked it more. Persil advertising has done this, nothing else. It's done it by being about people, not powder, about love, not washing.[3]

This is the ultimate aim of brand advertising, and it now forms the basis for advertising methodology, especially in this country. Advertisers, unwilling to tempt fate, affect false modesty about this, playing down the role that advertising plays in this compared to things like distribution and packaging. But they don't really mean it. Without advertising, branding would be impossible to achieve. This is the one thing that has given the business corporate credibility, and in an increasingly corporate decade, cultural respectability as well. It is not something the ad business is going to give up easily. Additionally, they argue that consumer good will is now more important than ever as products become more and more technically interchangeable, because markets quickly develop into battlegrounds of added rather than functional values:

> the sheer amount of competitive pressure in most markets continues to increase. What this means for the consumer is rapidly increasing choice. In fields where there is little real functional difference between the products on offer, the choice the consumer makes will be made largely on intangibles . . . on factors such as trust, service, reputation and

24

design. McDonalds have revolutionised the whole concept of take-away food in the UK. Of course they offer excellent products but the marketing strategy is clearly based on the concept of McDonalds as a brand, you buy the atmosphere, the optimism, the fun of McDonalds. 'There's a difference at McDonalds.'[4]

Brands are products that are famous. We have crystallised in our minds why they should be valued. We *know* them, even those we never buy, nor ever intend to buy. The experience of the last eighty years has been that famous products sell better than just ordinary ones. Many of the most famous existed long before explicit theories of branding, indeed, they actually supplied the experience on which, by a process of post-rationalisation, the theory evolved:

> What makes companies succeed is not products but brands. Arthur Guinness and Company prosper not because they brew stout, but because people want to drink Guinness. Lever Brothers are successful not because they make soaps and detergents, but because housewives like and buy Persil, Omo, Radiant, Surf and Lux . . . this is not just about playing with words. The difference between products and brands is fundamental. A product is something that is made, in a factory; a brand is something that is bought, by a customer. A product can be copied by a competitor; a brand is unique.[5]

The logic of branding reflects two things at once; first, how it is we apprehend objects; and secondly, the nature of consumer competition. A brand is a product defined by how we perceive it, a circular and probably inescapable process of cognition. After all, no account of an object is complete without considering the light in which it is seen.

Advertising exploits the idea that there is nothing we can't be made to feel good about, no limit to how good we can feel, and nothing we will not then do for those things that have us committed to them. Thirty years of mass-media, pop culture and pleasure hype have proved this again and again. The 80s has been *the* decade for actively, aggressively and acquisitively consuming things that you feel good about, and for realising that no one will ever consume what doesn't turn them on.

Added values are precisely what something looks like when made accountable to what makes you feel good.

ADDED VALUES

Brand advertising therefore sees its mission less as one of telling people facts about products than of adding value to them, helping them become, and endure, as brands. It's the advertiser's business to understand the complexities of consumer behaviour rather than to judge them. Branding is about matching a product with what is thought the most plausible and appealing relevance for its intended consumer. It offers a broader canvas on which to define products than that of function alone. The advertiser mediates between how we live our lives and how manufacturers set about manufacturing their products. That is because it is in the brand that consumerism and culture meet.

Understanding added values also means understanding how and why we consume. The mechanisms of pleasure, fantasy, our different selves, our social worlds and social status all colour and texture the larger sense that turns products into brands. Objects work in a number of different ways, all of which can form the basis for branding; they can be metaphors, analogies, totems, fetishes, metonyms, substitutes, catalysts, icons. . . . The one thing a brand can never be is just a box on the shelf.

Products are projected as microcosms not of their intended use, but of the world in which their use makes sense. As the ad adage goes, no one wants a quarter-inch drill – they want quarter-inch holes. In fact it should have gone even further, no one wants quarter-inch holes, they want something to hang their shelves up by, and they don't want shelves just to dump books and glass mermaids on, but to make their houses beautiful, to make them homes, to enhance the pleasure of being a home-owner, and the self-esteem of DIY well done.

The people who make drills pay ad agencies to tell them this, and to produce advertising that transforms power-tools into symbols for, and agents of, just such chains of means and ends. Things always stand for other values; and the advertiser is merely making sure the translation is vivid and to the product's advantage: 'the focus is on the additional advantage to be gained when advertising integrates tangible product characteristics with something else – *symbols, meanings, images, feelings* – to create a brand that is loved and wanted.[6]

What you create out of 'symbols, meanings, images, feelings' is a *theme* for a product, brought to life in an enduring, endearing way, and quickly becoming that product's most important equity.

Branding is also where the morality of advertising is at its most ambiguous. The real objection to advertising is not really that it tells lies, but that it sells objects pretentiously, in terms of values that are more important than it is, and to the detriment of those values. As Raymond Williams put it:

> We have a cultural pattern in which the objects are not enough, but must be validated in fantasy by association with social and personal meanings which in a different cultural pattern might be more directly available. . . . A washing-machine would be a useful machine to wash clothes rather than indication that we are forward-looking, or an object of envy to our neighbours.[7]

The fact that 'objects are not enough' is advertising's keystone, which, in a funny way makes it sound a profoundly non-materialist business. Take away Williams' tone of hostile condescension, and this process of grafting on social meanings to physical needs, would be one most advertisers would recognise and ringingly endorse.

> We cannot easily make progress in inventing new brands until we get some idea of the real motives that lie behind the system. Why for instance, do people want to wash clothes? What is the balance between their different desires, a crisp feel, avoidance of disease, prestige, expression of personality, and so on? What is the real significance of the whiteness? It is fairly clear that the simple answer – to get them clean – only scratches the surface.[8]

Between these two positions, which mark either extreme of those pro- and anti- advertising, there is plenty of scope to argue about the actual *status* of these non-functional values. Where do they come from? Are they inherent to a product, or added in an act of social conditioning? Have they got too exaggerated?

> We're marketing slippers as quintessential symbol of the nuclear family rather than slippers . . . first class stamps as

the turbo-chargers of vital business communications . . .
weed-killer as the humane outlet for territorial
aggression.[9]

A whimsical lament, but one that makes you wonder whether it
is actually possible ever not to see things as X-rather-than-Y,
after all, once you call something a 'weed', the word 'killer'
suddenly seems altogether legitimate.

Advertising works, therefore, by linking the product to an
image of consumer satisfaction that may not be a literal or
functional extension of it. The agency first discovers as much as
it can about how the product is used. It then decides what aspect
of that use should be the basis for the campaign. This is the
process of branding, the sexy smugness of driving a certain type
of car; the things that can happen after a certain type of bath;
the balm and bliss of keeping the family towels as soft as shag-
pile carpets; the culinary kudos of a certain mineral water. If
successful, that image will become a brand property forming the
basis for future theme advertising, a theme that the product will
slowly reabsorb back into itself as its unique brand value. A
brand is a product that has a personality that we relate to as
though in dialogue with it. The illusion of dialogue is sustained
by symbols, meanings, images and feelings.

They have all manner of sources. The most common follow
the marketing truism that *production* should mirror *consumption*.
People are not just interested in films at the cinema, they're
interested in entertainment. Hollywood survived the arrival of
television by understanding the difference, and by catering for
our love of entertainment by moving into television, music and
videos. Advertising bridges this gap; it communicates not just an
airline, but global mobility; not an anti-perspirant, but a release
from the anxieties of body odour. This is the source of that
particular breed of corporate speak that IBM uses when they sell
us 'not computers but solutions'.

Holidays, for example, became a mass-market product in the
seventies. The advertising this spawned was correspondingly
unsophisticated; sun, sea and sex – and all at bargain-basement
prices. Increasing competition and growing affluence have driven the concept of the holiday, like many others, more and more
upmarket, with the result that the ad campaigns are seeking out
more and more subtly compelling pictures of what we get from

travel. Operators are, in other words, working harder to come up with added values that reflect exactly what it is we look for in travel.

Flick through the pages of any colour supplement and the holiday ads offer a diverse range of promises; not just locations and fun, explicitly *not* here, *not* now, but broadened horizons; recharged batteries; a new you; living history; spiritual tranquillity; exoticism; personal challenges. All these are added values that work more indirectly than cost or convenience, and in turn reflect consumer discrimination that goes beyond the basic questions. This has the effect of translating the world into the terms of the tour operator's vocabulary of added values. The globe becomes a commodity, a myriad of advertising opportunities whose *loci classici* include the beach, the sea, the old city, the natives, their customs, 'authenticity' (i.e. unspoiledness); historical periods that are gentler and more courteous compared to modernity, palaces, mountains, food, weather, customs, souvenirs, doing-what-you like.

The question of whether or not to add value, and if so, which, is basic to all areas of production. In academic publishing for instance, it will always make sense to invest in expensive paper, elegant typography and lavish dust-jackets when you publish a prestigious historical monograph, not because it will make more people buy it, but because it will make the small, finite number of people who will buy it pay more for it, and appreciate it more. This is particularly so in periods of relative economic prosperity, where the demand for values in addition to the product becomes particularly inflated. It is not enough for a lager to deliver taste and texture, it also has to have a heritage, because if it doesn't then there are plenty of others that do. Added values are therefore relative to the time and place which produce them. There are moments when it is appropriate to project the notion of economy and value; later this may seem drab and need to be replaced with more glamorous or cosmopolitan values. These in turn may start to seem meretricious in a period concerned with notions of social responsibility, and so on.

It is advertising's job to communicate, if not actually create, the right added values. Sometimes if a campaign style is particularly successful it will itself become the added value. But advertising is only part of the process. Things like distribution, packaging, product reliability and after-sales service also help determine the larger picture. The whole marketing process, of which advertising is simply the loudest part, is designed to create a sense of displacement; the product seen in terms of something else – with the link being either one of synecdoche, symbol, analogy, corollary or syllogism. The hand-lotion *becomes* the good life; or it stands for the good life; or if you use this hand-lotion then you will be happy; or all beautiful women use hand-lotion, all beautiful women enjoy the good life, therefore to have the good life you have to use hand-lotion.

POSITIONING

The first stage of the branding process is therefore to find out as much as possible about the product in general, in all its guises. Coffee for instance, is a plethora of different drinks. It is, of course, a cash crop grown in certain parts of the world, which is then processed before being consumed in a variety of different ways. But that makes coffee more than just a versatile drink. It means that it becomes a different drink on each different occasion on which it is consumed. And each of those ways can form the basis for a different type of brand added value, each offers, in short, a different niche.

Coffee drunk before breakfast is about waking up with a bang, it's about energy, caffeine as a stimulant, about starting the day. Coffee drunk during the day is about a break from routine, about taking stock before recommencing your work. And drunk last thing at night, it forms the crowning moment for dinner parties, meals in restaurants and as pretext for seductions. Each moment involves a completely different mood, and each has been commandeered by a different coffee brand.

Maxwell House shifted the direction of its advertising with its GET THE MAX campaign. This featured a loud and rousing jingle around fast cut sequences of people (well, fashion photographers and the like) using coffee as their crack of dawn 'upper' before embarking on their demanding and glamorous days work. Kenco coffee's latest campaigns feature its product being drunk at moments of quiet respite during the day. And, most infamously of all, two of the late 80s most quintessential campaigns, for Red Mountain and Nescafé Gold Blend, with the latter giving us coffee as the elixir of late night bonding (the

Gold Blend couple finally kissing after three years of attudinising about their coffee). Red Mountain added another twist, ripping off an old *Not the Nine O'Clock News* sketch and having people make espresso machine noises while secretly merely using instant granules, acknowledging that coffee is not just *when* it is drunk, but *how* it is prepared.

The same logic applies to every product category. A product exists in a number of different contexts – but for convenience's sake, they tend to break down into two, crude, sorts; either where the product comes from, (its raw materials, its loving producers) or where the product gets consumed (in the home, the pub, the motorway fast lane). Guinness beer has over the last ten years tried them all. First Guinness sacked their agency J. Walter Thompson after decades of brilliant jokes (because apparently, although we all loved the ads, we were neverthless deserting stout for lager in our thousands). Their next campaign, from Ogilvy and Mather, was a paean to the barley and malt that Guinness is made from, scythed in mythic slow motion in order to be apotheosised into beer. But that didn't work, so Guinness took a 180-degree turn, sacked the agency, and got Allen Brady and Marsh to conjure up a convincing vision of the gregarious pubs that Guinness gets drunk in. This they did with two years of their 'Guinnless' campaign, playing on a rather limp piece of word-play. But the thing only came right when ABM too got sacked, and the account went back to Ogilvy and Mather, who then gave us that dark angel of consumer posturing, Rutger Hauer, mouthing both Guinness and cod metaphysics – 'It's easier being a dolphin.'

McDonalds, the hamburger chain, does something similar. Their advertising has always stressed the fun of visiting their restaurants, rather than what goes into their burgers (unlike Burger King's emphasis on the size of its whoppers). But inside the restaurants you find endless leaflets designed to placate our worries about healthy eating. Here, the stress is on demonstrating the basic foodstuffs that produce McDonalds fare, and once again we are served up displacement. Instead of focusing on burgers, fries and milk shakes the leaflets tell us about beef, potatoes and milk, the great triumvirate of food mythology. In between the 'fun' of the restaurant and the almost Biblical wholesomeness of such fundamental foodstuffs is the whole sociology of junk diets, neatly eschewed.

Researching all the nuances of how we use our products and how we envisage them is only half the battle. The other thing that the above examples make clear is that products do not exist in vacuums. There are always competitors, and they too, will have set out to understand, in general, the dynamics of their market. The trouble is, the agency's job is to sell a brand, and not a market; Ariel, not washing powder in general. (Unless the whole market is new, in which case you do; I can only be persuaded to buy an Amstrad fax/telephone/answering machine once I get used to the idea that a personal fax is a useful or desirable thing to have. Only then will I start caring *which* I should have. And, of course, at that point, I will turn to Amstrad rather than someone else only if Amstrad is already a credible brand in my mind, extrapolated from other markets and product precedents.)

Most markets are dominated by a company that enjoys a premier position; either the biggest selling, or the oldest, or somehow the company most associated in the public mind with a particular product or service. All the others have to take this as their starting point, and accommodate their advertising plans to this fact. Avis's 'We try harder' is the classic example of advertising making a virtue out of a position, in their case second to Hertz.

In the mid-80s, for instance, the Japanese company Toshiba, who make hifi and televisions, was a minor contender in a market dominated by companies like Sony, Hitachi, Philips and Ferguson. The agency Gold Greenlees Trott were given the job of remedying this. The campaign they come up with was premised on the observation that Toshiba's problem, in terms of its positioning, was one of awareness, not image. No one knew that, like Hitachi or Sony, Toshiba was a high-quality Japanese electronics manufacturer; given the very high esteem enjoyed by Japanese electronics manufacturers, this lack of awareness was costing them dear. Had Toshiba been a Norwegian electronics manufacturer, or a division of a company more famous for making photocopiers and cameras, its *position* would have been very different. The advertising job, too, would have been very different; it would have had to sell the idea that the Scandinavians make good electronics; or that these hifi and televisions were worth buying because their photocopiers were.

Instead, all the campaign had to do was raise spontaneous

awareness of Toshiba – the pre-eminence of its Japanese background would be enough. The campaign consequently selected two specific product stories (that Toshiba FST televisions offered higher quality viewing and that the hifi speakers did not distort sound at high volume). Again, the point here is one of positioning.

Toshiba FST television is not necessarily better than that of Sony or Hitachi – but neither of the others were bothering to tell people how much better FST was compared to traditional television technology. Toshiba could, and by doing so, would make this technological superiority seem their monopoly. The blue-print man, and his parody of Alexei Sayle's 'Hallo John, got a new motor' ('Say hello Tosh to a new Toshiba'), realised all this in a series of campaigns between 1986 and 1988.

This is the perennial problem besetting the advertiser – the creation of perceived *desirable* difference. The philosophy of the 50s and 60s was to burrow away into the minutiae of a product's technical specifications until something unique to it was found; this USP (unique selling proposition) would then form the basis for the advertising. Occasionally, of course, this is the most motivating reason to buy, but when products become more and more interchangeable, the hunt for the USP becomes more and more sterile, trivial and marginal.

Perceived difference allows you to concentrate on intangibles that you can control. If you make three types of whisky you advertise one as the one you pay a hefty premium for in order to give as a lavish present, to consummate very formal social gatherings, or to brandish as token of discrimination; the other as the one you bring out when a mate comes round, lubricating long evenings of convivial male bonding; and the third as the one you swill around your mouth when it's the peaty taste of Scotland you want to savour. These added values make the difference and are as integral to the advertising as they then become to the product. In other words, a brand is powerfully different to other brands because its advertising is different. The advertising is the USP.

Perceived difference is in effect more commercially important than providing an anthropologically expansive view of what makes people do what they do. The advertiser not only has to understand the whys and wherefores of consumer behaviour, but reconcile them to what everyone else is already doing in the market place.

STRATEGY

Products survive in the market-place only by dint of carefully cultivated brand properties. They can take any form:

> It may be a distinctive style of advertising (like Coke). It may be a visual device (like the Esso Tiger), or an aspirational attitude (like Martini). Whatever form it takes, that distinctiveness . . . forms an incalculable competitive advantage. . . . That advantage, even when it is product, as opposed to perception, based, owes much of its success to the contribution of advertising in establishing, reinforcing and guiding the necessary evolution of the 'property'.[10]

Brand properties give the advertiser a strong point of purchase in the shifting nature of the market and the consumer. The brand property, in effect, gives a business the chance to be *strategic*. Strategy is one of those privileged words that so often gets triumphantly polarised against its 'weaker' opposite. In the business-presentation language of overhead projector 'bullet points' (a violently dialectical one that maximises knowledge for easy and dramatic assimilation), strategy is the opposite of (mere) tactics; just as marketing is the opposite of (mere) selling. Strategy is detailed, assertive long-term thinking; a style of dealing with future imponderables that takes advertising out of the realm of one-off strokes of arbitrary magic, and places it within a whole spectrum of business disciplines that, we are repeatedly told, account for American and Japanese commercial success – disciplines at the heart of business as an academic subject. It has been key to the credibility that advertising has seized for itself over the last ten or so years.

Strategic thinking, with its overtones of war and simulation games, also gives people in the advertising business a sense of their own indispensibility, and has reapportioned to 'creativity' the role of finishing touch, rather than alchemic magic wand. Brand properties are what the advertiser moulds and bends to the large variety of tasks advertising can address. It is with brand properties that the advertiser will try to give longevity to a product, sustaining it through social changes and consumer fickleness (the product's 'natural' tendency to rise and fall in cycles).

It is at the level of personality that the product can be adapted in the consumer's imagination with changing times and mores and remain a relevant and desirable option. Food, for example, took on a vastly different light in the austere 50s, the hedonistic 60s, the recession-hit 70s, and the health-conscious 80s.

But a brand property successfully groomed and massaged can carry an unchanging product through all these shifts while striking relevant consumer chords at every turn. It is why bran products, so long positioned as medical products because of their laxative properties and the British obsession with their bowels, became central to the healthy-eating lifestyle equation that followed Audrey Eyton's pioneering 'F-Plan' diets of the early 80s. It can also offer security against occasional disasters. Perrier bounced back after its 1989 contamination scare because it was so firmly established as a brand.

Branding can take all manner of forms, but usually works as a type of rationalisation, a scenario built around the question 'why do people buy this sort of product?' Bird's Eye makes frozen food, which has a number of product advantages – the process makes types of food available that used to be just seasonal; it keeps them fresh almost indefinitely. But in terms of consumer satisfaction, the key thing is that they are easy to prepare. It is therefore a boon to people without much time; such people are short of time because they are rushed, busy, motivated, caught up in the busy business of getting ahead. Convenience food can therefore be styled as a type of *freedom* for aspirational rushers, and dramatised as part of a fast and pressurised lifestyle. This chain of syllogistic, yuppie logic 'for the way you live your life today', with its exultant 'bird of freedom' links convenience into a brand-view fully conversant with the needs of the modern active achiever. The links are tenuous, but the final package has compelling momentum, even if finally convenience, for all its glamorous alacrity, probably still means slumming it in front of the telly.

Strategy is different from tactics as marketing is different from selling. It is cool, long-term and reasoned; it is about control. Strategic thinking in advertising recognises that there is all the world of difference between *why do people use shampoo* and *why do they buy Timotei*. The advertising process straddles that gulf. It starts off with the rawest and most basic of marketing data with which to answer the first question, and through a process of transformative refinements, ends up with an advertisement that makes the answer to the latter question as compelling as possible.

This is, of course, a harder thing to do when it is not clear what the product is. We all know that all the different brands of petrol come over from Rotterdam in the same tanker, so there is no point pretending otherwise. All that the Shells and Essos of this world can do, therefore, is brand their retail outlets, the petrol stations. For years they did this with promotional gifts; then with unleaded petrol, and now, with tarted-up forecourts and garage shops. The latest venture has been Texaco's 'piggy-back' campaign (i.e. a brand using an issue of social concern to draw attention to its corporate benevolence). On this occasion it was a case of offering free reflector stickers for children to help protect them from winter traffic.

Airlines and financial services too, have to bolster up information about numbers of destinations and interest rates with other factors; the charm of the cabin crew or cashiers; or perhaps the (sanitised) characteristics of the airline's home country.

THE PLANNER

The custodian of this style of advertising rationale is the account planner. The rise of the planning department has its origins in the efforts of two agencies, Boase Massimmi Pollitt and J. Walter Thompson, but is now more or less universal. The planner works alongside the account handler, takes a longer-term, more expansive overview of the advertising task and acts as the mediator between the creative hair-trigger of the copywriter/art director, and the sluggish myopia of the over-burdened brand manager. Planners commission and analyse market research; they distil out of their qualitative surveys, tracking studies and rivers of statistical data, manageable pictures of what makes the consumer tick.

The planner's work culminates in what is called 'the creative brief'. This is the document that serves as the springboard for the ad campaign itself, the structure for the ad – or, if you like, the sub-text for which the ad becomes the allegory. It directs the creative team by giving them a sense of *who* the ad is aimed at; it tells them how to *position* the brand; it gives them the ad's *main proposition*, as well as the evidence on which to base it; it stipulates what the consumer is supposed to *take away* from the ad; and discusses *tone of voice*, creative guidelines and suggestions for emphasis.

The process starts, however, with another type of strategic prop – the planning cycle. Apart from focusing the mind, such a schema offers the powerful illusion of control, which if you work hard enough at, will probably be realised. It asks the advertiser to consider: where are we now? Where do we want to be? How will we get there? How will we know that we've got there?

What follows are a sequence of operations and questions that have become the staple of sound business practice. Advertising strategy has, above all, to be realistic. This means deciding the nature of the advertising task, which is in fact a varied one. Advertising gets used to do a number of quite different things. It gets used to increase the volume sold; to increase market share; to increase penetration; to increase the rate the product is used; to reduce price sensitivity or to address specific problems of consumer perception; to arrest declining volume or share, or to maintain distribution. Some campaigns are addressed to the retail trade and designed to make them take a product seriously. Others, to the staff and employees of a company to increase their morale.

Getting someone to buy more of a product; to buy a product more often; to buy it more often than he or she buys competing brands; to get the consumer to pay more for the product; or to use it more quickly; to get the product stocked in more shops, more prominently; to get consumers to reappraise the brand – all these will require different emphases in the final advertising.

Similarly, clients can take different attitudes towards their advertising campaigns. A brand can be invested in by expensive, long-term advertising for which the dividends are not immediately obvious. Or else the manufacturer can act defensively, merely maintaining a presence. And not uncommon is for a manufacturer merely to 'milk' a product, to let it slump but squeeze its last drops of profitability before consigning it to oblivion. Advertising strategies also take their place within a wider commercial frame, one that embraces pricing policy, packaging, dealings with the relevant retail trade, promotions as well as corporate PR in the largest sense, shoring up the share price and keeping hostile raiders at bay.

Clear and precise strategies also help the advertiser out of another dilemma, being able to prove the effectiveness of campaigns to clients. The clearer the evidence of success the more likely the client will stay with the agency – and the greater the esteem that advertising will enjoy in the corporate jungle. The evidence supplied by qualitative research, day-after recall, quantitative communication checks, continuous tracking studies, can all be easily related to the results sought – if the strategy is clear and geared to these criteria.

BRAND CAMPAIGN

The idea is that all of these elements should seamlessly come together to produce a perfectly fledged advertising campaign. Take Castlemaine XXXX for example, a new lager introduced to Britain for the first time in 1984. Allied Breweries, who were producing Castlemaine in this country, saw as their opportunity the developing taste for non-continental lagers. Initial research quickly pin-pointed that Australia was more than just an ethnic point of origin, but capable of providing strong 'heritage'. Australia – or rather Australians – had all the right credentials (vast consumers of lager; tough macho image; more like us than people in Europe). But there already existed a well-liked Australian lager – Fosters, branded by Paul Hogan. But Castlemaine outsold it in Australia, and had the virtue of strong gold and red livery and a name to get your teeth into.

How to exploit the fact that it sold better than Fosters? The fact alone is not particularly motivating, but Australians preferring this lager could be projected not as consumer discrimination, but as Australian lager drinking writ large. The launch poster translated this into the now notorious line 'Australians wouldn't give a XXXX for any other lager'. Backed up by tv commercials with their rugged hard-drinking outback Australians and their deadpan humour, preferring lager to everything, their mates, even their marriages, the brand became an enormous success, not only successfully differentiating itself against the other Australian brand, but against the continental and British ones too.

The Australian male's cheery callousness and single-minded pursuit of his lager was powerful enough to made the commercials credible and seductive for those it was aimed at. The strategy involved the transformation of three propositions. The first was the mundane fact that Castlemaine outsold other lagers in Australia. *Therefore* it was the lager Australians preferred. *Therefore* Australians don't give a Castlemaine XXXX for any other lager.

These three sentences adumbrate how advertising strategy moves from fact, to analysis, to creative treatment. This is how most campaigns work; a genesis of propositions that slowly cross the various idioms of the marketing process, culminating in that burst of creative derring-do which propels the product into our lives.

BRANDING THE 80s

But branding has come to dominate more than just the marketing of fast-moving packaged goods. The whole discipline of understanding consumer demand and matching it as assertively as possible has underwritten 80s enterprise culture. The last fifteen years have seen all manner of services and institutions having to negotiate with marketing for the first time, forcing them to move from undifferentiated anonymity into the spotlight of consumer exigency. The clearing banks, for example, existed fifteen years ago happily absorbed in their daily business of furnishing financial services in a sealed-off market place.

Deregulation and competition have entailed, since those dull days of rude bank managers and intimidating sepulchral spaces, an orgy of advertising and consumer solicitation. The banks now range not just through the colour spectrum, but the social – and the interactive. Lloyds recognised that its clientele was well heeled and based in the South and West, and consequently took the high road, 'A thoroughbred among banks', and by using Rumpole actor Leo McKern steered its august image, with the help of the totemic black horse, with whimsy-softened snobbery, into alignment with the others. NatWest became the action bank, Midland, the listening bank, Barclays the bank you're better off talking to and TSB the cheery place that always said yes.

The classic example has been that set by the big supermarket chains, Sainsbury, Tesco and Asda. They used to promote themselves on how cheap their various lines of merchandise were. But following the lead set by Sainsbury's and a campaign written by David Abbott, retail advertising entered a new phase, as the supermarket staked out its niche as central site of the civilised 80s good life. Tesco and to a lesser extent Asda have followed suit, branding themselves as the repositories of value, quality and a wholesome regard for the consumer with whom they have daily, direct contact.

The added values of the major brands stood out not primarily against each other but against the unadorned, cheaper lines manufactured by the retailers themselves. The most reductive of them all was the 'yellow' range offered by FineFare; products that shared the same yellow packaging, with generic names stencilled on the front, Baked Beans, Pet Food, Corn Flakes, not just non-brands, but anti-brands, attracting custom by being conspicuously cheaper, because free of the trappings of design and packaging and in so doing, shedding accusatory light on their trumped-up product neighbours (a device used to satiric effect in Alex Cox's *Repo Man*).

But since the early 80s, the retail chains have been investing in their own brands, moving away from a platform of cheapness and competing in terms of quality, to the consternation of the manufacturers. The point of branding the retail outlet was twofold; first, of course, it offered a necessary competitive edge over the other chains; but secondly and more importantly, served to enhance the chain's own label within the store, which would then in turn reflect back on the retailer in a process of circular reinforcement.

In this country, five or six grocery chains now account for around half the country's goods and packaged-goods sales. Around a third of grocery sales at the big supermarket chains are 'own-brand'. Marks and Spencer sells only own-brand goods, under the label St Michael, the most powerful brand name in Britain according to market research. Sainsbury enjoys 55 per cent of own-label sales, after being the first to make the move from cheaper than the manufacturers to better than the usual manufacturers; the others have copied. The most impressive shifts have occurred in areas where there were no existing market leaders and have been slower in areas dominated by established brands, like Kellogg, Pedigree Chum or Cadbury. However, even here, it is true to say that a company like Kellogg is regularly far more exercised by competition from own label than from other competitors, like Weetabix or Farmhouse Bran.

Retailers, of course, have advantages over the manufacturers; they control the selling environment; they can gauge the success of a line within hours rather than months; they do not have to invest in expensive plant when they make innovations and they have customers captive once through the doors.

It is no coincidence that advertising, so associated with bringing the 80s into being, at least as a decade of radical enterprise culture, should have marked that culture's every step. Brand values embody as closely and as luminously as possible why it is people consume; or rather, why it is they spend money doing the things they do. As protective barriers, old snobberies and protective immunities start collapsing, just about everything existing in the public sector has had to take a deep breath and put itself onto the supermarket shelf.

Museums, for example, have suffered, or enjoyed, depending on your point of view, complete recasting, away from sacrosanct repositories of historically valuable artefacts, into the up-market end of the leisure industry. Museums and galleries, deprived of government subsidy and relying on admission charges, or at least having to demonstrate a willingness to market themselves, have had to reassess what it is people think they are doing when they visit a cultural site. Their interpretation of those shifts have been illuminating. The Victoria and Albert in London, for example, famously tried to challenge the museum's forbidding middle-class image with its campaign through Saatchis. The strapline 'An ace caff with quite a nice museum attached' underwrote a series of *objets d'art*, juxtaposed with disarmingly paradoxical low-brow things – souvenir mugs, cream cakes – things you could buy, which rarefied consumption and made edification seem earthbound, even pleasantly visceral.

The thought behind trying to brand the museum was that in fact, people had started to seek out quality places to meet and drink and that just as expensive wine bars and cafes were cashing in by a veneer of artiness – so too museums were becoming acceptable places to hang out in. Instead of wrinkling up a pedagogical nose, the museum welcomed the shift, and with an artless piece of vernacular seemed to be trying to demystify itself, repositioning the museum away from the high-brow, and into the up-market. A move absolutely in tune with the times, right down to one particularly telling poster, running an old Indian fertility statue alongside a salad – 'Yeah, and the salad

41

dressing ain't bad either'; the mock salaciousness of the 'yeah', the 'rough trade' *frisson* of 'ain't bad either' made this exhibit at least seem little more than a louche piece of designer exotica.

Other industries and products have also had to discover what it is that turns us on about them, and the answer is not always that clear. Computers for example, have never really tried to broach the question of what, precisely, are the benefits on offer, and have instead opted for the darker proposition, that not only are they inevitable, but that anyone without one faces certain extinction. The IBM slogan, 'I think therefore IBM', goes the furthest; without one you don't even exist.

Nor, in fact, can you escape added values. In a market, the very presence of competing products changes the perception of your products, even if the new perception is just of your product being the one you never see advertised (which can occasionally be a positive). All products have a *position vis-à-vis* other products thrust on them. Advertising works by choosing and then creating the added values that make the most of the position occupied by the brand. Audi cars, regularly eclipsed by Mercedes and BMW, was the first German car to make its ethnicity, its Germanness, its main selling point and in so doing, gave the 80s a renewed sense of Germanness as added value, as cool sexual engineering, and assimilated that idiom exclusively to itself.

MAPPING BRANDS

But advertising only works because of the huge scope that exists for variation in added values and the way they are expressed. The distance between an ad that is conventional in its structure and execution and one that experiments with the conventions is enormous. Similarly, advertising strategies can vary a great deal, from being either completely mechanistic, to being richly humanistic.

If you take these two sets of criteria as axes to a grid, as *Campaign* magazine did first in August 1985, then it is possible to plot onto it where different campaigns lie, a kind of freeze-frame of the late 80s British consumer market-place (which I have updated and added to in figure 1).

The grid also shows up other patterns, in the way advertising has developed since the mid-50s. The bottom left-hand corner – conventional and mechanistic – is really where television

1 Branding map

commercials began, inherited from America and the progeny of the marketing giant Procter and Gamble, notorious for its creative inflexibility. This is the stuff we learnt to love to hate, patronising, brain-shatteringly dull and sexist, but effective when shown often and persistently enough. Moving up and to the right, we begin to enounter first of all products and services not confined to the kitchen/supermarket nexus; lagers, transport, cars, retail chains. The diagram sheds light not only on individual product categories (compare the relative positions of Daz and Persil for example) but on the history of advertising philosophy. We can also trace the history of that philosophy on it.

Crudely speaking, the 60s began bottom left (figure 2); the 70s began to learn the value of humanistic idioms; people we warmed to and identified with, a softer tone of voice, products as answers to more interesting problems. The decade's advertising consequently shifted its centre of gravity up towards the top left, conventional, but softer sell. The 80s and yuppie acquisitiveness promoted the trend for minimalist cool; lots of 'less is more', uncompromising efficiency and oneupmanship. The advent of the new 'hot' shops like Gold Greenlees Trott and Yellowhammer was signalled by a fashionable shift towards the bottom right; very creative, but very chilled. The late 80s, harbinger of the green 90s, have reinvested in creativity *and* human values, taking the dominant idiom of advertising back up to the top right-hand corner – the destination advertising has always given itself the credit for finding inevitable.

This pattern is reinforced when you consider individual campaigns. British Rail for example, since its early 80s days with Jimmy Savile and the 'Age of the train's' cheery populism, gave way to the mid-80s corporate accountability of 'We're getting there' and the 'real' footage of helpful BR guards lifting cases, directing lost children and actually saying sorry, in a way that quickly became a hostage to fortune. The latest British Rail campaign, from Saatchis, sacrifices anything remotely 'actual' for a drowsy fantasy called 'Relax', hauntingly shot by Tony Kaye and featuring softly photographed tableaux of interestingly-cast people reading, stretching out their tired feet, playing chess and simply whiling away their troubles to Leon Redbone's soporifically gruff music, set off against blue and sepia washes.

What British Rail realised was that credibility is not the same

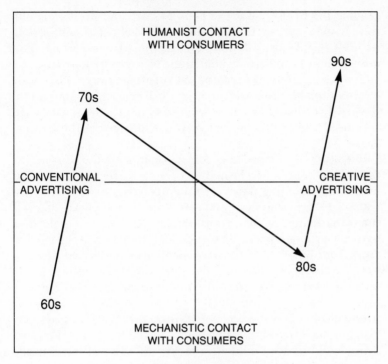

2 Branding map

thing as literalism. If you have good enough production values, based on a sound(ish) piece of research (people travelling on trains experience tremendous relief on finding and occupying their seats), then there is absolutely nothing to lose by *not* apologising for a service frequently criticised. There is scarcely a campaign style or a product category that has not moved up towards that top right-hand corner, in pursuit of ever more convincing part-of-everyday-larger-than-lifeness.

The way added values work depends also on the type of product. There is clearly a difference betweeen products that we use in a routine way and those, usually more indulgent, ones that are explicitly about 'how you feel about yourself', like make-up or clothes. But behind nearly every household name product and brand lies a successful manipulation of added values and positioning.

Dulux, the paint division of ICI, did some research that pin-pointed the British paradox about DIY; we love decorating our own homes, *but* are fantastically reticent about colour in our paints – people just will not paint anything beyond white! The answer was to produce a whole range of paints that are basically white, but suggestive of colour, the 'off-white' range, white with a hint of apple, rose, marigold, or whatever. Animations and a doctored version of Procul Harum's 'Whiter shade of pale' have produced one of the most successful campaigns of the last few years.

Rowntrees developed the Yorkie bar in response to research that found out how cheated people were feeling about the inexorable 'thinning down' of Cadbury's bars of chocolate. By usurping the position of bulkiness, Yorkie bars quickly entered the vernacular of popular confectionary. Audi cars were the first to turn Germanness into a positive, and thereby split the market away from BMW and Mercedes, neither of whom had thought to be explicit about their origins. Bottled water is another recent boom market. Perrier were the first to exploit the market and they did this by branding their water as a sophisticated alternative to alcohol and to sweet soft drinks. But as soon as concern over the quality of tap water began to reinforce this desire to drink bought water, bottled water positioned itself as in every sense the opposite of 'the mains'. Bottled water began to be retailed as though it were cheese, deriving from utterly specific regional sources, and boasting about those sources.

And on and on and on . . .

Added values work either as heritage, as a type of social bonding, as production values, as technical USP or as positioning statement. Which route you choose depends as much on what the competition is doing as it does on what your research tells you.

THE NEW EUROPEANS

The culture of brand advertising is now even higher up the agenda of Western and Japanese companies, as they struggle to adapt to the sweeping changes in Eastern Europe and what was the Soviet Union. Alongside the considerable short-term political and economic turmoil, however, these companies are beginning to ask longer-term questions about what sort of consumers the 'new Europeans' are likely to become, as this part of the world matures from being a low-cost manufacturing zone into a fully-fledged consumer culture.

> On September 29 1990, six hours of British TV programmes complete with TV commercials dubbed into Russian were shown on the main national Russian television channel. The estimated audience was 150–200 million. TV commercials were selected by J. Walter Thompson (London) including well-known ads for household products, toiletries and confectionery. . . . Subsequently, a sample of Muscovites who had seen the programme were interviewed on their attitudes to it, the commercials and their everyday lives.[11]

The complexities surrounding this exercise were enormous. Russian citizens were being monitored in the response to a form that more than any other symbolised the confusions and turmoil of their current situation, between the erosion of a state centrally-planned economy, and the rise of a market economy. As consumers, the Russians are doubly removed from their Western counterparts, accustomed to scarcity, lack of choice and a restriction to subsistence essentials, so while suspicious of materialism abroad, they are also resentful of conditions at home. And as consumers of contemporary Western advertising, they are similarly doubly removed. Russian advertising, such as it was, was heavily factual, utilitarian and unadorned. It did not imply choice. Ordinary Russians had not shared the thirty years of growing technical sophistication that have taken Western commercials from being crudely televised press ads to highly eliptical, art-directed vignettes. But, on the other hand, they had been subjected to political propaganda, also a cause for suspicion and hostility. In other words, advertising was a loaded concept, redolent of everything that the West possessed that the old USSR didn't, and yet also, perhaps, an indication of things to come, and something that was always going to produce grave ambivalence.

> The political and economic turmoil, the hardship, deprivation, loss of faith, the uncertainty, make viewers highly sensitive to the morality of advertising. Not to whether or not advertising should exist; it is known (and can be enjoyed) as part of the machinery of capitalism. But rather,

the moral values assumed in the construction of commercials.[12]

What emerged from the research was, if not a complete vindication of contemporary British commercials (the Russians did not shed their reservations about displays of conspicuous consumption, or irritation at seeing ads as Western propaganda gloating over Russian 'failure'), then vindication for the idea that brand-based advertising is liked (the Russians did enjoy ads that communicated with wit, and with story) and that ads that are liked ('defined by consumers as meaningful, pertinent, believable and worthwhile – and not merely entertaining') are more effective than those that aren't.

> Emotionally, commercials are capable of evoking two opposing kinds of responses. On the one hand, they give a quality catharsis – an escape from daily hardship into fantasy and dreams. On the other hand they are capable of causing deep resentment and a wish to distance oneself because the imagery is too painful and absurdly removed from current reality.[13]

So, far from being either naively gullible about advertising, or naively cynical about it, Russians proved themselves especially demanding. They wanted advertising to be liked, but to be trustworthy; to use symbolism and social relationships, but to avoid excess for the sake of it. They appreciated, after having been denied it, not only the brands themselves, but the langauge in which the commercials were couched. But they were also much less forgiving of anything that smacked of propaganda or of distortion. In a world where increasingly it is the advertising that separates one product from another, and where it is therefore crucial that ads produce a 'gratitude response', the balance of power seems to be swinging back to the consumer.

THE CONSUMER

Advertising is based on a problem; just how seriously are we supposed to take it? Unlike other professions, advertising has to win popular approval for what it does, it has to be liked even by those who don't pay for it. But by and large, immense enthusiasm for the industry's nuts and bolts is restricted to those who work in it, for only they think it is less important than it deserves to be. The rest of us are generally less impressed. We are hostile to the pretensions of the advertiser in two ways. On the one hand, things that *are* as important as they deserve to be, like art, culture, politics and personal identity are regarded as being sophisticated, complex and subtle. Advertising is of course by comparison cheap and crude. And on the other hand, advertising is full of things that we refuse to acknowledge as remotely important, like toothpaste, soap powder, or underarm deodorant. Advertising marries the bathos of trivial objects with the pretentiousness of our dearest social values.

Luckily for the advertising industry though, this disdain is only really skin-deep, a mantra we are good at reciting but can't possibly really believe. (Witness endless arguments about the technical merits of cars those arguing will never be able to afford, or the hankering by ex-pats for Marmite and corn flakes.)

The thing is that while we can look pretty nonplussed by hucksterism and image-mongering, our priorities are not always especially rarefied. We have endless views, actually, about how our washing smells, about bottled versus tap-water, about the difference between instant and ground coffee, about labels, product performance and personal gratification. We are very good at not making them sound very front-of-mind, and certainly they vanish when put on the spot about life's really important questions. But, nevertheless, we spend a quantity of our waking lives forming, nurturing and exercising these value-judgements. We also have pronounced views on the value of successful marketing. We are, most of us, consumers and employees. As consumers we care passionately about not being disappointed or ripped off. And as employees it is a matter of great concern that the people who employ us know how to sell.

Advertising's greatest 'crime' is its over-motivation, the way that the whole of life's intangible good things get identified with just one tiny product. But to take exception to this lack of proportion is to miss the point about how ads are consumed. It is to me as someone who needs to wash his hair that shampoo ads make their appeal. Clean hair and the promise of being transformed into a sexually irresistible person are only confused in the part of me that does spend forty to fifty seconds a fortnight in Sainsburys pondering the well-stocked shelves. And for the

49

fifty seconds I do let the shampoo-buying decision accrue other values; yes, I want my hair to look better for being washed, to make its contribution in so far as clean hair can, to the well-being created, as far as it is, by a well-groomed appearance. The ad therefore reduces the significance of life to the level of shampoo; but this hubris only makes sense in the context of the commercial's link with that buying moment that this hubris has any point. Outside that nexus, the ad's exaggerated conceit is meaningless. It is a case of relevance and appropriateness. And along with washing my hair, I could read this rationale into any of the plethora of products that clutter up my particular everyday existence, as many dozens do.

From each one of these isolated moments whole industries stand or fall. The makers of Nescafé are not embarrassed by their preoccupation with coffee, just as lawyers are not by theirs with jurisprudence. They know that coffee ultimately is not as important as thinking about the Middle East, or sex or the next election. And while it is occasionally gratifying to keep on reminding them of this, deep down we would not excuse a lousy cup of coffee because the manufacturer was actually thinking harder about more 'important' things.

Perversely, it is because we dislike being sold to so much that advertising has had to adapt to a climate hostile to selling and contemptuous of selling tools. This has forced advertisers down a different route, away from hard sell and straight product endorsement, and into an idiom far better researched and much more sympathetic.

But the times have been good for 80s advertisers; in one sense our attitudes to selling have hardened and got more bullish, but more crucially, our attitudes to buying, to shopping and to consuming have burgeoned spectacularly. We love buying, but hate selling; and UK advertising has been extremely well placed to exploit the discrepancy. Advertisers seized on the contradiction that while selling may be an alien thing to our culture, the brands we are familiar with are its very core.

This has meant that British advertisers have had to think longer and harder about how their campaigns should work. It has meant learning to live with the fact that consumer patterns do exist and that they are often far more complex than we would like to admit. There is far greater scope than the advertising sceptic would concede for researching even the most mundane parts of everyday life, not just how we use our products, but how we read and relate to advertising. There is no such thing as *just* drinking coffee, of going to the pub or washing clothes. Each act is rich with latent or ulterior elements, which the marketing strategist needs to know.

A corollary of this is that just as there is nothing self-evident about even the smallest social or personal act, nor is there anything remotely self-evident about who people are. Consequently market researchers have spent the last few years ever refining their pictures of different contemporary consumer-types.

TARGET AUDIENCES

This used to be done by the relatively crude criterion of the occupational standing of the head of household, the notorious As, Bs, C1s, C2s, Ds and Es. This was, until recently, the most sophisticated version of the type of marketing thrown up after the war:

> A major shift developed in the 1950s. Advertising gener-
> ally was firmly product-oriented until well after World War
> II, but in the 1950s it began to be directed increasingly
> towards people's desires, needs and wants. Marketing as a
> separate discipline had its greatest growth period in the
> competitive boom economies of the fifties and sixties.[14]

And ever since, the process of understanding the consumer, individually and collectively, has grown more and more refined. Of course, it had to, not only as people became more sophisti-cated consumers with more experience of how to spend money, but as society as a whole became more and more fragmented. The forefather, so to speak, of this approach to research is Ernest Dichter:

> In his book *Strategy of Desire*, Dichter explains that his aim is
> 'to go back to the reality of human behaviour'. There are,
> he wrote, two phases in motivational research. 'One is to
> find out why people behave as they do. The second is to
> prescribe a remedy and to determine how people might be
> motivated.' Dichter's next piece of research [was] an inves-
> tigation into car-buying habits . . . in which he came up

with the equation that convertibles are mistresses, sedan cars are wives.[15]

But since those heady days when saying these things had the power to shock, research has focused its attention even more closely (and usually a lot less sensationally) on what attitudes consumers have towards their products. After all brand personalities can only work if they reflect something subjective about the people they are aimed at.

> Beware all housewives target audiences – select your prime prospect . . . by painting a picture of him/her using all the attitudinal data that you can find. . . . Persil Automatic was not launched merely at 'front loading washing machine users', its success has demonstrated a precise and continuing understanding of the attitudes and lifestyles of the women who own such a machine.[16]

It is to lifestyle then that the advertiser turns his or her scrutiny. This is especially the case when developing a brand from scratch or in assessing how to relaunch a brand already in production. The logic flows back from the picture of the consumer attitudes being addressed to the product, and not the other way round. Similarly, in the research carried out to fathom our responses to brand personalities, it is from the whole that one starts, and not the parts:

> Even harder is the research which maps out the positions of the brands as a whole, as coherent totalities – which is what people buy. The most successful methods seem to be the simplest; that is asking respondents to imagine brands as people. . . . People are much more used to talking about people than things. [17]

The target audience is here partially defined by whatever aspect of its *consumerism-as-lifestyle* is strategically reckoned the most relevant to the branding link. Lifestyle categories are incorporated into the advertising by breaking them down into telling scenarios, stereotypical miniatures and by using high production values in the final execution. They have even been used as the basis for a complete map of consumer Britain, right down to the size of postal codes. This system is called ACORN (a classification of residential neighbourhoods), and boasts that it:

is possible to specify, for example, which group is most likely to drink a specific brand of coffee, or to most want to borrow money. What it does, said one marketing man, is to quantify much more scientifically something burglars have always known – that where people live is related to what they buy and own.[18]

Or there is VALS, (values and lifestyles), a typology that splits us up into different categories depending on how on top of our circumstances we claim to feel. A mid-80s report commissioned by ad agency McCann Erickson dissected the nature of women in the UK, with this as its rationale: 'We wanted to look at the whole woman and in particular, look at how attitudes, personalities and behaviour are clustered together in a complex modern society.'[19] Not surprisingly, the results vindicated the fact that society can be characterised in terms of broad stereotypical sweeps, suitable for further advertising accentuation:

> Is there anything real in the idea of the feminist? Of the Sloane? Or the Yuppie? And if there is, are there sufficient of them to make a real marketing target – or an aspirational target for advertising? . . . And the results confirm that British society is indeed highly complex and highly segmented – by personality, by beliefs and attitudes, by lifestyle and finally by demographics, all in interaction; no one kind of measurement today is enough to comprehend large groups of people.[20]

The resultant eight clusters broke down into four opposing pairs: 'two motivated by ideals or opinions, two identified by their self-awareness and independence of spirit, two driven by a questioning or seeking personality, and two marked principally by their lack of involvement.'[21] The purpose of research like this is to analyse each 'product field and look for positioning gaps', by making lifestyle and brand properties mutually significant.

More recently, the teenage market has also been subjected to this sort of breakdown. Here, two business psychologists from University College London have outlined twelve different categories: trendies (they want admiration); egoists (who want pleasure); cowboys (who want easy money); puritans (who want to feel virtuous); innovators (who want to make their mark); rebels (who want to make the world in their image); groupies (who want acceptance); drifters (who don't know what they want); dropouts (who want no commitment); traditionalists (who want stability and reassurance); utopians (who want the world to be a better place) and cynics, (who want to have something to complain about).

Anyone addressing this age-group would have to take these differences into account. If you were producing an anti-drugs campaign, then targeting it at drifters and dropouts would require a different creative treatment from targeting it at trendies or egoists. Similarly, an anti-acne cream is more likely to appeal to groupies or traditionalists than to rebels or cynics.

Both these are examples of 'psychographics'. As one of the authors of the teenager survey explains: 'Psychographics tries to classify consumers and segment markets in terms of psychological dimensions. Instead of looking at demographic attributes like age, sex and social class, it looks at the motivations, needs and attitudes of consumers.'[22] Although much of this may sound rather fanciful, the idea that people relate to the world and can be distinguished in terms of conformity (following mainstream trends; opting for minority trends or rejecting all trends altogether), control (do I control my destiny or not?) and pleasure (those who seek it versus those who disapprove of it), does make a lot of sense.

But not all consumer research is geared around providing quirky pigeonholes. The other driving force behind recent market research has been the growing recognition that people bring much more to their consumer decisions than simply questions of function or utility:

> Our starting point is that consumers endow the products and brand they buy and use with meanings, over and above their sheer functional value. It is the creative task to communicate these meanings in ways which motivate and reinforce. Research is to unlock them and make them available to the creative process. We are then making a clear distinction between the *ostensive* or face value aspects of brands, and their *latent* or symbolic values.[23]

Researching the right hand column in figure 3 requires new, and subtler research techniques for its findings, because brand advertising is about mobilising the symbolic rather than the literal, which by its very nature, lies furthest from explicit speech:

Researching the 'practical' is relatively straightforward . . . the 'symbolic', however, requires a different sort of probing, and much more time. . . . Unconscious wishes and identifications are often present which can be revealed by projective interviewing or careful observation of inconsistencies, slips, blaming etc. And there are the purely intuitive, playful properties of brands and advertising which take us into the inner world of consumer imagination. It is this inner world which can provide the sources of creative, and in our view, effective advertising.[24]

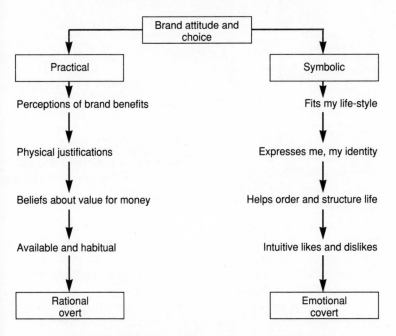

3 Practical and symbolic attitudes to buying brands

What is interesting about this style of psychological mind-plumbing is the way those in advertising who use it then make it sound less like 'hidden persuader' dabblings in the subliminal mind, and more akin to less tendentious schools of thought, like anthropology:

This 'model' is similar in some respects to the motivational ideas of the 1950s and early 1960s in pointing to unconscious, repressed and embarrassing motivations. The main difference . . . is the recognition of the *intuitive* level which is largely responsible for the inarticulate and active involvement consumers have with advertising. Whether it's strictly above or below the so-called unconscious level is arguable. In many respects we prefer to see it as a different order, at a tangent, reaching into cultural myths and archetypes.[25]

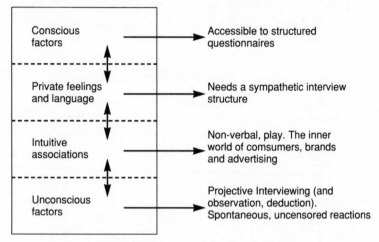

4 Researching symbolic attitudes to advertising; basic model

Myths and archetypes allow the researcher discontented with the merely literal the chance to read enormous significance into the advertising process, without incurring the bad karma of anything that sounds like mind-tampering.

But for most people in advertising, the resort to these more and more nuanced depictions of the target consumer has a much more basic motivation – they provide you with something to say when all else has failed. One of the most effective ways of talking your way out of the advertiser's most common dilemma (there's nothing to say about the product), is to transform the product into a living mirror of its consumer.

THE *OBSERVER* OBSERVED

For example, in a document produced as the intellectual hub to a 'pitch' for the *Observer*'s advertising account, which I worked on during my brief months in an ad agency, the planner gave the following background to his suggested advertising strategy:

> In terms of the overall form and content of *The Observer*, there is so little perceived difference between it and *The Sunday Times* that claiming a difference in those functional terms is more likely to arouse disbelief rather than interest. We believe that the greatest opportunity lies in promoting the overall personality of *The Observer* (which the contents substantiate), *through a reflection of the people who read it*. This enables us to flatter those who already read *The Observer* and encourage those who do not to join the same elite and attractive club.[26]

Having nothing to say *vis-à-vis* the market leader rival happily coincides with what the advertiser likes doing best anyway, producing a brand personality out of an emotional theme. Only here the emotional theme relies on mirroring the consumer. But what is important is that it is only *in* the advertising that the search for personality means 'there is nothing to say'. In its own right the *Observer* has much to say about itself, but once translated into the idiom of aspirational advertising it becomes merely a mirror of the reader, engaging him or her in an empty dialogue.

The *Observer* has a market position that makes impossible any advertising based on literal properties, because in the popular perception, these are the generic monopoly of the *Sunday Times* (as ascertained in prior research, which showed that for most people the two papers were indistinguishable, except for a vague sense of the *Observer* being thinner and perhaps a little less establishment-orientated). It is this relative position which dictates the strategy, and not the other way round.

In this case the strategy outlines its target as follows:

> The primary target-group is ABC1, 18–35 year olds . . . they are all going through the process of putting down roots and acquiring all those things which make life more comfortable, whether it's fitted kitchens, fast cars, or a partner to share it all with.[27]

More specifically to the *Observer*, the advertising is to be based less on what quality papers offer than on the lifestyle mind-set of the people attracted to them. The following definition trips off the planner's tongue, saved from irony only by being so awk-wardly formulaic (shouldn't it have been 'protective of their individualit*ies*', for example, or is this a fitting solecism?):

> They regard themselves as intelligent, aware people, and are protective of their own individuality. Although con-scious of trends in lifestyle, brands and even opinions, and aware that they might appear to be part of an identifiable social group, they would react against the suggestion that popular trends would affect their individual choice or their views. They are less afraid of being out of step than of being neatly categorised and overall they project self-confidence in their own abilities and beliefs.[28]

So the 'having-nothing-else-to-say' obliqueness of picturing the typical *Observer* reader, has to go one stage further, because the lifestyle values identified are those that explicitly resist easy formulation (in a rather paradoxical manner). The further twist involved another familiar piece of advertising legerdemain – not as many people buy product X as buy product Z; therefore those that do must be more discerning, less reducible to fashion, less predictable. So instead of just picturing yuppies, the resulting adverts had to portray wacky yuppies in a droll and intriguing way. The copywriters came up with a burlesque figure of the *faux-savant* cockney paper-boy, which attempted to make self-parody a way of seeming out of the ordinary, anarchic even, while actually pandering to the comfort of the familiar. The campaign didn't last very long, however, for all the intellectual calibre of its strategic positioning, and the *Observer* has since meandered indecisively from campaign to campaign.

THE MEDIA

The reasoning here seems more valid than with other sorts of products because our choice of newspaper does involve the question of social attitudes, our papers being, after all, source as well as reflection of those things from which we construct our view of the world. It isn't so far from the mark to make a distinction between the reader of the *Guardian*, and that of the *Sun*, in a way you cannot between people who buy Mars Bars, and those who buy Flakes, and a distinction that isn't just an index of the difference in price. There is already a mutually confirming rapport between product and consumer, a circularity if you like that is very close to the one branding in general aspires to achieve on behalf of products less attitudinally defined.

This fact influences more than just the vagaries of the newspaper market; it reflects on the other crucial aspect of advertising, the media department, the people who buy space and time in the media in which to place the ads. There is not all that much difference between the thinking that went into characterising the typical reader of the *Observer* in advertising terms, and that which goes into considering which newspapers are suitable for what sorts of advertising.

Choosing media is a crucial part of the advertising process for two reasons. First, it is advertising's front line, where it 'does' its work, the actual point of contact between the consumer and the advertiser. Any idea of how advertising works or how a particular campaign is intended to work has to take that point of contact into central consideration.

The second aspect of the strategic importance of media buying has already been alluded to. The 'media' are not anonymous vehicles; in a strange way they represent the consumer writ large because they are themselves 'consumed' in an archeypal way. To advertise in the *Daily Telegraph*, say, requires at the very least an implicit understanding of (i) how the printed word in a daily paper determines the 'stimulus' and (ii) how 'what sort of reader' the *Telegraph* attracts will vitally determine the nature of the response. A newspaper is read very differently from a magazine, which is in turn consumed very differently from the way a radio broadcast or a televised movie is consumed.

That is why the media have to advertise themselves to the advertisers in exactly the same way the advertisers will then use the media to promote their clients' products, namely, by a combination of product attribute and thematic personality. The end-benefit for the advertiser is the size and type of audience; and the media will sell themselves not in terms of content, but in terms of what type of readership or audience it can deliver, how committed that readership/audience is, what sort of disposable income they have and what sort of reading/viewing they do.

The *Guardian* stops being a left-of-centre, slightly non-conformist quality think-tank, and instead becomes where you can buy up hordes of tomorrow's captains of industry; and the

Guardian reader stops being a vaguely anti-consumerist conscience-plagued egg-head, and becomes someone *x* per cent more likely than the national average to drive a certain type of car, to have money invested in a building society and to take 1.7 holidays abroad per year. And alongside the established media, new media opportunities are being spawned and are hustling for attention – taxi doors, school jotters, blimps, even the speaking clock.

This is at the root of the debate about the future of broadcasting. The concept of 'what the advertiser wants' is a contentious one. Traditonal Reithians suspect that it amounts to little more than lumpen, craven numbers, deliverd by programmes that match, while the advertisers themselves preach a line more in tune with the late 80s, castigating ITV for not delivering quality minorities who, after all, pay attention to what they watch, and are therefore going to be more attentive to the ads.

The quality/quantity debate has become more and more important, as the old criteria of the media departments are, we keep being told, being shed in favour of more sophisticated, and more culture-friendly yardsticks. Agencies are probably not being insincere when they confess to having junked the old fixation with 'cost per thousand' (the marginal cost of reaching a certain number of the right consumer/viewers). Today, the cost of media has become prohibitive, and this penalises lack of discrimination. But more importantly, the agencies are becoming more and more confident in their ability to assimilate the philosophy of branding and marketing into the purchase of space and time, even if, no sooner than managing to understand the complexities of niche marketing, they are now going to have to deal with the challenge posed by direct mail and the assertion of some of its champions, that we are now able to market to the individual, and not just the social group.[29]

2

DESIGNER DECADES
Advertising and the 80s

iDaDs

Of all the valedictions to the 80s, perhaps none was so appropriate as the one published by Penguin in conjunction with *iD* magazine, entitled *iDeas*. And just as museums tend to become their own biggest exhibits (think of Stephen Bayley's Design Museum, for example) so anthologies become their own biggest entries. But what this obituary to the decade had in common with all the others from less epochal organs was the central place given to ADVERTISING in its rememberance of things past.

> If you wanted to know what was really happening in the 80s, you watched the ads. Paranoia about hidden persuaders took a back seat as ads were celebrated as a non-stop carnival of images which didn't just sell, but also crystallised contemporary aspirations, fantasies, moods and fears[1]

It was only when the media began to write up the end of the 80s that it became clear just how scripted the decade seemed to be. Beginning as agitprop, turning into soap and ending up as morality play, this was a potent ten years. The modern had become the postmodern.

There is nothing new about this sort of epochal self-consciousness, but what was interesting about the 80s was the prominence enjoyed by advertising. It wasn't the first time that advertising had been symptomatic of the society that produced it – but it was the first time that it was acknowledged as so being. And this observation worked more retrospectively than over the course of the preceding ten years. BBC 2's series *Washes Whiter* was a high-profile, densely produced social history of Britain

61

since the mid-50s which used television commercials exclusively for its data. Transmitted in the spring of 1990, the five part series explored thematically the ways in which ads had changed between 1956 and the present day.

By collecting an enormous archive of ads (which took the production team literally years to do), the series could pack together an astonishingly rich cross-section of commercials. Selling to women, to men, to teenagers, the use of fantasy, sex, household mores – all yielded up, through the shifting production values of the ads, a vision of Britain as resonant as any inferable from more established media, but more compelling for having been so ignored. Nicholas Barker, the series producer, justified the method on the grounds that commercials had a vested interest in getting their reflections of contemporary attitudes and desires right, and would consequently change more deftly than less accountable media.

What was significant about the series, from the 80s point of view, was that something had clearly happened to the status of the television commercial to make the BBC take it seriously as an index of social attitudes (or maybe something had happened to the BBC). But, the series itself stuck to being fairly empirical and reflective in its method. The ads of the 60s reflected 60s 'givens' in a fairly straightforward way.

What however was different about ads in the 80s was the self-consciousness with which they typified and expressed their surrounding culture. They became doubly reflective, not only in content but in form also. The sales propositon at the heart of any ad must always correlate in some way with people's opinions, but it was only in the mid-80s that advertising as a form began to be less overshadowed by the media it had before parodied and plagiarised. The inflation in production values, the two-way traffic between pop promos and movies helped to break down the cultural divides between them, and the growth of computer graphics and special effects that only advertisers could afford to use began to challenge the production superiority of television and film. What had started out as a supermarket theory – add cultural and symbolic value to a brand – started to look like a whole view of culture. Advertising became acknowledged as being a sophisticated cultural product at a time when that was how both 'popular' and 'high' culture were being explored and consumed.

Advertising spent the 80s becoming a force to be reckoned with. The last ten years have seen an unprecedented expansion in both influence and prestige. Ad budgets soared. Production budgets followed suit and by the end of the decade it had become almost routine for commercials to cost many hundreds of thousands of pounds, more expensive second by second than even the most lavish of feature films, let alone television programmes. Britain now invests the second highest proportion of its GNP on advertising in the world, second only to the USA. The stock market began to reward companies who invested in branding their products with extravagant campaigns. There was even a move made by companies like Rank Hovis McDougall to have the intangible value of their brands incorporated into the share price.

New companies began to advertise for the first time, each making their debut with bigger and more ambitious campaigns – computer companies, clearing banks, insurance companies – and most notably of all, Her Majesty's Government. Smaller bodies too, took to the hoardings; local government, the GLC, the new towns, charities and the armed forces.

The number of advertising agencies grew, as well as their billings. The bigger, older agencies spawned newer, more ambitious agencies, like Abbott Mead and Vickers, or Gold Greenlees Trott. A whole host of even smaller agency set-ups followed these in the mid-80s, dubbed 'third wave' agencies, they had the customary conflation of tongue-twisting names and plenty of radical creative ambitions (although few of them have really had the impact of their predecessors). The larger, American-owned agencies like J. Walter Thompson and McCann Erickson too self-consciously tried to recapture the creative and analytical high ground from their upstart rivals.

An increasing proportion of advertising had moved on from being just jingles and fibs; it became art direction, wit, the loving manipulation of fantasies and desire that set the template for the decade's growing preoccupation with retail architecture, service industries and new patterns of consumption. In addition to the challenge being posed by the big new look of the ads was their new cultural pretentiousness. The rise in enterprise culture had the effect of making advertising more and more central to key social questions. The conclusion was permeating the whole of culture; in order to understand the cultural importance of something it was necessary to understand how (and more importantly why) it was being consumed. And the ad agencies too, were quick to get involved in this sort of inquiry, touting their research as closer to public opinion than anything sociology or political polls could offer, and their ads as better, more potent embodiments of contemporary desires than other parts of the media.

SOFT SELL

The story of 80s advertising is really the story of two agencies, Saatchi and Saatchi, and Bartle Bogle Hegarty. But before considering them, we first of all have to understand what happened to the *look* of advertising, to the language it spoke, responding as it did to the perception that consumerism had become a radical force in society, that it had real cutting edge.

Despite its air of sophistication, brand advertising is embarrassed advertising. Soft sell has always used humour and oblique images of lifestyle to cast a veil over the central pitch, displacing a characteristically British antipathy to trade, selling and huckstering by producing advertising that is reticent, whimsical and irreverent. This is in contrast to what we take American advertising to be about, with its much more tangible and uncompromising view of products, products and more products lurching out of the screen at us. Our sales messages have tended to be diffused and coyly packaged as part of something larger, be it humour, 'life' or even just advertising itself, perhaps because we inherited from sterner times a strict code for the ways in which commerce could solicit our business. The British have always given themselves the credit for being decorous consumers, and have traditionally expected advertisers to respect this:

> [we] make poor capitalists (or so we are informed); to begin with, [we] distrust, even despise advertising. . . . In this country . . . the appeal of television commercials (by repute the best in the world) is often measured by the success with which their directors and copywriters have contrived to *disguise* the purely mercantile nature of the product – by which I mean, not the article being promoted but the commercial itself. . . . In a fair proportion of British TV commercials the product on offer becomes almost a

McGuffin, as Hitchcock would say, a narrative factor of no great significance in itself except insofar as it generates a brief fragment of fiction.[2]

As we become more and more familiar with the stories that adverts tell us, with their densely crafted added values, it is easy to forget that all ads are by necessity variations of one basic theme – 'we want your business'. Indeed that is what makes an ad an ad. The reason we have advertising at all is because companies *need* to make this request, and need to make it well. This is the point of origin behind all the traditional liberal defences of advertising as a democratic practice, that it invites accountability and devolves the real power onto the consumer.

But most advertising is not that blunt. Advertisers are after more than wallets, they also want our *custom*. A quest, in essence, for credibility, trust. They want us to be their friends, their confidantes, to feel good about them as well as glutted on their products. Soft sell then, is about seeking out business, but also respect, the willingness just for a few seconds, to take a household purchase one iota more seriously than of course it would otherwise deserve, dear bashful iconoclasts that we are. Implicit to soft sell is a very British insecurity. We are *above* the hedonistic delight that consumer products give us. And we are above it because it makes us feel guilty, and superciliousness is the way to feel good about what makes you feel bad. And the way to win over people hung up on what makes them feel good is camp, that giddy hybrid of high seriousness and absurdity, the classic defensive/assertive mode of those who need to make an exhibition of their own maligned peripheralness. The serious and the absurd are the qualities between which British advertising has, much more than American, to walk warily.

But all this changed in the 80s. In both advertising style and social context there was a hardness and lack of inhibition about consumerism. Advertising isolated consumer values from a sense of their social consequences. Those in work enjoyed not only more spending power than ever before, but an ethos in which to exercise it, most graphically dramatised by the rise of the yuppie, who took over from the Sloane the mantle of most conspicuously profiting from inequality.

The 80s brought new markets to the advertisers, as well as new idioms for their commercials. Financial services in particular were booming, and danced to a loud and competititve drum. Share flotations and privatisations brought together older Thatcherite notions of suburban share ownership with the market-making activities of seriously rich young men in red braces.

The enterprise culture was one in which high-tech and designer self-consciousness collaborated to reshape not just our electronic media-world, but our view of consumer durables and the high-street retailers who provided it with both form and content. And all of these things were manifested in how ad agencies themselves styled their own commercial culture, decked out with power notions of being a 'people industry', and bristling with their own 'floated' city status.

CONDOM CULTURE

There was a new hardness in the air, particularly manifest in the images we confronted in the ads. Lifestyle had become a commodity in its own right. Take Smirnoff, the vodka that for years sent itself up with a campaign style that was the epitome of camp (all those 'I thought X was Y until I discovered Smirnoff'). 'Just good friends' has, however, thrown this all over. This was 80s consumerism in its new guise.

For a start it looks different; its production values are affected anti-glam, and the strapline throwaway cryptic. It is a louche vignette of scandal laughed off. There are three levels of alarm at being 'caught out', from the simian leer on the left to her gleeful glaze on the right. There is a narrative of sorts. A nightclub, an off-the-cuff incriminatory photo, rebuffed by man in shades to the tune of the old lie 'just good friends' lipsticked across the bottom. But being caught out is the business. This is yuppie intrigue, framed as we are by the visual into obssessive interest in this lifestyle that we have stalked and here tried to capture and disrupt. This is self-conscious voyeurism turned in on itself, a flash-point shunning of the public (private?) eye. And we have our prurient question – is their pleasure guilty? – both thrown back in our face, and at the same time teased back out into the open. Sex is dangerous, and needs to be tracked down, with a punitive public gaze. We share the guilt with our own auto-eroticism – we are 'flashing' at them. This is life underground, on the edge, on the up, utter self-confidence even when

3 Smirnoff advertisement, 1987

narcissistically threatened. The image draws us in by turfing us out; a strong, heady expulsion for the photographer, and implicitly, the non-drinker.

We see three mouths, no eyes and varying degrees of grimace. Just the snarl and upraised palm knocking the over-exposed glare of flasher/voyeur off-balance. The logo conceals their identity, while proclaiming these the faces of have-it-all guilty pleasure. It is a picture of flagrant anti-shame; incriminated at the very moment of shame brushed aside, coolly disporting a hedonism made artfully subterranean. The guilt, the spontaneity, the moment, all transmute into studied self-projection, the buzz of alcohol inside your head turned into that of lifestyle as public consumption.

In this lifestyle of pleasure there is inevitably something to feel guilty about, just as there is also immunity to be had in exultantly riding that guilt. It is lifestyle in which friends are 'just' guilty sex partners, who assuage their guilt with sex that is just better than everybody else's. The spectator's point of entry into this picture is a rapacious, vicarious and clumsy one, that of the gutter journalist/private dick behind the flash. Momentarily we share all that this entails, this image of how other people's lifetstyle gets invaded, syringed dry of intrigue and then fed into a public appetite for both glamour *and* scandal.

The lifestyle/sexual elixir of the vodka gives us a double fix of pleasure *and* guilt, of private conscience become public shame, garish with defiance. 'Just good friends' – the fuck they are. And just as they are more than just good friends, so Smirnoff is more than good vodka, and the ad, more than just a good ad. Both brandish a whole new language of guilt and pleasure. Behind this ad is a new sense of social value, that in guilt, precisely in guilt, lies pleasure. It is this which has replaced the old reticence, the one that fought shy of hard sell because in pleasure lay guilt.

But on a more macabre level, the easy usurpation of guilt by pleasure, most potently symbolised in sex, was brought sharply to a halt by AIDS, which has produced new resonances and silences around old subjects. The Smirnoff ad is a case in point. In a climate getting more and more used to being cool on sex, 'just good friends' needed new pleasures to derive their guilty (safe) danger from. Danger needs its prophylactics just as does sex.

This has its echoes in the movies. This ad was after all a preemptive dead ringer for that moment of *Zeitgeist* crisis so chillingly captured by Adrian Lyne in *Fatal Attraction*, a nightmarish allegory for what happens when you stop being 'just good friends'. Strange as it may sound, while this is a film much trumpeted as an allegory for AIDS, it has as much to say about consumerism, about ads. This is not just because Adrian Lyne is the quintessential movie-maker-who-started-in-commercials (didn't they all), but because it so shows.

Never mind characters as individual personality/psychologies, perhaps warrantably linked into larger themes; the fact is, movies just *are* how culture creates the discourses of gender, disease, sexual morality. And as such, *Fatal Attraction* was paramount. It made its intervention into these things not by face-value individual characterisations, but by archetype and genre. Judith Williamson picked this up in her *New Statesman* review:

> Last year I thought I had identified a new stereotype in American movies – the Single Working Woman. . . . Glenn Close . . . appears as an SWW much closer to the archetype, with snaky locks that give her the appearance of a Medusa. However *Fatal Attraction* doesn't just feature Glenn Close as the classically screwed-up SWW – it features the SWW as the AIDS virus.[3]

What made this sort of alarmist conjecture so interesting however, was not so much the bald, superficial misogynism with which the SWW gets persecuted, but the generic images of all that is her opposite, the opposite, in allegorical terms, if Williamson is right, of AIDS. On the most obvious level, what stands contrasted to AIDS-darkened sex, is matrimonial sex, the family Dan and Beth are trying to protect. But that has no real purchase either, not just because the way Dan and Beth are played is too overburdened with saccharine contrivance to be credible, but because, ultimately, such values mean nothing outside of the material lifestyle which supports them. This is a film, then, in form and content, about consumerism, not sex – or rather the polarities it plays between aren't those of promiscuous versus familial sex, but sex-as-consumerism and consumerism-as-sex. It was a film about ads – not AIDS.

Williamson went some of the way to this conclusion, but stopped short:

Lyne came to movies from commercials and not only is the whole film a continuous ad for family life (or condoms, which ever way you look at it), its component scenes are actually identifiable as specific ad types. There is the underwear ad where we see how much Dan really fancies his wife. There is the 'people like you' ad where the Gallaghers go out bowling. There are the after-dinner coffee ads where their friends chat delightfully round the polished table. There is the 'listening bank' ad where they paint their new home wearing dungarees and perched cutely on step-ladders.[4]

Ostensibly then, the language of commercials got used to paint a shorthand picture of everything that Alex did not have, and everything that she in turn threatened. But this was not just materialist covetousness − Alex had the 'things', and in abundance. But in her life they just did not come real, her life stayed a dead inventory of things, all props and no commercial. Dan's, on the other hand, was hagiographic testimony to the fact that *the commercials are right*.

Nor was the film the morality play critics said it was. Alex was not the AIDS virus, because the film used much cruder means than this to deliver its anti-promiscuity message. The film taught Dan that casual sex was a no-no, not because there's a plague out there, but because women aren't capable of it. Alex's problem, her sexual shortcomings, are not pathological in the physical sense. There is no imagery of infection, or disease, or physical wasting away, the hall-marks of the language of AIDS. Instead, we have a picture of a neurotic, psychotic, fucked-up spinster who hasn't the mental wherewithal to be casual. The opposite of relaxed, 'discreet' (her word), is not wifely devotion, but out-of-control harpie nightmare. And Beth is of course constitutionally incapable of countenancing casual sex, well, because she's Beth, and it's unthinkable.

Dan's choice then was between two type of female incapacity to countenance casual sex, and he chose the Beth version rather than the Alex one. Women are joy, women are venom, the problem of guilt and pleasure lies with them, and not with any virus. But what gave this old, old message its contemporary patina was its imagery of lifestyle. The opposite of AIDS is ads. Lifestyle is life turned into an ad with sex; displaced into consumerism. Individual gratification mediated through the glow of family life, buying things for those you love, there happiness lies. This is a profoundly conservative formula, which uses the family as both the sanction for the anti-individualism of reactionary values (privileging it as a unit above social equality) and as a repository for those values of rampant individualism which spit on the grave of post-war consensus.

Even the sex act itself is now in thrall to a new commodity, the condom. As Sean French pointed out:

> it is now becoming clear that anything can be turned into advertising. The big new subject is sex. . . . I had naively assumed that there was at least one remaining area of human activity that was outside the world of commodities and consumption. As I had originally understood it, condoms were being advertised on television as a rather desperate strategy to prevent the spread of AIDS. But, of course, sex is a huge market for the company that can create a demand for the appropriate status symbols. And now Richard Branson has got his foot in the bedroom door and is offering us a sort of Filofax for the willy.[5]

With 'Mates' we really can be 'just good friends'. They also help explain why it is that AIDS is more and more beginning to seem the ultimately unyuppie thing to have, tainted increasingly by 'underclass' images of drugs and sex, by people barred from the consumer lifestyle of displaced guilt/pleasure, condemned to a regime of dirty needles and infected phalluses.

HERE TODAY AND GONE TOMORROW

It is amazing how little it took to set the tone for a period. Our 80s preoccupation with the winners of enterprise culture 'can-do' took striking form in a clutch of hard-nosed cynical campaigns oriented toward the world of business. If sex is the language of what you get out of life, then business has taken over from war as the language of what winners put into it – and that of losers who want to be winners:

> the current emphasis on 'caring' is misplaced, and that in 'Labour Leads' the party needs to project a far more aggressive, go-getting image to appeal to Labour's lost

71

voters . . . current trends in advertising, for example the Vauxhall Cavalier, British Airways 'red eye' and 'If everything was as reliable as a Volkswagen' commercials, also suggest that ruthlessness is a selling point among consumers.[6]

The axis on which our culture revolves shifted, and at its heart lay a new brazenness, a new eulogistic swagger in the marketplace. The Midlands Bank 'Credo' ad, was at the fore of this new style of hard-nosed cynical campaign. The commercial's production values, long silences, no music and frank, hostile interchanges set the style for many others, but no more so than in its depiction of success emerging from its sting in the tail denouement. (The ad features an executive being made redundant by his slimy boss, who fobs him off with what is obviously a large cheque. The sacked executive, however, turns the tables on his now ex-boss, by confessing to having planned his move all along, and smugly informing him that the cheque will do only too nicely as set-up money for *his* new company.)

> The new ads are selling the new Mean Chic benefits of business life – greed, competition, treachery and the big money that follows. They define an emerging perception of businessmen – the style the PR woman in *Serious Money* describes as Sexy Greedy.[7]

But of course it had to be like this. The ad agency responsible will have discovered in the course of its research that most small businesses are set up by people who have just been made redundant. How then, do you make someone who has been sacked seem like a winner? You give them vulpine prescience and maverick coolness.

> BBA Club World and all the other New Businessmen's ads feature the advertising industry's new vision of Thatcherite Britain – a romance compounded from popular newspapers' ideas of yuppiedom; the agency world's own recent and rather partial experience of the City; a swift bone-up on the American 'Success Through Intimidation' type of bestseller, and the art director's recce in Docklands, where design and money have gone ape.[8]

It would be just the same if you were to try and advertise the services of an estate agent. Most people who buy property do so in the aftermath of a broken relationship. At some stage then, your campaign would have to make capital out of this fact, which would mean focusing on the type of person who can triumph from the end of an affair.

Funnily enough it is precisely this scenario that figures in that other apogee of the hard-line Thatcherite ad, the VW Golf commercial, done to the strains of the 'Here today, gone tomorrow'; *Oh What a Lovely War*'s recasting of the old hymn, 'What a friend we have in Jesus' (and banned from being transmitted on Sundays because of it). This commercial boasts its own uncomfortable irony, perhaps also symptomatic of our times, in having been shot by David Bailey. The last ad he did was a highly praised, hard-hitting poster for the anti-fur league, featuring a model dragging a blood soaked fur coat along behind her, to the line 'It takes forty dumb animals to make a fur coat, but only one to wear it', which gave us the chance to be misogynistic and ecological at the same time. The prominent role played in this VW commercial by a fur coat caused its share of comment, and while hypocrisy was strongly rebutted (the coat was artificial apparently), its use as an unquestioned sign of glamour has its own story to tell.

Hell hath no fury like a dumped Sloane, and our woman of slender means soon lets us know what she thinks about being 'just good friends' – yes, but only with my car. Her haughty, magnificent rage takes delicious pains in peeling of marital baubles and discarding them with fabulously implacable pique. But then – the car – the key, dangling over the gutter . . . and a small smile of self-mastery, resolving itself with a bright crescendo of music, and a compact gesture of solidarity behind the windscreen wipers, patting the steering-wheel, and off, to greener mews, sweet with the quiet inner arrogance of being worth more than any relationship. If only everything was as reliable. . . . Moods are mutable, human relationships are quicksilver, but the human/car bond transcends them all – a reliable car to get attached to, to confide in.

Not like the Renault ads, however, which project their cars as servicable accoutrements to a fast-moving, wacky lifestyle. The Golf is a reliable friend in a life with *these* sorts of upsets, relationships consummated in gifts and wrecked by incompatibilities we can only guess at. 'Here today and gone tomorrow', the lush maudlin stoicness of those whose privilege it is to be able to see as merely transient the durables of human life. And doubly so; what's always here today is privilege, and what's gone, for the moment, is no more than today's sugar-daddy:

> Our heroine of the mews is no financially independent woman; she clearly leaves *his* house; jettisons *his* baubles; and dumps *his* coat. But she has definitely read the 'stand on your own two feet' communiqué in the divide-and-rule-society. . . . Volkswagen woman has no children, no commitment, no conscience, no basis in truth.[9]

And female erotica is back with a vengeance, of the two steps forward, three steps back variety. A recent Cadbury's Flake ad drew a few raised eye-brows, particularly as it had been thought that the account's move out of Leo Burnett, into Gold Greenlees Trott would have spelt the end for all those hail fellatio well met swoonings. But not a bit of it. We get a heat of the night chateau, and a silken, languid woman chasing away her longeurs with vulnerable chocolate, with thrashing music and a telephone ringing unanswered while a lizard darts across the dial. But what is unusual about this old scenario is that if there is any opposition of male and female sexuality going on, it is in the contrast between the urgent, screaming phone, to which she will not bring relief, and the remote intensity with which she pursues her own pleasures to an entirely different tempo. Sex is the high-point of guilty pleasure. Unless, of course, you make do with self-worth, a shake of the head and your ex-lover's Volkswagen.

Or it's independence not just of sex, but *with* sex. Like the glamorous bundle whose fan-belt goes, only to be coolly replaced by a stocking stripped from her upper thigh with sensual gusto. Now that *is* icy, and radical, even if it does culminate in a triumphant triptych of images – the jaguar on the car; the nine out of ten cats (bathetic) joke, and our driver – three predatorial pussies purring into the hard late 80s.

MILES BETTER (THAN WHAT?)

But on a less hostile and nasty footing, advertising does undeniably seem consistent with today's personal and corporate ethos. The decision to advertise is taken by many companies in the spirit of complete corporate overhaul, and is often the most visible aspect of having taken to heart the advice of various types of management consultancy. Advertising is both the cue for, and embodiment of, the new management initiatives that burgeon out of companies born again amid torrents of new logos, mission statements and zealous commitments to 'being number one', or 'excellence in the community', etc. etc. Advertising expresses, and emerges from, that type of strategic overview which makes companies try to line up their internal structures with an accurate, imaginative answer to the question 'what business are we in' (not always as easy a question to answer as it might look). These resolve themselves typically into a whirligig of self- and consumer-motivating principles, rationales, planning-cycles and slogans. Advertising, then, is not just something to bolt on as a marketing extra, but has become the most visible expression of a management fixation with strategy, structure and consultancy.

Similarly, with individuals, there is enormous contemporary incentive to invest heavily in the question 'what lifestyle am I in?'. Aerobics, healthy eating, 'feeling good', all are part of an ethos of life-management, making an exhibition of internal vigilance and external effectiveness. Our bodies and our environments come together as seamless, coherent wholes, all of a piece, and all branded with ourselves as individuals. These two strands meet iconographically at least, in the much-maligned filofax, the perfect nexus between corporate and individualist notions of mastery through management skills. In size and texture, the filofax has become the new bible, heavily reminiscent of those dog-eared leather tomes that evangelical fists used to brandish from bygone pulpits.

And all around us, too, advertising both expresses and embodies what for the 80s is seen as the way forward. This is particularly symbolised by Glasgow, a city whose turn-around in popular perception from urban hell to chic, rugged authenticity, has become a byword for what imaginative PR and civic pride can achieve in these times of benighted industrial decline. Advertising occupies an unusual place between two orders of social existence, between the language of necessities (groceries and the like) and yuppie accessories, reflected in that of the nation as a whole, locked as it is into a period of terrible transition, one that separates winners from losers, the out-moded from the up-to-the-minute. This then is Glasgow:

75

Over the past few years ... some marvellous and intriguing things have been happening to the city. Epidemics of stone-cleaning and tree-planting have transformed its former blackness into chequer-works of salmon pink, yellow and green ... Optimists ... say that Glasgow has become Britain's first post-industrial success; a city that has weathered the recessionary gale to emerge into the sunlight – microchips and macrobottles of house white – which has swept along behind. People who describe themselves as realists say there is still some way to go. Pessimists insist that all it amounts to is a grandiose exercise in self-delusion, a placebo which offers no cure for a terminally ruined economy and the wretchedness of mass-unemployment.[10]

So, between the optimists, realists and pessimists lies a real estimate of how effective this attempt at regeneration has been. Glasgow has seen real efforts being made, packaged and energised by an imaginative advertising campaign, and its 'vision' of new possibilities (wine-bars, festival shopping, converted warehouses – the city as (a) living commercial):

Advertising men and public-relations consultants were hired ... (and) the *Glasgow's Miles Better* campaign was born at a cost of £500,000. Today the city advertises itself to the world as a 'centre'; a business and conference centre, an educational centre, a tourist centre. The manufacturer's plates have been replaced by a comic figure (Mr Happy, on loan from Roger Hargreaves and his *Mister Men* books) and a stick-on slogan that can mean everything and nothing.[11]

The common currency here is *aspiration*, on a personal, a civic, a corporate and a national level – as well as a lexicon of other Tory abstractions for those with the stomach for them: 'What has happened in Glasgow, as in the rest of Britain, is that the class system has been startlingly simplified. Ewan Marwick put it like this: "There are the people who aspire and the people who don't or can't".'[12] In other words, in a period of transition it is advertising which dramatises most starkly the wedge that is driven in between those who aspire and those who can't/don't. So for the moment, all one can do with Glasgow is wait and see, measuring up with the passage of time, in the spirit of critical ambivalence, who among the optimists, the realists and the pessimists is right.

In so many ways, then, advertising has secured for itself a new legitimacy, representing in spirit a sign of the times, as well as providing, in the letter, details of the new world awaiting us, as always, just around the next corner.

And it goes deeper than that. Another result of the sort of thinking I have outlined in the previous two chapters is a crisis in our capacity to ascribe values with any certainty of validity or good faith. What, surprisingly perhaps, has been most put at issue, has been the ability to gain some sort of ethical grasp on advertising and consumerism. After all, if Lannon is at all right, then the whole notion of brand values acquires a convenient validity where before lay a surreptitious roguishness in the fictions of adspeak. The old charges just don't stick any more.

AN ACE GALLERY WITH QUITE A NICE AGENCY ATTACHED

The three biggest things that happened to advertising during the 80s were its politicisation, its commercialisation and its assumption of the status of art-form. In other words it became more controversial, more lucrative and more pretentious than it had ever been before. And one agency name has more to answer for for this than any other. Actually it's two names. Saatchi and Saatchi.

Between 1986 and 1989 they were the world's largest agency group, before being overtaken by WPP, a company run by Martin Sorrell, the man who, ironically, had helped Saatchis take over the world. But Saatchis were always more than their size. For most people they are the only agency they have ever heard of. With no Madison Avenue in London, their name *became* advertising.

Unlike any other agency, Saatchi and Saatchi entered the collective unconscious of 80s UK culture. And even more than just standing for 'every-agency' they have taken the credit – and the blame – for all that advertising has done to the culture over the last ten years. Their name became the flash-point between politics, culture, media and the market-place, none of which will ever be the same again.

It wasn't just that they advertised better and bigger than anyone else. What Saatchis did, not always intentionally, was spearhead the more controversial aspects of enterprise culture and lend a sense of crisis to all those traditional assumptions that stood in their way. By the end of the 80s it was just impossible to talk about politics without talking about communication, about consuming policies . . . it was impossible to talk about cultural institutions without asking what it was people got out of them . . . it was impossible to talk about collecting art without taking into account the role of the private collector and the market.

These were shifts not just in attitude but in cultural values that left no one untouched, and somehow, somewhere, Saatchis were always bound to turn up. Even to the advertising industry itself, Saatchis proved a maverick force, challenging and recasting deeply-held views about the proprieties of selling, and the etiquette of self-promotion. They embodied ten years of violently polarised views about advertising and its proper place in the scheme of things.

The brothers set up in 1970 with little more than Charles's creative renown and £1m. worth of business. In those days advertising was dominated by American owned agencies and an ethos that paralysed even this, the glitziest of businesses, with the full dead-weight of English anti-selling phobia. It took ten years before their outspoken ambitions to take the world of advertising by storm were taken seriously.

Their first big break was, of course, their appointment in 1978 to handle the Tory Party account, a relationship quickly consummated with the notorious 'Labour isn't working' poster, generally attributed with having made Callaghan crucially postpone the election. . . .

The early identification with Thatcher took a plethora of inter-related forms. At a crude level the 'packaging' of Mrs Thatcher drew advertising into the 'image–reality' debate at its most contentious, drawing from opposition politicians the automatic chorus-line of contemptuous scorn, selling statesmen as though they were baked beans, breakfast cereals or (the favourite) soap powder.

The myths soon started to proliferate. Thatcher looked, *par excellence*, a 'packaged product', which horribly jarred with what were supposed to be conviction politics. And Saatchis were lionised (and vilified) as those reponsible. Insiders maintain that they never had anything like this sort of input, and, indeed, barely even met her. But the two radical things that they did give the early election campaign were first, a respect for researching voter attitudes in far greater detail than had ever been done before; and second, that their advertising expressed the appeal of the Tory Party in stark emotional terms, and not in the jargon of policy details.

For the left, of course, the Saatchis were anathema, although a useful way of explaining away Thatcher's cross-class appeal and their own failure. Writhing at the aggression, the entirely negative contempt for them so brutally expressed in the campaign posters, all they could do was appeal to some supposed moral high-ground where true politics survived untainted by the language of the marketer. The old liberal intelligentsia, as despised by Thatcherism as the Labour Party was, also looked on in horror as alien forces hijacked the influence of the great and the good. While for the general public, there was something rather irresistible about a politics they thought they weren't allowed to have, selfish, acquisitive and yet also patriotic. It is tribute to the power of that campaign that Saatchis are *still* glossed as 'the people who sold us Thatcher', as though in 1979 we were all content with high inflation and the winter of discontent, and only subterfuge of the highest order seduced us into voting Tory.

For both the embittered left, and, of course, political satirists, the Saatchis were perfect foils. Foreign, shameless, brothers, hucksters – they were a blissfully easy target. Advertising's stress on image and reality (the stuff of satire too) ensured the brothers immortality as 'the Corsican Twins' in *Private Eye*, as bullshit henchmen in Steve Bell's vitriolic cartoons, and as the only admen who have ever made it onto *Spitting Image*.

As the Thatcher project took off, the Saatchis became even more mythically implicated. The Tories had reinvented the language of election campaigns, aggressive, compressed and emotive. But they also espoused advertising not just as the visible skein of enterprise culture, but as a tool of public policy, not least in privatisation campaigns. And Saatchis supplied the template for these with British Airways, the account they snatched from US agency FCB ('We'll take more care of you') and transformed via the Spielbergish extravaganza 'Manhattan' into a symbol for Britain at its globe-eating new best. This was a political battle being waged not only at the centre of 80s culture, but for control of it too.

And fuelling the move of enterprise into the high streets and living rooms of mid-80s Britain was what was happening to international finance. Here too London was storming the globe.

Going public, then global, Saatchi and Saatchi took full advantage of the new money, and were the first agency to sell the advertising sector to a city previously sceptical. By 1986 they were, following a pyrrhic buy-out of Ted Bates, a major world contender in their own right, the largest agency group in the world – sixteen years after first setting up business in tiny Golden Square offices.

Saatchis took advertising and all it stood for from inside a tiny media village and made it, and themselves, not just one of the world's most visible businesses, but also one of the world's most visible new business disciplines. It was Saatchis who made advertising not just consistent with, but actually indispensable to, areas of policy making, corporate and governmental, previously far above mere selling. Having brought advertising to electioneering (or so it seemed) and then to politics in general, Saatchis was behind (or again, so it seemed) every invasion of advertising into areas previously unbesmirched.

Above all they were the agency people went to when they needed help; the egg marketing board after the salmonella scare; the Turkish government seeking admission to the EEC but with a dodgy human rights record; charities; the Victoria and Albert Museum; as well as the usual crop of the world's biggest blue-chip companies, like Procter and Gamble, ICI, British Airways – one by one they all succumbed to Saatchis swaggering, single-minded populist battle cries. And, as inevitably, furnished yet more parts of the media with evidence of our cultural collapse.

The word 'Saatchify' entered the language as the basis for a new breed of conspiracy theory. As marketing invaded parts of society not previously subject to the indignity of actually justifying themselves, so the Saatchi factor spread further and further. Saatchi chairman Tim Bell became a close confidante of senior Tories, at a time when advertising was used more and more by government, and not just during elections. Privatisations, public announcements, ministry logos, all used and reflected the values of the ad agency. The government became one of the largest advertising clients in the country; between 1983 and 1988 expenditure on advertising rose five fold, and now rests somewhere around £150m. Quite unfairly given how little government work Saatchis actually did, they nevertheless became the name we all associated with this changing political landscape. As long ago as

1982, the NME in its review of the year spoke of the Falklands War as 'Saatchi art-directed'.

In 1989 for example, Glasgow, elected European City of Culture for 1990 wanted to appoint an ad agency. Three pitched, two Scottish agencies, and Saatchis in London. Saatchis won, to immediate controversy. The losing agencies accused Glasgow of copping out, while to the rest of Glasgow it only confirmed their misgivings that the rehabilitation of their city was going to be used as a piece of Whitehall PR. There was a botched repitch, but once again Saatchis won.

The Glasgow council insisted that the decision was based on the Saatchis' line 'There's a lot Glasgowing on', not because of its self-evident genius, but because of its sound basis in research – namely that to the majority of Glaswegians, all that could be said for being City of Culture 1990 was that it meant there would be lots of things to see and do. . . . But typically the name Saatchis implied some sort of whitewash, some sort of government dissi-mulation, disguising the political as cultural.

By the general election of 1987, so great was the Saatchi factor that it seemed the only issue worth discussing was which agency was doing what, how much Neil Kinnock had copied them, and whether Saatchis was going to be dumped before or after the election. In the event, the severance came sooner rather than later, and Saatchis did their best to make it look a case of jumping rather than getting pushed (they sued the BBC for implying it was the latter). What was even more strange, though, was that it hardly seemed to matter, so powerful was their sense of influence – it was abundantly clear that even the Labour Party were up to their eyeballs in strategies, briefs, top-drawer direc-tors and cliff-top presidential biopics . . .

And advertising became not only more politicised than it had ever been, but more commercial too. The brothers became business heroes in an age that now lionised, even eroticised the tycoon, a figure they themselves gave most iconic expression to in their later BA ad 'Boardroom'. There was a sense of (para-doxical) cultural invigoration coming out of Charlotte St, the chill wind of wide-awake, unfettered derring-do, scandalising an established order for whom traditionally selling was at best an evil necessity.

By their mid-80s heyday, it could be said that the whole notion of *selling* would never be the same again. They had shown us how to sell politics, how to sell advertising, and even how to sell selling. But what they never quite got the chance to do, though, was sell themselves, because at the crucial moment, it all started to go wrong.

As the boom-years of the 80s came to their inevitable conclusion (probably about 1988), the Saatchis again took poll position, only this time as sacrifical victims, not heroes, to the decade which had started to falter so badly following the October 1987 stock market crash. This, allied to their own loss of senior management, their disastrous bid for the Midland Bank, and the slow but inevitable realisation of the folly of many of their wild acquisitions, made the slow-down in their business as symptomatic of general economic malaise as its rise had been symptomatic of economic boom.

Before the 90s were even a few months old, we were all learning a new script, gloating self-righteously over the over-reachers, the Saatchi brothers, along with others of their ilk like Sophie Mirman, George Davies and Ralph Halpern.

And it all now seems so clear. Those who live by greed die by it. Rarely can one decade have so quickly despatched the truisms of the prior decade. And Saatchis were not giving up without a fight. On 8 January 1990, the Berlin Wall, which once had been the divider of East and West, but now stood as the most tangible divider of 80s and 90s, had adhered to it an enormous poster proclaiming 'Saatchi and Saatchi: First over the Wall'. For a mere £5000 it represented the latest in a long line of classic Saatchi gestures, bold chutzpah easy to despise but hard to quarrel with. But opinion remains much more bitterly divided about the propriety of this bid to hijack the new decade. And the agency's latest British Airways commercial has five thousand schoolchildren forming the shape of a face and a globe shot from Hugh Hudson's helicopter, and forming the lavish background to a multi-ethnic crowd hug orgy.

But as the share price continues to dive, these sorts of gesture are failing to convince. What remains is an ambivalent legacy. Thanks to Saatchis, the 80s were forced to reconsider how class works, what the importance of consumerism is, how people need to be communicated with, just where power and influence really lie. We were forced to reconsider our untested assumptions about selling, presentation, accountability, as well as chauvinism, manipulation and ambition. It is the ambiguity that suggests we are sitting on the cutting edge of new social attitudes. But as the new orthodoxies of the 90s settle into place, and as the excesses of the 80s become more and more transparently obvious, there is the sense that once again, things are too cosy, too vested in the market-place.

CHARITY ADVERTISING

Two other strands central to advertising in the 80s and all that the decade stood for, culminated in 1989 with two ads, called 'Sky to Tap' and 'Toilet'. They each climax with a child, white, male, of about five years of age, having a drink of water. The first stretches his hand into the crystal cascade pouring from his kitchen tap, filling his glass with not-quite-yet privatised English water. His gesture forms the innocent vindication to the government's multi-million pound campaign to sell off the ten water and sewage authorities of England and Wales, perhaps the most contentious, and certainly the most lavish of the government advertising extravaganzas that have lined the ad agencies' pockets and placed them at the centre of the political process.

The second child stars in an ad that could hardly be more different, not least because the drink of water he has is out of a filthy public toilet bowl. This ad, in conception and screening, is one of the most powerful in another great 80s genre, the charity ad. Written and funded by one of London's top copywriters, Dave Trott, it confronted head-on the problem of Third World infant mortality.

Between them they span the extremes of advertising's new role as the language of social policy, representing the limits of public life made answerable to the ethos of the thirty-second commercial, the poles of what consumerism thinks it can now do politically. There has been an enormous increase in the amount of money spent by the big charities on advertising campaigns since the days of innocent flag-day appeals, and variety club cinema audience button-holings. Responding to the greater political emphasis on the voluntary sector, the increased competition between different charities and the general sense of marketing gone ape, nearly all the major charities have invested in advertising. And most have followed the example set by the Salvation Army's 1967 poster 'For God's sake care', and vied with one another in producing ever bleaker, more arresting ads.

It is over the last six years or so that the genre has really taken off. Spurred on by the increasing regularity with which this style of hard-hitting pathos has carried off industry awards (the path to fame and glory for copywriters), their creators, unleashed from the infantile bathos of mainstream campaigns, have pushed the limits of what we are prepared to be shocked by further and further back, producing ever more effective 'charity nasties'. The genre promises to become even more important, following the IBA's decision in August 1989 to relax the rules that prohibited charity ads from being shown on television.

Illness, handicap and political causes all became grist to a new philanthropic mill. Public apathy was being assaulted as never before, and the adman's skills showcased with more self-importance than ever before. And while no advertiser is ever going to get rich doing this sort of work, it isn't difficult to see what each side gets out of it; the charity gains higher public profile, while the ad agency creative and moral prestige. But it is the neatness, some would say cosiness, of this relationship, that has created disquiet.

For a crusading maverick like Dave Trott, it is utterly a case of the ends justifying the means.

'We got some footage of the concentration camps in the Second World War, gassed Jews being bulldozed into mass graves, and being shovelled off the back of lorries and we want to intercut that with images of Third World starvation, when the same thing is happening, little children, skin and bones, being buried, and they look remarkably similar to the bodies in the camps.'

'Don't you think people will find that comparison to be completely tasteless?'

'Yeah, okay, shall we do five million children dying in a tasteful way? Maybe I'm not doing it in the right way, but at least I'm doing it; a lot of people who are criticising me are sitting there doing nothing.'[13]

But outside such uncompromising zeal lie the stark realities of the market place. The campaign produced by BMP–DDB for the Multiple Sclerosis Society has become a classic of the genre. The agency has held the account for over twelve years, but it has only been in the last three that they gave MS its most distinctive campaign style. This takes the form of vandalising various body beautiful photographs with a loud and ugly tear across eyes, limbs, nerves.

The device works on two levels. Most simply it is a branding device, separating MS in our mind's eye from other debilitating illnesses, ensuring we no longer confuse it with, say, muscular dystrophy or spina bifida. And secondly, it illustrates the hideous seriousness of the condition without resorting to the more literal images of disability and pathos, the monochrome uniformity of passive figures immobilised in their wheelchairs.

This tackles head-on the ambiguity that lurks at the heart of charity advertising, the contradiction between means and ends. The genre's now numerous critics point first and foremost to the incompatiblity between raising funds and raising awareness. You raise money by shocking and chastening, with images of abject affliction. But these images confound the longer-term aims of integrating, enfranchising and legislating for people with disabilities. The funds from charity ads therefore come at a price, not least the sense that the voluntary sector is being delegated too many jobs by a government squirming out of its responsibilities.

The dynamic behind such campaigns, the shock and guilt leading to the instant catharsis of the money in the tin, is too short-lived and self-contained to work in the longer term and fundamentally less sensational business of disability politics.

The intractable problem with charity advertising is, it seems, the fact that the relationship between agency and charity is too close, too cosy.

The problem is one of representation: what do you have to do to an individual to make them the centrepiece of a charity ad? Basically you have to make them symbolise all the reasons why we should take the charity seriously. At the very least the person depicted will not only have to manifest an affliction, but do so in a manner that prompts the right sort of emotional response. That individual then becomes, literally, smaller than his or her disability. But who wants to be an object of charity?

The problem isn't just one of individual sensibilities. According to Susan Scott-Parker, whose report for the King's Fund entitled *They're Not in the Brief* analysed the limitations of charity advertising, it compromises the whole charity project. Charity advertising emerges, she contends, from a belief that the charity and the agency are the only ones who need to be involved. Significantly the feelings of those represented are not made central. Neither agency nor charity tend to make the question of imagery paramount, above the more orthodox marketing objectives of an advertising campaign.

> Advertising agencies and charities have a unique relationship, part business, part philanthropy, part mutual aid. While their way of working together is superficially modelled on the usual commercial relationship of agency and advertiser, there are important differences in the way things are done . . . the major difficulties arise simply because the commercial framework has no room in it for a human product: Fiesta cars do not complain that their job prospects are damaged by Ford ads. . . . The entire relationship can be described without reference to people with disabilities. They are not clients, not audience, not product, not customer. Often even the people who actually feature in the campaigns are 'able-bodied' models.[14]

One notorious example of this was a campaign mounted by the schizophrenia charity SANE, which produced a cinema commercial, and follow-up poster ads which depicted schizophrenia as the delusions of a disturbed mind.

> He thinks he's Jesus
> You think he's insane
> They think he's fine.
> Stop the madness. S.A.N.E.

These ads produced furious responses from the other leading mental illness charity, MIND, who argued, not unjustly, that the campaign was confusing and inflammatory. SANE's attempt to have schizophrenia recognised as a dangerous illness was a challenge to the government's Community Care Programme that was taking schizophrenics out of hospitals, rather than a bid to create hostility and mistrust towards the mentally ill. But it was a clear example of how a specific political purpose can be confused with a more general intent, and create enormous resentment and ill-feeling.

The charity/lobby group SHELTER are also adamant that they will only use advertising with extreme caution. In the early 80s the agency FCB produced a famous ad for them. It featured the picture of a white nuclear family sitting huddled and devastated on a park bench, obviously dispossessed, under the strapline 'Just because you're out and down doesn't mean that you're down and out'. But SHELTER soon regretted the ad, convinced that its depiction of the classic 'deserving poor' distorted their larger commitment to all homeless people, not all of whom so neatly coincide with our picture of those worthy of sympathy. To this day, the charity prefers to compromise funds rather than collude in the myth that some homeless people deserve help more than others.

This is a political thing. For SHELTER, having a home is, or should be, a political right. It is not something that should be contingent on the attitudes of those not living rough. Any campaigning that they do has to justify itself either by addressing a specific theme (like social security provisions, or the housing act) or by illustrating the wider truth that the problems faced by a charity's client group are those that society creates.

Questions of employment policy, transport, access, mobility and even language are starting to appear much more often and more explicitly the focus of charity ads at the expense of the traditional pathos of the suffering individual. The shift in emphasis has now brought into the debate more aesthetic matters. The use of black and white (the staple idiom of disaster beautified) and the use of models are now key issues. There is even talk of following the American example of including disabled people within mainstream ads. Levis, McDonalds and IBM have all done this, though their failure to do it outside the USA suggests less corporate idealism than the accommodation of what is a particularly vociferous lobby in one particular market.

The attraction of this sector to the advertiser is that its demands are the opposite of those posed by mainstream advertising. Charity ads are about giving, not getting; they depict people worse off than those who read the ads, and not, as is usual, better off. But what the admen are being made to face up to is that these are real problems, not just the stuff of creative challenge that their usual clients don't give them.

But if charity advertising has forced us to rethink the propriety of private solutions to public problems, it was the spate of share-ownership campaigns that really tested the limits of what consumerism's political agenda should be. These privatisation campaigns – BA, British Gas ('Tell Sid'), British Telecom, BP

('Be part of it'), the regional water authorities ('Be an H$_2$Owner') and, most recently, the electricity boards ('Buy into what you plug into') – were not only among the biggest of the decade, they were also the most controversial.

The rewards such work offers the ad agencies are enormous. Not only are the budgets huge (the government spent an estimated £20m. selling off the water authorities), but there was guaranteed media attention as well as political dividends. The creative challenge too (despite the government being a difficult client) is irresistible. The campaigns begin with great chest-beating corporate hymns to self-evidently useful things (water, electricity, telecommunications), and culminate in frenzies of hucksterism as the final day of share applications approaches.

The water privatisation campaign of 1989 was one of the hardest for the advertisers to crack, coinciding as it did with a whole series of public water supply pollution stories and scandals. It was also the campaign that had the hardest initial proposition – that the water system was in superb working order, an engineering marvel, *but* that it could receive its only too necessary renovations by private, not public, investment. Given that the present water system's origin was as a reaction to the cholera endemic to the system that preceded it, then it is clear why it doesn't automatically work as a symbol for the folly of nationalised endeavours.

The campaign broke into three main sections. The first tried to make us rethink how we take water for granted; milkmen were seen delivering the number of bottles of water the average house uses in a day; the countryside yielded up its buried pipes and sewers. The second stage was to then turn up the volume on our appreciation of the wonders of the water infrastructure, while the third urged and hectored us to buy the shares that were then on offer. It was the second stage that gave birth to 'Sky to tap', over a million pounds worth of state-of-the-art production values.

What was interesting about this commercial was the way it mingled nature, technology and mysticism. It traces the journey from the middle of a rain-cloud to an ordinary kitchen sink of one drop of water. That odyssey takes us from the sky, to the river, through a dizzying virtual world of pipes, dams and systems. The music and the casting are pure Spielberg (the child's world of high-tech ravishing wonder were established early on in this style of advertising as the main imprimatur), and the sense of crescendo, of nature harnessed by an infrastructure of stone and computer graphics, suggests rational quibbles have been left a long way behind. The drop's voyage continues, beneath the feet of two yuppies kissing in the rain, past a new-born baby held aloft in a silvery halo of water, past a Yeatsian golden crow, forged and doused before pointing up new horizons from its perch at the top of a gloriously English church steeple, before arriving in the glass of our thirsty child. All the while our commentary gave us a flow of pseudo-facts, tautologously complete: 'Every one of the 2000 million gallons a day to every factory, every office, every home we supply, means you can be sure that every time you turn on the tap, there's water.'

This is the apotheosis of 80s advertising. It is all very baptismal. It is language that literally brooks no dissent, that taps an irrational capacity for wonder, and drowns us in non-negotiable streams of consciousness, not communication but communion, a corporate requiem for advertising itself.

THE GREEN WATERSHED

Advertising has to evolve different directions and as the decade drew to an end, we started to get some clues about what those were going to be. Campaigns for such paragon 80s products as Apple computers and Audi cars, shook off their earlier hard-edged patina, and played new, gentler games with us. Since the mid-80s, Audi, through their agency BBH, have sold us their cars with a combination of Geoffrey Palmer's rich, plummy voice-over, images of cold calculating aspiration, and the strap-line 'Vorsprung durch Technik'. The combination came to epitomise the product fascism of the 'me' decade.

The seminal Audi campaign reached its zenith in Spring 1989 with a commercial set in New York City. The Audi Coupe 'tested in the Arctic and the Sahara' gets its toughest initiation on the 'world's meanest streets', the urban wasteland of pothole-pocked rubbish-strewn inner Manhattan. The car's technical prowess is displayed as the car ducks and weaves its way through the armies of Manhattan's dispossessed, its underclass of beggars who try to earn a living washing the windscreens of cars while they wait at red lights (privatised 'sponging' that works as a threatening perversion of enterprise culture). All these things serve only to test the car's capacity to steer, brake and accelerate around them, leaving New York City's urban flotsam standing, mouthing dispossessed profanities.

The second half of the commercial takes us a notch upmarket. The driver has a valet from the restaurant he is visiting drive the car away to be parked, only for us to see the uniformed prole so seduced by his taste of the high life that he flees New York in it. It's a truism worthy of Tom Wolfe that while you can protect yourself from the envy of the really downtrodden, you'll always be vulnerable to the serving classes, but it's worth it if only for the vindication these peccadillos offer for life's larger truths – like 'Vorsprung durch Technik'. In a sense the 80s commercial had no further to go. The 'Bonfire of the Vanities' fantasy it traded on, beautiful foreign car as emblem for and shield against our most pernicious image of urban iniquity, flaunts it all.

But between Spring 1989 and October 1989, when the next Audi commercial hit our screens, something had changed, and if the advertisers were to be believed, changed utterly. Crudely, it was the six months in which green added values began to make their presence felt. Nappies, batteries, unleaded petrol and CFCs in aerosols all got implicated in the first stage of what looked like becoming a consumer revolution.

These ecological issues were at the sharp end of what ideologues in the advertising industry were starting to call 'usism'. At their most literal the campaigns dealing with aerosols and nappies offered straightforward new product information. CFCs and dioxins in nappies were the two villains in a gathering story of the planet's impending poisoning. Nappy manufacturers removed chlorine, battery manufacturers removed cadmium, aerosols dropped their CFCs and petrol shed its lead. This looked like presaging a new consumer awareness, although, apart from nappies (whose proximity to babies makes them particularly vulnerable to consumer concern), they were the results of legislation rather than consumer lobbying.

But taken together they signalled a new appetite for change; it seemed that simply dropping a chemical meant making a gratifying gesture of solidarity with an increasingly distressed planet and still holding onto product performance. And the marketing gurus were quick to extrapolate a larger shift behind all this –

one that by embracing the planet was perhaps trying to become less egotistical:

> But now, as we approach the 1990s, there is a clear shift away from . . . individualistic (and narcissistic) lifestyle to a much more collective attitude. . . . In a world which is constantly changing and constantly being affected by the ravages of pollution, environmental decay, the AIDS virus, consumer overload and ever-expanding choice, the need for group responsibility and group caring is fast becoming less easy to sidestep . . .[15]

With years of eco-panic now gelling into a coherent and urgent sense of consumer disquiet, the summer of 1989 genuinely witnessed the media turning a conceptual corner. And the marketers sought to understand where this left them, especially those manufacturing environmentally unfriendly products. The message coming from the ad agencies was, don't panic, there's too much to be gained from taking it seriously:

> If you happen to command a large consumer franchise, your feelings about the Green Tidal Wave probably lie in a range from Mild Apprehension to Outright Panic. . . . This paper seeks to present and justify a specific point-of-view on 'Green-ism'; essentially, that every manufacturer should – must – approach the issues in a positive frame of mind, and that there is every reason to do so.[16]

The green lobbyists were just as quick to spell it out to the advertisers – their time was up. The culture of more more more was bankrupt, and for once it all started to seem less and less an empty threat.

But the escape clause to all these predictions of zero-growth economies, and consumerism turned anathema was implicit in all that 80s advertising had been about. The development of added-value-based marketing made advertisers more and more adept at absorbing and using intangible values. And the advent of green consciousness was only in one sense a threat. The green consumer was very much an opportunity.

Green consumers, whether confused, stubborn, born-again zealots or yuppie faddists, all have in common a preoccupation with quality, not just in the product, but in the values associated with the product. The environment quickly became a new anthology of added values. The more prescient marketers saw in green consumerism a happy identity with upmarket consumerism; less is more means both anti-consumerism and paradoxically quality consumerism. The advantages of the latter include among others, higher margins. So the ads have now embraced the new piety with gusto.

The petrol retailers went rural; yards of nature footage got snapped up and pumped out as a beguiling correlative to the petrol that no one actually wanted before the Chancellor reduced the duty on it. Tesco became the 'greener grocer' by virtue of labelling and stocking less ecologically pernicious household cleaning products, and products everywhere became kinder to the environment, better for the planet, ecologically healthy, gentler to nature. Imagery of science and nature turned turtle. Silkience shampoo cut out of their commercial the figure of the white coated scientist because research linked him in the consumer's mind with Chernobyl. Nature became something we were kind to rather than something advertisers had invented as being kind to us.

And Audi took the plunge more pretentiouly than anyone with a commercial called, mock portentously, 'In the nick of time'. In this ad, urban wasteland gives over to a Eurosomething eco-wonderland. Instead of prowling the streets in search of an expensive restaurant, the ad's protagonist is on the most important family mission for new man to be embarked upon, the dash to the maternity ward. Sweeping up his older son and pirouetting past revolving leitmotifs of zoescopes and carousels, the car breaks the most important convention of car advertising, that the cars we see arrowing their way down Northumbrian roads and round quarries are never on their way anywhere, they are simply exhibiting the platonic ideal of carness that real journeys merely compromise.

And in so doing it became a metaphor for Audi's own audacious bid to hijack the 90s – this is a journey towards a repudiation of everything we thought consumerism was about. This is advertising participating in its own demise, acknowledging that we buy things for reasons bigger than those of mere consumerism. While you might argue that so exemplary a new man might actually have taken the trouble to be at the birth itself, there is no doubt that we are being plugged into new values, wonderment, heart and mind coalescing in taking the world into a new generation.

Forfeiting Geoffrey Palmers arch and plummy cadences is one thing, but to replace one of 80s advertising's most seminal tones of voice with a woman's (albeit cold and steely) emphasises the ad's desire to be seen as a rite of passage from one era of advertising to another. The Greed is Good axiom of 80s advertising became Green is Good at its most clinically aspirational.

HARD TIMES

The 80s brilliantly exploited the link between commerce and a new ethic of self, but it is a link whose heyday is arguably over. There is a sense of come-uppance in the air, as though the price we have to pay for the 80s is now becoming all too clear:

> *SPRING 1988*: the retail boom is at its height and the yob and the yuppie are icons of the new materialism. Harry Enfield's bragging London plasterer, Loadsamoney, is working-class affluence personified . . . his upmarket soul-mate, the yuppie, is hero and heroine of the style manuals and financial markets. A mythical creature of the boom – part agent, part victim – with a lifestyle ruthlessly dedicated to consuming.
> *AUTUMN 1989*: falling house prices and a sales slump in the shops; the symbolic failure of retailing's NEXT and advertising's Saatchi and Saatchi. Suddenly Loads is very much last year's hero. . . . Like all good things, the boom is running out of steam.[17]

But if environmentalism posed one challenge to the confidence of 80s advertising, then it was as nothing compared to the gloom and despair that descended on adland during 1990. Having survived previous recessions pretty well, it came as something of a blow to discover that this time, advertising was not going to be so lucky. Job losses have mounted, share prices for the by now large number of publicly quoted companies, plummeted. Even WPP, the company everyone had hailed as the one that would show Saatchis how really to take the world by storm, took hard blows below its water-line. As the recession bit, the stock market started to rethink the emphasis it had placed on companies which spend large amounts of money advertising high-premium consumer desirables. All those things that had contributed to advertising's spectacular success in the 80s started to unravel, and the headlines in *Campaign* became gloomier and gloomier. Production budgets, agency commissions, salaries, perks – all the material trappings of a boom industry were now in distinct jeopardy.

But the darkest cloud of all, even darker than the prospects of more, intrusive legislation from the EEC (tobacco advertising bans for one), and the fragmentation of our (up till now) coherent television systems, is the possibility of a watershed in people's attitudes. Has the quality of life question left advertising behind? Are we about to see an anti-consumer backlash?

Brand advertising enjoyed a different status in Britain than it did in other European countries. In Germany, for example, although the magazines are bursting with ads, there is a profound difference in how advertising is regarded from how it is here. On German television the advertising is restricted to long 'ghettos' between the programmes. They are announced ('Werbung') and run for upwards of eight minutes at a trot. And in between each ad, the television networks run short animated stings, clearly in an attempt to lubricate the ads for that small minority of people who didn't take the ample hint and leave their living rooms in order to put on the kettle. German commercials seem extremely perfunctory, compared with British commercials. It is obvious that they simply do not enjoy anything like the cultural prestige they do here. Curiously, the ads do not communicate a sense that this is a culture in which quality consumerism is so central a preoccupation; it's lucky for Europe's most powerful economy that they don't make cars like their ads.

In other words, Germans do not look to the commercials to teach them their consumer preferences. In this country, however, advertising in the 80s was a radical force, because British culture was not previously accustomed to the highest standards of design and construction in cars, clothes or furniture. In German, French and Italian cultures, they did not need advertising to be radical, because they already knew what to expect from food, design and engineering.

British advertising developed not just because ours was a culture that habitually produced some of the world's best pop music and television, but because until the 80s, our experience of consumerism was relatively restricted to those two areas. The new worlds of European consumerism (cars, lagers, clothes) became available over a relatively concentrated period of time. These formed the cutting edge for a new appreciation of what the market had to offer, and it was advertising that delivered it. Agencies like Saatchis and BBH showed us just how radical advertising could be; BBH at the level of imagery, and Saatchis at the level of what jobs advertising felt itself entitled to do. BBH left us with feeling that advertising could produce popular culture sublimes as powerful as anything pop or television could – while Saatchis left us thinking that just about every job in the public sphere was essentially an advertising one. In short, advertising was used by consumers as part of their social agenda, setting cues to lifestyle, innovation and self-expression. But the educative potential of advertising as a whole must be finite. And when we have learnt from advertising all we want to learn about the consumer agenda in general, then it is plausible that advertising will revert to specific product information, the role it has in other cultures.

That is why it now seems rather easier to speculate that the era of branding by advertising is over. While branding still remains one of the key business disciplines of the 90s, there are challenges. The first is from those who argue a shift in consumer preference away from what is merely lifestyle accoutrement. And then there are those, like American marketing guru Stan Rapp, who argue that we are entering the era of direct marketing, where computer databases and personalised media will obviate the need for advertising in the media.

It seems difficult to believe that the watershed in our attitudes to consumerism heralded at the end of the 70s will be very easily reversed; people aren't going to wake up not wanting things any more. But cause for concern in advertising circles is the fact that in Britain – unlike in Germany, France or Italy – our experiment with quality consumerism was an image-led thing. This makes it more vulnerable to a cultural backlash than it would be had it been created by something more substantial. The danger for advertising now, post-Thatcher, is that the old austerity and mediocrity that characterised the British marketplace of the 70s, will re-emerge, vindicating itself as a rejection of all that trashy style-culture.

One answer to this dilemma is to expand on the added values

at the heart of our commercials. Nationwide Building Society, for example. produced a lavish commercial through Leagas Delaney in November 1990, in which a woman ruminates on how her life's priorities have changed from, rather Karen Blixen-like, wanting to 'travel to Africa' (under black and white footage of Egyptian fishermen passed overhead by an old Catalina seaplane), to marriage (a large Jewish wedding), to family ('I became family') and caring about her 'daughter's right to be, to achieve'. All this as preamble to the proposition that opening a savings account in a building society is a way of securing life-enhancing dreams. But the trouble with this (apart from bathos) is that advertising that teaches us consumerism's larger lessons will leave (mere) products behind. The danger (for the advertiser anyway) is that we will buy the advertising and *not* the products.

After all, seeing an ad for trainers in which an actor runs exhilaratedly through a beautiful park prompts two reactions; either, a desire for the individual gratification of buying the product; or, a collective recognition that good urban parks are a desirable thing, and why aren't there any? Trainer manufacturers are hardly likely to invest their advertising dollars stirring up social discontent that wants *social* remedies.

But one thing remains abundantly clear; advertising agencies have spent the last ten years investing in getting as close to contemporary culture as it can, and as values threaten to evolve in new directions, then that preoccupation can only get more intense. But it is a preoccupation that advertisers paradoxically share with their bitterest opponents, a fact which ensures that 'culture' remains the site of advertising's bitterest contest.

3

MARTIAN POSTCARDS
Culture as critique

Craig Raine's poem 'A martian sends a postcard home' deftly exploits the role played by culture in our knowledge of the world. His 'martian', or cultural outsider, explores the world stripped of its (obfuscatory) familiarity, 'defamiliarised' as the formalists say, returned to us clothed in wonder, as the romantic would put it:

> Caxtons are mechanical birds with many wings
> and some are treasured for their markings
>
> they cause the eyes to melt
> or the body to shriek without pain.
>
> Only the young are allowed to suffer
> openly. Adults go to a punishment room
>
> with water and nothing to eat.
> they lock the door and suffer the noises
>
> alone. No one is exempt
> and everyone's pain has a different smell[1]

And if objects as prosaic as books or lavatories present these sorts of possibilities, just imagine how much more indispensable cultural context is, to more complex areas of our experience. Imagine trying to describe anorexia to your martian. How do you describe a psychological/physiological syndrome without at the same time accounting for why only some people seem prone to it, why only in the last couple of decades, and why different periods in history and different societies have such seemingly specific types of psychological problem (like hysteria in the nineteenth century)?

And what about AIDS, where we are all of us in a position as vulnerable to misunderstanding as our ficional extra-terrestial. Here the boundaries between scientific and cultural criteria are horrendously fraught, the site for perhaps the most important and far-reaching piece of personal and social re-evaluation yet undertaken by contemporary society. Never mind just getting the *medicine* right, it's coming to terms with the social consequences, in lifestyle, language, our whole conception of relationships, disease, 'us' and 'them', plague years, personal integrity, sex and death, that is proving just as hard.

The mere enumeration of some of the ways AIDS has been characterised suggests its enormous power to generate meanings:

1 An irreversible, untreatable and invariably fatal infectious disease which threatens to wipe out the whole world.
2 A creation of the media which has sensationalised a minor health problem for its own profit and pleasure.
3 A creation of the state to legitimise widespread invasion of peoples' lives and sexual practices.
4 A gay plague, probably emanating from San Francisco.
5 A condemnation to celibacy or death.
6 An imperialist plot to destroy the Third World.
7 A fascist plot to destroy homosexuals.
8 A capitalist plot to create new market for pharmaceutical products.
9 A Soviet plot to destroy capitalists.
10 The result of moral decay and a major force destroying the Boy Scouts.
11 America's Ideal Death Sentence.
12 An infectious agent that has suppressed our immunity from guilt.
13 A sign that the end of the world is at hand.
14 God's punishment for our weaknesses.
15 God's test for our strengths.
16 The price paid for the 60s.
17 The price paid for anal intercourse.
18 An absolutely unique disease for which there is no precedent.
19 Just another venereal disease.
20 Science fiction.
21 Stranger than science fiction.

22 A terrible and expensive way to die.[2]

No wonder every new campaign from the Health Education Council is heralded by such agonising about what is being said about whom to whom.

Over the last thirty years or so there has arisen a new interest in the role played by our material circumstances in such things as how our minds develop, how we learn to communicate, and, even, how it is that we establish a sense of who we are – things that used to seem so distinct from notions of context. Philosophy, psychology, literary studies and sociology all have – and now readily acknowledge – their shared frontiers which meet in culture. A good example of this is a 1987 social psychology book called *Toys as Culture*,[3] which tries to provide as full a description as possible of the place enjoyed by toys, as artefacts, by our children in our society. The book breaks down into four sections; family, technology and science, education, and lastly, the marketplace. To understand toys in culture is to see them from a variety of different perspectives, indeed, to use them as a metaphor for the culture from which they take their meaning: 'we enter a culture through one tiny vantage-point, one small peephole, and much else comes into view.'[4] And advertising too has started to take note. Because advertising sells artefacts to people as social values, it more than any other cultural industry has a vested interest in understanding and *working* the relationship between people, artefacts and society.

To study culture is to study meaning – where it comes from and what role it plays in our lives. Or, one could put it the other way round and say that today, to study meaning, in whatever form (psychological, economic, historical, semantic), is necessarily, at some level, to be involved in a consideration of culture. But this is no static academic exercise – just witness the energy with which both left and right have always fought for domination of the word, evidence of how they each, in their different ways, conceive the relationship between people, artefacts and society (the bottom line, after all, of socialism and capitalism).

MY CULTURE – RIGHT OR LEFT

On the right, writers from Coleridge to Roger Scruton and Peregrine Worsthorne have used the concept as a stalking-horse for the spiritual health of the nation, a way of sounding off about hierarchy and nationalism, using it as the formaldehyde for the decaying tissue of shared history (to shunt the metaphor on a bit). Their 'culture' is the guarantor of national identity, of standards and values. It is the chauvinism of Shakespearian pentameters and the wistful self-absorption of Elgar's melancholic chords:

> (Culture) includes all the characteristic activities and interests of a people: Derby Day, Henley Regatta, Cowes, the 12th August, a cup final, the dog races, boiled cabbage cut into sections, beetroot in vinegar, nineteenth-century Gothic and the music of Elgar.[5]

Thus the worthiest old Possum of them all, T.S. Eliot in his *Notes Towards the Definition of Culture*. This is a new way of summing up a national character or spirit of a nation, or call it what you will. Instead of talking about civilisation or society, instead of mustering grandiloquent historical generalisations or reams of social statistics, Eliot embroiders a resonant list of things, all in their way trivial, but capable of conjuring up images of the essential Englishness of English culture. The sureness with which the reader moves from detail to larger picture, and the supposed sense of belonging in doing so, is source for Eliot of immense satisfaction and security. Of course, the longer these traditions take to assume their characteristic shape and their place in our repertoire of 'English' things, the more effective their capacity to represent us to ourselves and to the outside world. And in a much humbler guise, this is the sort of thing a market researcher like Mary Goodyear means when she says on the Channel 4 programme *The Marketing Mix* that advertising gives us a context in which to make sense of our lives, that it is a language of objects forming a safe and familiar universe.

On the left, however, the word 'culture' is used much more combatively, not to celebrate the status quo, but to query it. The concern here is to see how it is we know our 'place' in the world, which is as much about inequality and hierarchy as it is about time and space or symbolic allegiance to common knowledge. In a recent *Observer* article, for example, Neal Ascherson gave a spirited and cutting apologia for his approach to journalism: 'the guiding thread I have tried to run through all these columns is an approach which is not "cultured" or "cultivated" but *cultural*.'[6] 'Culture' in this sense has a breadth and moment to it that the more precious notions of the cultured or cultivated do not. To show what this entails, he drives home a further distinction between styles of Anglo-American and central European journalism:

> But in central Europe, there grew up long ago a different sort of column, usually known by the French word *feuilleton*. The best way to describe this form is to say that it regards all social phenomena, including politics, as something to be reviewed like a play. When a Minister makes a speech the *feuilleton* writer does not ask how the speech affects the next election but what it reveals about the sort of society we live in and the myths on which that society rests. A new public building, a quarrel among historians, a royal procession, the installing of a new police computer – these are the right starting-points for an investigation of a national and political culture.[7]

The issue is one of where you *locate* the cultural in relation to the political. The traditional use of the word denotes a realm of artefacts and ideas outside the *ad hoc* contingencies of the mundane. But Ascherson's 'feuilleton' (a branch of what has been called 'cultural politics' or 'cultural materialism'), is designed to contest various assumptions traditionally regarded as dear to the right, namely the ability of forces like 'tradition' or the 'aesthetic' to lift cultural phenomena beyond the jurisdiction of politics. But while it is the left that has been particularly energetic in examining concepts that have previously been regarded as 'self-evident', like 'the family', or 'beauty', or 'Englishness', and been reviled by the right for doing so, nevertheless the right are no strangers to the idea that social institutions have powerful symbolic (and therefore, political) dimensions that need vigorous assertion and defending.

Mac Daly, for instance, cites the House of Lords debate on the infamous Clause 28 of the Local Government Bill (on the 'promotion of homosexuality'), which

> has shown how directly the promotion of literature, for example, is tailored to underwrite certain key notions thought necessary for the maintenance of the present social order – in this case, the notion that normality equals

heterosexuality, and that behaviour which fails to under-write that normality is a threatening deviance which ought to be strictly controlled.[8]

And any last vestige of faith in the idea that the right believes 'culture belongs in a self-regulating realm' is scotched the moment you hear how their Lordships debate such matters as the British Council, or the BBC external service. It is chastening to be reminded just how synonymous culture in this sense has always been with political prestige and influence, with military, and latterly, commercial aggrandisement.

CLASHING SYMBOLS

So, both left and right do agree, to varying degrees, and for very different reasons, that it is in the realm of 'culture' where many of the most politically important symbolic battles get fought. 'Culture' can therefore no longer be regarded as autonomous. Instead, 'culture' is where society locates its enabling values. This has led to some interesting clashes of cultural interpretation, 'contested' symbols pulled left and right. For example, the old red telephone box. This is Roger Scruton's description of it:

> In every English village there is one object that stands out as the prime focus of the traveller's attention, and the fitting representative of the stable government beneath whose mantle he journeys. This object is the telephone booth: a cast-iron structure in imperial red; classical in outline, but with an interesting suggestion of Bauhaus naughtiness in its fenestration . . . the door, divided into three parts by its mullions, has a brass handle, set into the cast iron frame, and above the cornice, a little crown is embossed, symbol of national identity, and promise of enduring government. So suitable has this form proved to the streets, countryside and villages of England that it now appears on Christmas-card snow scenes, beside the Gothic spire, the gabled cottage and the five-barred gate.[9]

Scruton doesn't miss a trick. The process by which the telephone box became this rich a symbol, in addition to design and con-struction, is itself a model for all cultural signification. It has the royal seal 'embossed' onto it, a logo of royal assent, authorising us to see in it a microcosm of 'national identity' and 'enduring government'. But in case that sounds too coercive and crude a thing for a monarch to do, like Caligula stamping his face monomaniacally on all the statues of Rome, it is aided and abetted by a more popular process, 'So suitable has this form proved to the streets and villages of England' . . . that we have all, unconsciously, elevated the humble kiosk into a national totem, but one that far from propelling us into the tangible here and now, abandons us to an England that is explicitly one of artifice (and cliché) the 'Christmas-card snow scenes, beside the Gothic spire, the gabled cottage and the five-barred gate'.

In no way could you describe this as a disinterested piece of cultural analysis. It tells us more about Scruton's own agenda than it does about 'England' (or the 'England' that stands outside his agenda). Tom Nairn contrasts Scruton's paean to 'Ukania' with this:

> readers will note one or two . . . features missing from this impassioned plea. There were (for example) never enough of the old booths. Though easily findable by the village green, they were rare in the more deprived urban areas where – obviously – most likely users were located. Disguised by mumblings about cost and maintenance, this corresponded in fact to the highest spiritual strategy of Christmas-card and *Salisbury Review* Britain: it simply did not do to provide the sub-elite with over-easy, cheap, re-liable communication. No, the spirit of 'class' was best maintained by a sense of solidly Crown-bestowed privilege. And where better to ram this message home than in the sensitive nodes of a public communication-system – the exposed nervous system of the lower orders . . . the mess-age of the little embossed Crown-boxes is profoundly different: as well as stability, longevity, loyalty, decency, what they proclaimed was something like – '*You* belong to the class for which this sort of thing is good enough; but you may nevertheless, if lucky and in possession of the correct H.M. coinage, make a call here'.[10]

This is an alternative agenda; one that situates itself on the housing estate, not the village; among the deprived, rather than the privileged; and one suspicious of the *status quo*, and its proclivity to sustain not 'continuity' but inequality.

Or take the filofax. In 1988, Arthur Scargill made a telling symbolic protest at the Labour Party Conference, when he brandished a filofax in one hand, and a party card in the other. The gesture was not hard to decipher. He was implying that the Labour Party was betraying its roots, by capitulating to all that the filofax epitomised, a yuppie politics of champagne socialism. The two things, the filofax (because of its guilt by association) and the Party card (because of its history) were incompatible. This was a warning against modernity and consumerism from someone committed to Labour Party tradition. But, argue Bea Campbell and Wendy Wheeler, the gesture goes both ways. The filofax's combination of diary, notebook and address book, with space for all sorts of other information is not just a symbol of 'loadsamoney ideology', the party card of 80s 'me' generation, but a commodity that helps you organise your public life:

> that's the point about the filofax – it signifies a public rather than a private life, a social rather than a solely private citizen. More important it signifies a social citizen whose life is not serviced by subordinates. Like Arthur Scargill, all of us are busy, participating people. The boundaries between our private and public, professional and political worlds, are blurred. But most important of all, unlike Arthur Scargill we have to do it all ourselves. We are not serviced by an army of secretaries and wives who arrange our diaries and dinners, our private and public responsibilities. This is where not only class but sex comes in: this personal organiser is only a commodity, it is not a hierarchy of social and sexual relations based on service and subordination. . . . It is this nexus of sex and power which is masked by Scargill's scorn for the filofax.[11]

That scorn is reinforced by a general scorn for consuming as a female domain. It has echoes in the condescension produced by the left for all the icons and machines of the consumerist age, the fridge, the washing machine, the television:

> Within a male-dominated Left there has been a certain purism which has set itself against consumption, or if not consumption itself, then against a self-aware politics of consumption. . . . Arthur is well known to have been the proud owner of Jaguars. We can understand his passion

for exquisite engineering, his need, as a travelling man, for maximum comfort, and his belief that nothing is too good for the workers. But compared with the front loading washing machine, the telephone, or, dare we say it, the filofax, the Jaguar is irredeemably both phallic and conspicuous consumption. . . . Clearly there are Real Men's Commodities which are excluded from that certain puritanism. . . . Maybe it's because filofaxes – unlike Jaguars or secretaries – are about personal *responsibility*, rather than personal *power*.[12]

Just as interesting as these specific cultural debates about what particular commodities mean, is the sense that arguing about culture is inevitably to argue about such potent 'discourses' of social experience as class, gender and race. Both left and right use culture in order to consolidate their differing views on these categories; both are cultural materialists for precisely this reason. 'Culture' is never a static concept, but a forum for the bitterest political and ideological contests.

ROLAND BARTHES

Central to this sort of special pleading are the notions of myth and power. It is therefore no coincidence that Neal Ascherson should point to the French for an example of what engaged citizenry might look like, because the outstanding luminary in this tradition, at least in the last twenty years, was the late Roland Barthes. He taught us to read culture by teaching us to do two things; to 'read' objects as though they were 'texts', and 'texts' as *mythologies*, patterns of belief whose individual components rarely ever get probed or justified. More than anyone he broke down the mechanisms of iconic shorthand, the associations and language of images and stereotypes:

A garment, an automobile, a dish of cooked food, a film, a piece of music, an advertising image, – all are signs. When I walk through the streets – or through life – and encounter these objects, I apply to all of them, if need be without realising it, one and the same activity, which is that of a certain reading. . . . Modern man . . . reads . . . images, gestures, behaviours: the car tells me the social status of the owner, this garment tells me quite precisely the degree of its owner's conformism, or eccentricity, this aperitif . . . reveals my hostess' lifestyle. Even with regard to the written text, we are constantly given a second message to read between the lines of the first; if I read the headline: Paul VI Afraid, this also means *if you read this, you will find out why*.[13]

But what made this sort of critical virtuosity more than just a fashionable attention to detail was its growing preoccupation with the workings of power and ideology. In his vastly influential book *Mythologies*, Barthes prises out of everyday things complex social narratives, as microcosms for how our culture works. For instance, the language of soap-powder commercials: 'to say that Omo cleans in depth is to assume that linen is deep, which no one had previously thought . . . as for foam, it is well-known that it signifies luxury . . . foam can even be the sign of a certain spirituality.'[14]

Or, about 'Blue Guides':

> For the 'Blue Guide', men exist only as 'types'. In Spain, for instance, the Basque is an adventurous sailor, the Levantine a light-hearted gardener. . . . The ethnic reality of Spain is thus reduced to a vast classical ballet, a nice neat commedia dell'arte, whose improbable typology serves to mask the real spectacle of conditions, classes and professions.[15]

This then is the world that we used to divide so categorically between *things* and *words*, but which has now collapsed (or been liberated, depending on how you look at it) into a galaxy of *signs*, some linguistic, some not. The thing about signs is their artificiality, both in experience and in representations of experience. This has radically influenced the major subjects of social study, history, social relations, linguistics and psychology (we have already seen its impact on politics). Once recast as sign-systems, as story, myth, game or text, they take on a completely new guise.

To try to understand the meaning of experience is, it would seem, to ask a certain type of question. In the Middle Ages it was a religious or a theological question. Nearer our own time it became a scientific one, while today, I would argue that it is a question of culture in its largest sense. From facial expressions to magazine horoscopes, from 'A' Level practical criticism to

poring over love-letters; we are all actively and passively involved in negotiating with, and through, shared knowledge.

But what is perhaps new is the stress that we place on the
conditions that make meaning possible. To quiz the nature of
experience requires, in the wake of Barthes, greater self-
consciousness than it did before. In other words, the question
has become *meta-critical*, that is, it takes equal account not just of
the substance of its inquiry, but the terms in which the inquiry is
carried out. In practical terms, this has meant paying far greater
attention to the *medium*, because:

> ours is a mediacratic age. Media do not report reality, they
> make it. 'Events' which do not constitute reality take shape
> through the media; some have none other but media exist-
> ence. And media-created reality is essentially dramatic; it
> consists of repeatable . . . episodes . . . it exists in a frame
> . . . which protects it from tests other than internal
> plausibility.[16]

Two recent examples of this are biographies of high profile
media giants, personalities inextricable from the electronic,
celluloid industries which created and sustained them, and at
odds with an inner reality (if such there actually is) in ways at
once personally sad, and globally monstrous. The first, a biography of Marilyn Monroe, is, according to the blurb:

> much more than a biography . . . it explores the ways in
> which her life was interwoven with the images that were
> constructed of her and the myths that were spun around
> her. . . . [The author] analyses the writings of the (mostly
> male) biographers who, he argues, represent Monroe as
> other than she was or wanted to be.[17]

The other book is a biography of Ronald Reagan, by Garry
Wills, called *Reagan's America*,[18] which was reviewed by Peter
Conrad:

> The man is himself a myth, and that – as Wills deconstructs
> him – means a fiction, a fraud, an amiable emptiness. But a
> vitally necessary one on which America depends for its
> sense of invented identity. . . . Reagan, reducible to what
> Barthes calls a 'bundle of meanings', is made from such

contradictions. . . . In his person he embodies the American myth.[19]

At the base then of this new critical dispensation, is the sense that the things and values we live by, are, in a special way, man-made – and all too often just that, *man*-made. Human situations yield up their real significance only when viewed formally, that is, in terms of the conventions of genres. Clifford Geertz, the American anthropologist, argues that the analogies with which we explain the unfamiliar are now derived not from the physical sciences, as they used to be, but 'more and more from the contrivances of cultural performance . . . from theater, painting, grammar, literature, law, play'.[20] All of these cast creative light on to aspects and patterns of cultural behaviour, and show us that both human life and attempts to describe it share similar generic roots, indeed, can no longer really be distinguished in the old positivist way. This will come as no great surprise to the advertiser who has for years quite unselfconsciously dramatised products in scenarios as life-strategies, social props and borrowed meanings.

All this puts culture at the head of a long list of things people throughout history have asserted as the context for knowledge. It used to be religion, in the light of which all other questions made sense. With the rise of the scientific method, and its complement in a recognisably modern preoccupation with how the mind knows things, God got displaced for a less transcendent power, that of human deductive reason, for the first time equal to the task of mathematically understanding the universe. This view reached its apogee in Kant's categorical basis of human understanding.

But the sufficiency of mental logic came under attack from those who, at the turn of this century, argued for due acknowledgement to be made to the role played by language, the most basic medium of awareness:

> most of our encounters with the world are not . . . direct encounters . . . the 'realities' of the society and the social life are themselves most often products of linguistic use as represented in such speech acts as promising, abjuring, legitimising, christening, and so on.[21]

This means, if taken to its logical conclusion, that no description of the world can be complete which does not at the same time take into account the medium used. And this is most true of language, with its unique capacity to:

> create and stipulate realities of its own, its *constitutiveness*. We create realities by warning, encouraging, by dubbing with titles, by naming, and by the manner in which words invite us to create 'realities' in the world to correspond with them . . . for example, the law, gross national product, anti-matter, the renaissance . . . converting our mental processes into products and endowing them with a reality in some world. . . . The constitutiveness of language as more than one anthropologist has insisted, creates and transmits culture and locates our place in it.[22]

Language is that without which experience would not exist – perhaps even, could not exist. Out of language we create text, and out of text, reality, and not, as the old literalists used to think, the other way round. Actually, this is not a new idea, merely one in a new shape:

> The most general form of this new paradigm or encyclope-diac model is the notion that reality is a text, an elaborate system of codes for decipherment . . . the Middle Ages regarded reality as itself a text, or more precisely, as two texts – the Book of Nature and the Book of Divine Revelation – both written by the same author (God) to convey his message in two different media. Contemporary pantextualism, similarly, has two books, one of science, and one of culture, both written by the same author (the human race).[23]

This shift is best seen as the move from the traditional concern of philosophers with epistemology – how it is we know things – to a concern with 'the broader question of how we come to endow experience with meaning – which is the question that preoccupies the poet and the story-teller'.[24] And not just 'poets and story-tellers' – or even just advertisers – but every one of us, because if this view of culture has anything to tell us, then it is that

> it is through stories that we understand and live in the world. As Nigel Harris points out, even the question, 'What

is a chair?' makes sense only within a system of meanings; otherwise a chair might be a bundle of sticks for making a fire, or beating an enemy about the head with.[25]

And as would quickly become obvious were we to write many more postcards back to Mars, 'There are stories everywhere' –

in speech and behaviour as well as formal narrative. In the media, they are not just in the articles and programmes labelled 'fiction' and 'drama', but in those on current affairs, sport, party politics, science, religion, the arts, and those specified as education and for children. They are in the advertisements.[26]

Interpreting these stories for us are a new generation of journalists and writers, indeed, what is tantamount to a new culture industry. New magazines sprang up, dedicated to culture and its trappings (the so-called, 'style' press, like *iD* or *The Face*, distinctly more Holland Park than the ponderous old philosophers. These glitzy emcees of life in the fast-stream all take their cue, some more explicitly than others, from Barthes – suave Peter York, wistful Gilbert Adair, grumpy Paul Morley in particular. They found their habitat in the new style of media pages that began to abound in our increasingly self-conscious fashion(able) press, as well as the explosion in magazine television programmes, from *The Media Show*, to *The Late Show*, to *Without Walls*, with even the old battle horses like *The South Bank Show* and *Omnibus* capitulating to doing whole programmes on popular culture. There are rich pickings for this sort of observation, because advertising in particular has flooded the world with opportunities to signify. Ever since wearing trainers *meant* 'wearing trainers', for example, there were 1500 words of copy, and a nine-minute item on *The Late Show* to be screwed out of the fact.

Academics too turned their hand to this sort of pop culture attudinising. Paul Fussell, the author of the masterpiece of critical history *The Great War and Modern Memory*, a haunting and unique account of the culture of World War I and those who fought in it, later published *Class: Style and Status in the USA*, a book that took the mechanisms of advertising as its central methodology:

All proles have a high respect for advertising and brand names. By knowing about such things you can display smartness and up-to-dateness, as well as associate yourself with the success of the products advertised. Drinking an identifiable bottle of Coca-Cola outside on a hot day is not just drinking a Coke: it's participating in a paradigm deemed desirable not just by your betters – the Coca Cola company – but by your neighbors, who perceive you are doing something all-American and super-wonderful.[27]

But what has made this more than just up-market journalism was the move beyond 'language' to 'power' as the key element of cultural phenomena. There is nothing new about the view that society uses seemingly apolitical forms to legitimise itself; 'hegemonic systems' are as old as history itself:

> Historically, the idea that religion was invented by the powerful to keep other men in subjection is untrue. Religion, like any other ideological formation, had an inception much more complex. Nevertheless, that it has historically served to legitimate systems of power and subjection is indubitable, and what was happening in the Elizabethan period was of the utmost historical importance: religion was increasingly being perceived in terms of such legitimation. . . . [And] what Machiavelli did for religion, Montaigne did . . . for law: 'Lawes are . . . maintained in credit, not because they are essentially just, but because they are lawes. It is the mystical foundation of their authority; they have none other.'[28]

At the heart of this view, is the concept of history as artifice – the sense that the values and structures with which we live are produced *by* the status quo, rather than merely reflected in it. After all, when we recall how staged were the great show-trials of history and how prestigiously we now view political PR, we can see just how malleable to political expedient the great humanist ideals have always been. Perhaps the surprise is not that this should be so, but that something, in the last hundred years or so, has made us forget it.

And what historians are doing to the cultures of the past, critics, post Marx, are doing to the 'discourses' of the present, with particular vehemence and edge in the case of feminism, and its critique of how we conceive social relations. Gloria Steinem has used the stigma attached to menstruation to show the pivotal role myths play in the oppression of one group by another. None of our stereotypical views, it would appear, emerge from things demonstrably *there*, but from the need to give hierarchy the dignity of psychological irresistibility:

> So what would happen if suddenly, magically, men could menstruate and women could not? Clearly, menstruation would become an enviable, boast-worthy, masculine event. . . . Sanitary supplies would be federally funded and free. Of course some men would still pay for the prestige of such commercial brands as Paul Newman tampons, Muhammad Ali's Rope-a-Dope pads. . . . 'for those light bachelor days' . . . Generals, right-wing politicians and religious funda-mentalists would cite menstruation (*men*-struation) as proof that only men could serve God and country in combat ('You have to give blood to take blood').[29]

And so on and so on, a whole panoply of arbitrary justifications and post-rationalisations for a deeply unjust state of affairs, one in which surprisingly she sees advertising playing a powerful part. Actually, this style of counter-intuitive polemic is also a source for some very good ads. Saatchis first hit the headlines with its family planning ad, with the picture of a pregnant man whose rhetorical question ('Suppose it was you that got pregnant?') worked in much the same way. There is little so effective as the turning on its head of dearly held 'natural' views, which, once inverted, make us wince at just how cruelly relative are the mechanisms of prejudice, just how ingenious and self-serving the creation of consensus and 'self-evidentness'. It shows us that in all the important ways, *we* are the martians in our own homes, victims of what is sometimes called 'Orwell's paradox' – the odd business of seeming to know so little in the face of such over-whelming evidence.

So, neither language nor history is disinterested. This fact has altered how it is we read things. Traditionally, 'reading' involved one of two activities; saying interesting things about a text or a picture, or trying to see what it was that the text or picture said about the world. Semiotics and cultural theory have, however, made this one and the same thing. The old way of reading used to make its links between how a text or picture worked, and a larger sense of what it said about life, in terms of something called 'lived experience'. Today the emphasis has moved; what is relevant to us is what *in terms of ideology* things say about the world. If reality is story-bound, then *stories* are not the frivolous contrivances we used to think. Theirs is the very real business of order and authority. Culture is an industry, and its products are signs and stories – but its market is power, power that is everywhere:

> not because it embraces everything but because it comes from everywhere . . . the manifold relations of force that take shape and come into play in the machinery of production, in families, in groups and institutions, are the basis of effects of domination that run through the entire social body.[30]

Images are no longer just pictures, but constructions designed to communicate, and consolidate, ideological 'truths'. Chris Weedon analyses an advert for sportswear in this light. The ad's image is of a white, nuclear family, a man, his wife, a boy and a girl. They are opening presents in front of a Christmas tree. The mother is looking slightly off-camera, holding her smiling daughter on her knee, while the son, football in hand, looks at her; the father, meanwhile, at the back, and taller than they looks the camera straight in the eye:

> At the back of the picture, rising slightly above his wife and children, is the father who symbolically encompasses, protects and controls his family. The son is invested with the promise of his father's power by his position directly in front of his father who confronts the camera straight on. The wife is positioned sideways to the camera. Her body faces inwards towards her family. She holds her daughter closely on her knee in a posture which is as traditionally motherly as the father is fatherly. Patriarchal this image may be, but it is immensely seductive.[31]

This type of analysis breaks down 'cultural' images and texts into their constituent 'discourses', in this case the patriarchal 'discourse' of the nuclear family. Once thus broken down, it is available to be used as part of a particular political agenda, in this case that of

> radical-feminist theory, where the biologically based subordination of women is seen as the fundamental form of

oppression, prior to class or race, (where) . . . the family is identified as the key instrument in the oppression of women through sexual slavery and forced motherhood.[32]

One can dissolve society into a lexicon of cultural signs, but, conversely, one must acknowledge their potent materiality. The more disinterested the appearance of a sign, the more likely it is to be up to its neck in political legitimation. Roland Barthes used as his example the cover of an issue of *Paris-Match*, in which a black soldier salutes the French flag. More than just a picture, it is a powerful endorsement of certain colonialist assumptions prevailing at the time. The language of signs and stories, of texts and images, is therefore intimately bound up in how the State polices culture:

> States, if the pun be forgiven, *state*: the arcane rituals of a court of law, the formulae of royal assent to an Act of Parliament, visits of school inspectors, are all statements. They define, in great detail, acceptable forms and images of social activity and individual and collective identity. Indeed, in this sense the 'State' never stops talking.[33]

It would be a mistake to see culture as *just* a text, or social relations as *just* the 'constitutiveness' of words. Cultures don't just grow like crystals, they get forged into shapes – and not just by any language, but by the language with the power behind it. All language may be 'constitutive', it is just that some aspects of language are more 'constitutive' than others. After all we as individuals owe much of our public social identity to what it is society tells us we are:

> as citizens, voters, taxpayers, ratepayers, jurors, parents, consumers, homeowners, individuals . . . such cultural formations are made to appear as – to quote Herbert Butterfield on the whig interpretation of history – 'part of English life, like our country lanes or our November mists, or our historic inns'.[34]

SOCIAL INFERENCES

So, just as someone telling you that they love you willy-nilly turns you into the beloved (or at least makes you have to play out the role), so any judgement of what is natural, 'part of life', creates a role for the person being addressed in its own light. Advertising does much the same, because it is the language of consumer persuasion, the parameters of consumer culture from which we derive our sense of who we are, indeed, *why* we are. This is the other aspect of statements about culture – in a strange sort of way they create what they set out merely to reflect.

T.S. Eliot's list that I quoted at the beginning of this chapter is a good example of how, in culture, we create an 'us' and a 'them'. His list works precisely because it is a list of English things and the sum total of English 'things' is culture. Our culture is a shared language, a shared sense of meanings, what it is considered natural for a group of people to know and care about.

This of course raises the question of perspective, for just as these things will seem different when looked at by, say, an American, or an aborigine, so they will look different when looked at by different groups *within* a notional, national group. The questions Eliot rather ponderously begs are those of class, race and gender. As Gill Seidel points out:

> That 'culture' for Eliot subsumes a list of activities and interests decidedly white and Christian, and frequently gender- and class-specific into the bargain . . . it reflects the ubiquity of ethnocentrism, racism and sexism in 'our' dominant socio-cultural constructions.[35]

And in those omissions lie the mechanisms of power that Eliot *is* trying to promote.

Statements like Eliot's take their place in larger types of rhetoric – in this case, that of right-wing deliberations on culture, racial integrity and sexual hierarchy. Just because the status quo is richly evocable does not make it less open to critique. So, objects and acts have meanings which in their hypothetical totality represent culture. But within those meanings lie other divisions and patterns discernible to us precisely by looking at how different people make sense of them. Things connote 'Englishness' or 'feminity' or 'working-classness', but this fact only half explains what the concepts 'Englishness', 'feminity' or 'working-classness' mean in their turn.

High heels may signify 'woman', but what does being a woman mean, particularly if high heels are its *sine qua non*? When we recall that high heels are highly impractical, painful shoes, designed to present the female ankle to the male gaze, and that as such they are consistent with large aspects of fashion and images of sexuality, we can see that such things don't passively reflect a concept of feminity already in natural existence, but one that we have constructed, and carved into our repertoire of what it is natural to believe. Signs merely tell us the first half of the story; semiology is a one-way interpretative act. In other words, we still have to ask, what does it mean for these things to mean what they do?

This is a worry well beyond the remit of advertising research, except in the fraught business of trying to avoid offensive imagery or insinuations. At the start of the chapter I talked about a book called *Toys as Culture*, which tried to show from every conceivable angle what toys, in their totality, look like. Although this was an academic study, it is nevertheless similar to the sort of research that the modern advertiser would undertake. In other words, if this book had come out of an ad agency, conspicuous by its absence would have been the fourth part, that of the market-place. The book would have happily shown, for example, that toys are powerfully involved in family relations; they cater for the child's need to explore, through irrationality and novelty, the limits of their experience; they are powerful companions to growth and development; they perform vital educational roles; they involve humanoid projections. From these, the agency would pluck the most relevant and dramatise the toy's added values in terms of it. But it would most certainly not have addressed its own role in making toys what they are, precisely because of its reluctance to relinquish a passive, reflective sense of its relationship to reality.

In each of these considerations there is an answer of sorts to the question 'what does it mean for toys to mean what they do', and one could go on at digressionary length about the mechanisms of family life, of play as psychological therapy or of the growing child's relationship to the world of possibilities and limitations. And there are academic researchers aplenty doing just this. But where that question takes on the most relevance is in the final section, the market-place. It is here where suddenly the stakes become much higher, where there is the possibility of much more serious and contentious answers to why it is toys are made to mean what they do. As soon as it is massively in someone's interests that things seem the way they do, then cultural significance is entirely secondary:

> mainly what the controversy shows is that commercials . . . have a pervasive rather than a decisive effect. Which is to say, few particular commercials necessarily compel all children and all parents to respond with active purchasing, but in general these commercials establish in the minds of parents and children the 'orthodoxy' of what play is all about.[36]

And it is precisely here where the advertiser's public account of the cultural totality of the toy, as social artefact, would, publicly at least, stop short. From the marketing point of view, it would obviously be important to consider, when advertising toys, these different types of connotations, which taken together show how revealing of culture something like 'toys' are. But the one set of connotations not taken into account by the advertising researcher are those of the market-place, or of advertising as *itself* a culture. So what the market understands, and what we understand by the market, are two different views of cultural value. And as soon as something enters the market, and derives from it vital aspects of its social identity, then you know that it's in the grip of forces larger than those of the ebb and flow of cultural whim.

What then does it mean for *advertising* to mean what it does – how would you explain consumerism to your curious martian? I suppose that you would have to get anthropological about it, which is precisely what I would like to do in the next chapter.

4

REASONING THE NEED
Advertising, art and junk

There is a crucial and poignant moment towards the middle of *King Lear* where he makes his famous plea:

> O reason not the need! Our basest beggars
> Are in the poorest thing superfluous.
> Allow not nature more than nature needs –
> Man's life is as cheap as beast's.[1]

This is literature's most explicit injunction to take as central to the human lot all that lies beyond mere necessity. To put it like this, of course, is to shear it from its context, to make too neat an incision into a wound bloody with ambiguity and irony. This is after all, the last-ditch whinge of a man beaten in his own power-game. But the point stands. Mess with symbols by turning them to the wrong sort of account, and life degenerates into rationalist nightmare.

Similarly there is a moment, in that other literary expedition to the essential frontiers of nature and culture, where Robinson Crusoe attudinises on what there remains for him to value once physical needs have been requited:

> But all I could make use of was All that was valuable. I had enough to eat, and to supply my Wants, and, what was all the rest to me? If I kill'd more Flesh than I could eat, the Dog must eat it, or the Vermin. . . . In a Word, The Nature and Experience of things of this World, are no farther good to us, than they are for our Use; and that whatever we may heap up indeed to give others, we enjoy just as much as we can use, and no more.[2]

Not much, it would seem. From a utilitarian point of view, all

118

else is *literally* rubbish, to be thrown to the vermin. And it can happen to people as well as things, the fate that Lear feels has been sealed for him too, transformed by his two older daughters into a piece of metaphorical trash, for which the only fitting thing left for him to do is wrench off his clothes and pity 'poor wretches'.

But Crusoe is wrong of course. Neither his actions, nor those of his author's, nor of his author's culture, remotely endorse this means/end rationality. Indeed they all stand it on its head, giving birth as the book does to the three nascent strands of consumer capitalism that make ironic nonsense of his hymn to physical needs sufficiency – Man Friday, new colonies and the rise of the novel. All of these represent a legacy of new worlds to conquer still powerfully resonant to us today, and recognisable as First/Third World relations, international markets and commodified pleasure.

The irreducibility of human values to abstraction has long been a major literary theme, not surprisingly since literature is itself a powerfully over-motivated discourse. After all, as a supreme example of artifice in which social meanings are conflated with the pleasures of imaginative stimulation, it is little wonder literature engages with the role, the violently equivocal role, played by meaning and pleasure in human affairs. And, lately, these have been acknowledged as central to the workings of *consumerist* cultures, as well as just to imagined literary ones:

> It would appear that consumption, being a form of economic conduct, should be placed at the opposite pole of life from all that we generally regard as 'romantic'. The reasonableness of this contrast is deceptive, however; something which becomes apparent once we recognize that there is one significant modern phenomenon which does indeed directly link the two. . . . This, of course is advertising. . . . The assumption which has largely prevailed . . . however, has been that it is the advertisers who have chosen to make use of this material in an attempt to promote the interests of the producers they represent and consequently that the relationship should be seen as one in which 'romantic' beliefs, aspirations and attitudes are put to work in the interests of a 'consumer society' . . . [but] the reverse relationship should also be taken seriously, with the

119

'romantic' ingredient in culture regarded as having had a crucial part to play in the development of modern consumerism itself . . . indeed it could be argued that Romanticism itself played a critical role in facilitating the Industrial Revolution and therefore the character of the modern economy.[3]

Art and culture both express the extent to which the relationship between people, artefacts and society is born not of utility and rationality, but from a principle of creativity in excess of physical need. This is an anthropological view of life, for which culture is the broad category, art the apogee, and rubbish the symptomatic anti-type. Culture is whatever it is that at any particular time, most motivates us. It used to be religion; or going to war. Now, it's consumerism. Advertising is both a window on, and a product of, this new drive. Just one more example of a much wider theory of how society is human-desire-writ-large, which at its most expansive looks like this:

> Civilisation is not merely an imitation of nature, but the process of making a total human form out of nature. . . .
> The desire for food and shelter is not content with roots and caves; it produces the human forms of nature that we call farming and architecture. . . . It is neither limited to, nor satisfied by, objects but is the energy that leads human society to develop its own form.[4]

For 'civilisation' read culture. And what's sauce for the goose is sauce for propaganda. John Treasure, an advertising big cheese, quotes Professor Levitt in making a similar point, as he exalts advertising's elemental role in civilisation:

> 'One does not need a doctorate in social anthropology to see that the purposeful transmutation of nature's primeval state occupies all people in all cultures and all societies in all stages of development. Everybody everywhere wants to modify, transform, embellish, enrich and reconstruct the world around him. . . . Civilisation is man's attempt to transcend his ancient animality; and this includes both art and advertising.'[5]

Treasure concludes with a rousing piece of extraordinary semiology: 'There is nothing artificial or accidental in this process . . .

advertising is a special case of a general social process whereby reality is turned into images.'[6] I don't know how he came to the conclusion that creating images was not a process of artifice, but letting that pass, this is heady rhapsody. Social meaning of objects and the pleasure those meanings give are the two most obvious indications that consumerism is a deeply cultural thing, that is, a phenomenon that resists reductive description. Advertising is more than a market strategy.

THE BRAND AS ANTHROPOLOGY

None of which has passed the advertiser by. Judie Lannon, creative research director of J. Walter Thompson, had this as her subject in a long article written in October 1985's issue of *Admap* (for decision makers in advertising and marketing). In it she set out to show what impact these 'new ways of seeing' (or what she construed as being 'new ways of seeing') had on the business and its methodology.

Her article was called 'Advertising research: new ways of seeing', and it picked up on some of the arguments put forward by the British anthropologist Mary Douglas in an essay called 'Goods as a system of communication'.[7] The link in titles between new ways of seeing and objects as processes of culture places this article at the heart of what I have been trying to describe as a new critical dispensation. Although specifically concerned with techniques used to evaluate advertising effectiveness, she does have some portentous things to say about what sort of cultural practice advertising has become.

Her real beef, then, was with how the business judges its own effectiveness. This has traditionally been a rather crude affair, measuring a thing called 'recall'. Success was thought to depend on the number of people who could demonstrate recalling the ad, and roughly what it said. Conservative commercial interests take great comfort in this sort of tangible counter. But it does rather inhibit creativity, and make for some appalling advertising – advertising that Lannon argues, is based on a model of communication which is clumsy and antagonistic.

But where the debate really begins to simmer is in her bold contention that what is at issue is not just methodological nuts and bolts, but culture itself. Because out of the seemingly profession-specific question 'what is effective advertising?'

emerges enormous imponderables – what is communication? What is culture? How are they *linked*?

> The last fifteen years or so have seen what futurologists are fond of describing as a 'paradigm shift' in the way advertising is made and evaluated in Britain. New ways of seeing have produced both new theories and links between old theories and marketing practice, resulting in genuinely fresh concepts and metaphors.[8]

She pulls these 'new ways of seeing' together to form a model for what brand advertising looks like *as* culture, a view highly sceptical of the context in which 'recall' prevails, dependent as it is on 'transportation models':

> the term includes all of the hierarchy of effects models in all their variations and draws primarily from learning theory and perceptual psychology. The assumptions they have in common are; that advertising acts on an inert audience, that effects operate in a stepwise manner, and that measurements can be applied to each step in the process; the underlying metaphor is mechanistic and atomistic.[9]

All depressingly reductive. Surely advertising works with more sumptuous gusto than this, threading images, feelings, symbols and meanings through the eye of the beholding consumer, and producing a sense of mythology around a product, an aura of extra-functional significance which is deeply rooted in our personal and social mores. The questions advertisers need to ask therefore, should not be how many people remembered a product message, but the much wider one of what role does advertising play in culture, in people's lives? What is the relationship between people, artefacts and society? And have we even been asking the question *the right way about*?

> the earliest, linear sequential models of the advertising process ask what advertising does *to* people, focuses on the properties of the stimulus and tends to imply a fair amount of rational choice. Furthermore, this perspective assumes that advertisements carry the power to convert and therefore places heavy reliance on recall of advertising as a measure of effectiveness. The new perspective turns the

question around and asks what do people do *with* advertising – what do people use it *for*?[10]

In terms heavily familiar from those littering the previous chapter, Lannon diagnoses where this shift leaves the advertiser:

> The answer links the practical preoccupation of the marketing world with psychology, sociology and social anthropology, acknowledgeing that advertising ... turns products into brands, and shifts the emphasis away from the performance-based properties of what the manufacturer makes to the meanings and values delivered by what the consumer buys.[11]

Marketing has found powerful new allies in these -ologies, and their preoccupation with the formal man-madeness of things. In this case, it is the mundane business of consuming which is shown to be the inner dynamic of cultural genesis – because we don't buy *things*, we buy *values*, brands not products. Branding taken to its logical conclusion then, becomes the largest mythology of all – that our products *are* our culture, because it is in consumerism that we most express our sense of social belonging:

> so that the answer to why people personify brands is the same as the answer to why people need symbols to help in structuring social relationships, domestic behaviour and other aspects of life. And if advertising contributes to the meaning of inanimate goods, then the study of these values and meanings is of prime importance ... the prospective of research must be what people use advertising for.[12]

Well, so what is the answer then, why *do* people 'need symbols to help in structuring' their lives? Perhaps this is just one more way of begging this chapter's fundamental question; if society is man-made, as I, and all these others, have been suggesting, then *what with*? And the answer must be, with 'social relationships, domestic behaviour and other aspects of life', which are in their turn composed of 'symbols', more readily understood as 'personified brands'. These are what we recognise as the social meaning of objects, the types of pleasure we pursue in our purchases, and the interactive dramas/texts/games we use them in. The difference between a *product* and a *brand* has become a paradigm for this new way of understanding culture – and use of culture as a way of understanding people through their artefacts. Culture is the society we build with our brands.

Advertising becomes the expression of our consumerist being-in-the-world, by parodying the idea that our world is the world we choose to describe. It is created out of mythologies, forms and symbols, *into* a type of communication that, in holistic micro-cosm, reflects how culture itself grows and evolves: '[this] com-munication metaphor [is] described as embodied in myth and ritual (that we call holistic and cultural), so that communication is seen as a process through which a culture is created, modified and transformed.'[13]

All of which shows us how much our products transcend their literal function, that they are as much a part of our social nature as of our physical need – and that they are certainly more than just the manipulative figments of the copywriter/witch-doctor's imagination.

> Mass goods represent culture, not because they are merely there as the environment within which we operate, but because they are an integral part of that process of objecti-fication by which we create ourselves as an industrial so-ciety: our identities, our social affiliations, our lived everyday practices. The authenticity of artefacts of culture derives, not from their relationship to some historical style or manufacturing process – in other words there is no truth or falsity immanent in them – but rather from their active participation in a process of social self-creation in which they are directly constitutive of our understanding of ourselves and others.[14]

THE BRAND AS CULTURAL ARTEFACT

So advertising is, and is about, what it is for something to be cultural. It has this resonance because so do objects when under-stood anthropologically. Our products have a communicative, performative role to play, and advertising highlights this. In other words advertising is committed to the fact that *things* embody ways of seeing, that they harbour within them a sense of the world outside, and that furthermore, it is precisely here, in their formal in-excess of physical need where (according to the new paradigm) they most express their cultural humanness. It used to be the work of art that stood as archetype for this, now it is the commodity, the brand. And standing opposed to the work of art has traditionally been junk, or rubbish. Between them they gave us confidence in the validity of our value-judgments, a secure frame for discriminating the worthwhile from the tawdry. But anthropology – and its more combative cousin, cultural politics, of which more later – have, in their 'ways of seeing' dismantled and unnerved this confidence. They both study how it is people are linked to society through their arte-facts, but at the expense of aesthetic discriminations. And in so doing, have contrived to invert the metaphorical basis of art and the literal basis of rubbish. In other words, a culture's art is merely an indication of social values; and its material rubbish revealing evidence of relative world-views. The difference be-tween them is thoroughness; the anthropologist learns about culture through ascertaining the pattern between people and their artefacts, and leaves it at that, while the student of cultural politics is on the hunt for evidence of hegemony and mystification.

But they both set up the *brand* as the icon with most to tell us. Both relegate art from its erstwhile, premier position, and in its place substitute commodity aesthetics, albeit to very different ends. Ironically though, this is a move that has taken as much of its impetus from within art as from hostile external criticism, an impetus that has recast art's relationship to advertising *and* to cultural politics, creating paradoxical confusions in the minds of the critics. The brand then, sits at the complex juncture between advertising, anthropology, art and cultural politics, and I would like to spend the rest of the chapter following the threads.

What sort of cultural object is the brand? Culturally speaking it is a hybrid between art and junk. In other words it is a disposable object laced with associations and powers normally accredited to works of art (i.e. endowed with enduring qualities, and expressive of the world around it). A brand, then, is an object nestling rather uneasily between the opposing extremes of art and junk. Works of art embody ways of seeing that are metaphorically in excess of the literal, while bits of junk are literally in excess of what we need, and therefore discardable. They police the diametric extremes of our world of objects. In fact one could say that we have now reached the stage where it is the brand, the consumer commodity, which supplies us with our terms for working out what art and junk are, and not the other way round.

RUBBISH AND SYSTEM

Defining something as art or as junk used to seem a straight-forward thing to do, and with it, placing advertising (somewhere beneath tabloid newspapers but slightly above pornographic magazines). Everything had its place, Rembrandt (*et al.*) at the top; dinner-table mats, much lower. But our world of objects has at its fringes things whose perceived value fluctuates hugely, creating a sense of unnerving relativity in the whole business of ascribing value. This can work both ways, with yesterday's *objets d'art* consigned to oblivion, and cult status being conferred on the humblest of bygone knick-knacks. It can happen to whole periods, whose memorabilia ride and plummet waves of hyped interest. And values are linked to us as individuals. I would be surprised to see holiday snaps in the Tate (actually, I don't suppose that I would), but that doesn't mean that I think *mine* are without value. On the contrary, they are among some of the dearest things I possess. Or things acquire high added value through association. Like the blouse worn by Marilyn Monroe when she made *Bus Stop*, so of course its auction merits a photo on the front page of the national press.

Much more interesting than any particular definition of value is the fact that the question is inescapably as much about culture as it is about 'things'; as Jonathan Culler puts it, with reference once again to another work by Mary Douglas:

> Reflections on rubbish might begin with one of the classics of social anthropology, Mary Douglas's *Purity and Danger* . . . 'Where there is dirt, there is system', she writes. . . . She argues that dirt is vital evidence for the total structure of thought in a culture because it is an omnibus category for everything that is out of place.[15]

Getting a handle on what it is we characteristically choose to value as art, or spurn as rubbish, is something for which 'semio-tics' is especially adept, because of all the ways of looking at things-as-culture, this is the one most accustomed to linking their formal properties with their social meanings and comprehending which types of value a culture particularly prizes. Culler identifies a basic polarity behind what we think of objects:

> (there are) two general categories in which we place cultural objects, the *transient* and the *durable*. Objects placed in the transient class are thought of as having finite life-spans and as decreasing in value over time. Objects viewed as durable are endowed with, ideally, infinite life-spans and retain their value, or even increase their value, over time. A ham sandwich is transient, while a diamond is durable – this much is obvious – but for a wide range of objects class membership is determined by social forces as much by the physical character of an object; a vase may be placed either in the transient category or in the durable category (viewed as secondhand or as an antique).[16]

It is the shifting proportions behind 'transient' objects achieving 'durable' status where we find the inscrutable pulse of fashion and cult. The ambiguities are of more than passing interest, as they take us to the heart of how values are created, in a process in which advertising is implicated in a number of complex but related ways.

This is particularly so when we remember that this spread of values is not just *relative*, but *hierarchical*. Things seen as art are feted, while the other sort are reviled – as are the people associated with them. This is a vicious, powerful scale on which advertising is in two ways the traditional loser. First, it is itself considered of little intrinsic merit, ephemeral, trashy, inconsequential, both as 'art', and as mercenary ally of grubby commerce, disingenuous and pretentious. Second, this view is compounded by the way advertising sells 'transient' products in terms of intangible 'durables', and only in order to speed up that contemporary materialist process in which even 'durables' get devoured in a never-ending sequence of consumer craving.

JUNK ART

But this hierarchical pecking order is under attack. And not least from within art itself, with advertising (not surprisingly) the iconoclastic paragon. Advertising's artistic relationship to the 'fine arts' got turned on its head in any case – originally commissioning some of the great graphic artists to produce advertising work, but lately providing artists with *their* raw material and ethos. In the 50s, this scandalous besottedness with 'junk' gave art a new bottom line in camp irony, one whose most famous icon Robert Hughes describes here:

> Hamilton exhibited a small but densely prophetic collage called 'Just What Is It That Makes Today's Homes So Different, So Appealing?', 1956. This collage fulfilled almost to the letter what Hamilton wrote down as the desiderata of Pop Art in 1957, . . . Pop, he declared, should be:
>
> > Popular (designed for a mass audience)
> > Transient (short-term solution)
> > Expendable (easily forgotten)
> > Low-cost
> > Mass-produced
> > Young (aimed at youth)
> > Witty
> > Sexy
> > Gimmicky
> > Glamorous
> > Big Business
>
> Such an art could not be made by the people; it was not folk art. It came out of . . . 'a new landscape of secondary, filtered material'. . . . It was done to the people. It grew by analogy to what it admired, advertising and the media through which advertisements were replicated.[17]

Art, in other words, should be more like advertising than advertising itself by cannibalising advertising's own 'added values' and using them not to promote an absent product, but as consumer product themselves. But in a sense all that this anarchic levelling of high and mass culture did, apart from perhaps loosening the traditional 'apartheid' separating the enduring from the ephemeral, was make a fetish out of the *museum* in whose context (and only in whose context) this narcissistic alchemy could take place. But it did neverthless succeed in making us reassess the significance of junk, endowing it with a new formal status.

> Through Pop Art, happenings, Artaud and fringe theatre, Underground poetry, and the new respect shown to tele-

vision and popular music, traditional notions of critical authority fell into confusion. 'Art', 'literature' and 'poetry' looked like grafitti, advertisements, comics and pop songs. . . . So art became like advertising, and advertising like art: you could buy poster copies of great masters and there was a soup advertisement alluding to Andy Warhol. Avant-garde techniques, visual and verbal, became standard fare in advertising and pop music; it is hard to tell where art begins and ends.[18]

COMMODITY AESTHETICS AND 'WAYS OF SEEING'

This then was the age of the leveller, debunking the old verities, the unquestioned sense of hierarchy at whose pinnacle stood vaguely Romantic notions of the sublimity of artistic expression, the non-negotiability of genius, the self-authenticating disinter-estedness of aesthetic contemplation, gloating over art's fall from grace. And from outside the gallery, the challenge was reinforced by critics like John Berger, whose critique of art took cult form in his hugely influential BBC TV series and subsequent book *Ways of Seeing*.[19] The most significant legacy of this book, and all the others in the same tradition has been the ruthless distinction made between what art *symbolises* as spiritual expression of timeless intangibles, and what it *epitomises* as the repository for elitist values, rubbishing the former in a virulent critique of the latter.

> Aesthetics . . . finds itself equally embarrassed by the Marxist challenge. Its notions of purity, autonomy, and timeless significance seem remarkably vulnerable to historical deconstruction. One need not be a vulgar Marxist to see some force in the claim that 'aesthetics' is an elitist rationalisation, a mystification of cult objects that (especially in the visual arts) have an 'aura' about them that smells of money.[20]

Berger's aim was to satirise artistic 'ways of seeing' as tacit endorsements of an unequal society. His critique of the great artistic tradition so embedded in our assumptions about art and art galleries culminates in a condemnation of advertising's dupli-citious sell-out. His target is, by implication, the traditional view embodied by Kenneth Clark's *Civilisation*,[21] and where it really 'bites' is in Berger's controversial use of advertising (or 'publicity' as he calls it) as a retrospective model for all that he thought was wrong with art and our fawning appreciation of it. His 'ways of seeing' linked formal artistic properties to an ideologically unjust world in which aesthetic values are not exempt from the material world, and in which the 'sublime' is as compromised as any man-made concept.

Whether one thinks it fair to see in advertising a perverted parody of art, and art as little more than an allegory, in form and content, of power and property, he is certainly right about one thing. Admen may derive some weird kind of kudos, even if only by default, for their industry, parading its cult-status as clever junk, or as pseudo-anthropologically legitimate in-excess, like art, of physical need. But their *use* of art more than vindicates Berger's glumly reductive view. Here we find a slavish literalness which fully bears out his suggestion that advertisers understand art better than the connoisseurs do, and that at the core of art lies a material/spiritual nexus especially vulnerable to commercial pillage.

Art, according to the romantics, is sublime, standing in redemptive excess to all that is utilitarian and abstract. But it is precisely this that tends to get taken literally – and in two different ways – by the advertiser and by the consumer. For the advertiser, art's elevated status is the property of those able to appreciate it, a capacity itself literally in excess of physical need, born of wealth and leisure and quickly synonymous with them – becoming an 'added value' to privilege and self-serving social prominence. This is the John Berger view, now a reductive axiom in radical views of art's social value:

> Any work of art 'quoted' by publicity serves two purposes. Art is a sign of affluence; it belongs to the good life; it is part of the furnishing which the world gives to the rich and the beautiful. But a work of art also suggests a cultural authority, a form of dignity, even of wisdom, which is superior to any vulgar material interest; . . . it denotes wealth *and* spirituality.[22]

And to the consumer, romanticism has become literal in what Colin Campbell describes as the hedonism of consumption:

the individual . . . becomes not merely a virtuoso in feeling but also in pleasure, something he must prove by creating cultural products which yield pleasure to others . . . this self-illusory hedonism is characterized by a longing to experience in reality those pleasures created and enjoyed in imagination, a longing which results in the ceaseless consumption of novelty . . . [but] it still remains the case that Romanticism's connection with modern consumerism must be viewed as ironic, for although the Romantics certainly did intend both to provide pleasure and to promote daydreaming, they cannot be regarded as having sought an outcome in which these combined to facilitate the restless pursuit of goods and services.[23]

Art is a doubly rich source of assurance for the advertiser, socially and formally, as Judith Williamson points out:

[ads rely] on systems of value already in existence as sources for the 'auras', at once intangible and precise, which must be associated with the goods for sale. . . . Advertising pitches its products at specific social classes . . . yet, as with Art, choice and taste must appear as personal attributes of the individual. So 'Art' is a particularly appropriate system for ads: while appearing to be 'above' social distinctions, it provides a distinct set of social codes which we all understand.[24]

The chief villain in this is Andy Warhol, whose *Campbell's Soup Cans* still enjoys chic notoriety (and reminds us of the importance of the *brand* in all this – it is not a coincidence that this image should be of a branded soup, rather than just arbitrary tins, in its search for the paradox of art depicting banality):

Warhol's work in the early sixties was a baleful mimicry of advertising, without the gloss. It was about the way advertising promises that the same pap with different labels, will give you special, unrepeatable gratifications. Advertising flatters people that they have something in common with artists; the consumer is rare, discriminating, a connoisseur of sensation.[25]

But nor should we get snobby about this. After all, the idea of the artist as endowed with something to aspire towards is itself a myth. There is also the point that art gets commercially hijacked by the most rarefied markets, every bit as much as by the perfume and booze brigade, and to precisely the same effect, the easy, profitable adding of value. The high point of my days in academic publishing were the dust-jackets, four-colour sallies into the finest galleries in the world, gracing the -ologies and -istics with the full gamut of Western masterpieces. And occasionally with relevance to the title. One book, on aesthetics, was called *But is it Art?* and underscored its point with those damn Tate Gallery bricks; while another, a linguistic study of clichés and neologisms, was from the outset, destined to have the *Mona Lisa* on the front. Any irony in these, was, in both senses, merely academic.

MONA LISA AND THOSE TATE GALLERY BRICKS

Those bricks, and that *Mona Lisa* show us what art looks like as commercial language, providing the idioms of connoisseurship and social elitism; the amusing irrelevance of (useless) art to the real business of material life; the language of authenticity and 'presence'; and lastly, cryptic visual puzzles.

Just as Warhol has been famous for a lot longer than the fifteen minutes on whose epigrammatic animus he became the 1960s Mr Hypegeist, so this transient heap of bricks has enyoyed its own brand of 'durability' as a byword for the foolish, meaningless excesses of modern, minimalist art, exuding proof of philistine truisms. Witness the Lloyds Bank ad on the following page. There is deflationary whimsy here, of a gently philistine sort; the work of art (*that* work of 'art', of course) is here more effectively trivialised and undermined by the ad's sheer mediocrity, than ever it was by professional critical scorn. Those poor old bricks get damned not by our seeing how far short of a true work of art they fall, but with a sense of how far short they fall of being a garden patio! Even if it is rather odd that an ad for a bank loan should have DIY chores as its reward (of all ads, these are the least shackled in the images of consumer pleasure they can link to borrowed money), its use of useless art as an antithetical image for what it can offer is appropriate. A loan is, after all, unrealised money (or else you wouldn't have to borrow it) with which to perform self-improvements of a down-to-earth

"That reminds me, I must get a loan from Lloyds Bank to lay that patio."

With the approach of spring a young man's fancy lightly turns to...

Yes, all those jobs the winter weather has quite properly allowed him to postpone.

A replacement for the hut that passes for a shed. A more welcoming porch. A roof that stays put in the wind.

Of course, apart from finding the time for such tasks, you have to find the money.

That couldn't be more straightforward.

Through a Personal Loan, Lloyds Bank will lend the money for anything from new curtains, to a new extension to hang them in.

If you want as little as £500, that's fine by us. And only your ability to repay the loan limits how much we'll lend.

We're flexible, too, when it comes to the repayment period. Up to 5 years if you want.

So you can choose the repayment level that suits you best. And there's no penalty if you then decide to pay off the loan early.

Just visit any branch of Lloyds Bank, (you won't need to see the manager), fill in the coupon or call Freephone 0800 400470.

We'll tell you right away if we can help. And if we can you'll have your money, in full, without delay.

At a very competitive rate of interest. Currently 1.5% per month (APR 19.5%).

Now what was that job you've been meaning to do for so long?

REPAYMENTS FOR A £2,000 LOAN			
	12 months	36 months	60 months
Total cost of Loan	£2,200.32	£2,603.16	£3,047.40
Monthly Repayments	£183.36	£72.31	£50.79

To: Ken Sankey, Lloyds Bank Plc, FREEPOST, London SE1 2YZ.
Please send me further details and an application form for a Personal Loan.

FULL NAME (Mr/Mrs/Miss/Ms)_____

ADDRESS_____

_____POSTCODE_____

I am/am not a customer of Lloyds Bank.   01

Lloyds Bank

A THOROUGHBRED AMONGST BANKS.

Personal Loans are available to people aged 18 or over and at the Bank's discretion. Insurance advice is provided by Lloyds Bank Insurance Services Limited. Written details available from Lloyds Bank Plc, 71 Lombard Street, London EC3P 3BS.

4 Lloyds Bank advertisement, 1987

bourgeois kind. As ads go, bank-loan ads offer a kind of paradigm of their own, selling not just consumer objects, but the means with which to purchase them, and all the added values that the hitherto unattainable have in such mesmerising abundance.

The bricks lie there, not only roped off, but framed (i) by the attention of the couple, bemused and sceptical, unable to find in art anything other than an ironic echo of more important, mundane concerns, (ii) by the catalogue which is trying to explain what they are to make of this pile of bricks, (iii) by the museum, with its reassuringly spare, expressionist interior (site of all those adventures of the ravenous spirit), (iv) by the ad's visual, which is telling *us* what to make of the bricks, urging us to construe out of them an analogy for our own unrealised aspirations for which a bank loan is the answer, (v) by the ad as a whole, placing scepticism about art in a wider context of optimism about the efficacy of loans and DIY to provide autonomous and real self-improvement and (vi) by a quarter of a page of a Sunday paper, which itself occupies that middle-ground, half museum half allotment, between abstract recreational self-improvement and the literal odd jobs for which the leisure of Sunday is the archetypal, suburban frame.

From this concantenation of contexts emerges the limp afterthought, 'That reminds me, I must get a loan from Lloyds Bank to lay that patio'. What it does remind him (it is *him*, isn't it, he's holding the catalogue, and she his arm, her left leg sensually half genuflecting to his masterfully tongue-in-cheek powers of free association), is that without money, that is all that these bricks will remain, a fenced off pile of bricks, another unrealised intention. It makes you wonder why Lloyds have bothered to use so potentially powerful a conflation of values, if this is all that happens, although it does interestingly link the work of art, a DIY patio, and the idea of an interest loan as examples of how nature gets transformed into the material patterns of life and culture. What we have here then, is an example of the multitude of different ways this new paradigm informs our lives, and that art, advertising, capital and domestic DIY all derive their impetus from it.

The most celebrated collision of art and advertising was the Benson and Hedges campaign from Collett Dickenson Pearce in the late 70s. The agency produced, in 1977, a press and poster ad featuring the gold B&H pack lying in wait outside a mousehole gnawed beautifully out of a white skirting-board. This was the first in a campaign not only still running, but copied the world over. It was followed by a bird-cage with the pack sitting on the perch, but casting the shadow of a canary against the wall; by Stonehenge at sunrise with a pack supporting one of the plinths; by a diagonal pack set in the middle of the pyramids, and so on. The latest example is a pack pressed up against a bicycle inner tube, and then bursting.

Beautifully composed, art-directed and photographed, they were the first ads to be so clever with art, to appear to make such demands of the onlooker. The ads these replaced were, of course, very different, and immediately seemed very ordinary, and out of date; all those smokers reeking glamour or clean outdoor wholesomeness. These ads not only gratify the onlooker in ways that ads had never done before, they also, of course, flattered by being so 'difficult' to place or understand.

The question, therefore, of 'why art?' is simple. It attaches an aura of the exclusive, the intellectually demanding, the aesthetically gratifying, to a product that otherwise would have none of these things. But why surrealism – the perversest of recognisable modern art idioms? Here too, the answer is all too simple, because new restrictions had been put in place that made the methods used in earlier ads illegal. Suddenly the advertiser wasn't allowed to imply that cigarettes made men more virile, or (interestingly) women more independent; you weren't allowed to show people reaching for a cigarette too eagerly, or cigarettes being consumed in too 'natural' a setting.

And on and on. Cigarettes were made to abdicate their added values. The move to surrealism was therefore strategically brilliant, in one go it not only side-stepped the regulations but produced advertising history in so doing. Other implications were also there for the picking. Surrealism implied a sophistication in the person who appreciated it. It also gave this new taboo an interesting cultural history, putting it up there with all those other interesting pleasures that we have been led to believe forced surrealists into a language outside rules and conformities in the first place, flouting repression.

Surrealism is in terms of popular culture very much the 'clever', forbidden art, the most visual and also, reassuringly, the most vacuous. Alongside the two other widely familiar painterly codes used by advertisers (the lavish and opulent still-life, and the impressionist idyll), it is the art we know connotes forbidden subjects and dangerous elisions. This campaign brilliantly responded to having to incorporate absence in the ads – cigs having had their signifying contexts forfeited – and turned it into avant-garde virtue.

This contest between code and art-form became even more explicit after the imposition of compulsory health-warnings onto all tobacco advertisements. Far from disrupting, or chastening, the promotional images, these didactic banners curiously seem to reinforce them. For one thing it gave the advertisers even more license for obscurity. The warning, after all, automatically told you what the product was, and even exactly what strength of tobacco was involved. Two discourses are in combat in these ads, the most illegible of art image against the baldest and starkest of prose. Perhaps this too is a losing battle, because the health warning merely reinforces in our minds that association that equates pleasure (especially dangerous pleasure) with imaginatively ravishing imagery, and admonishments with language that steadfastly refuses to court us.

More traditional, of course, was that painting that signifies 'art' (and all that) more than any other – the *Mona Lisa*. Her lingering smile has come to epitomise all that art can signify; its own commodity 'presence', as something incredibly *mysterious*, incredibly *expensive*, incredibly *there*. Judith Williamson's look at a dairy cream ad is exemplary of this. The ad featured a sequence of three Mona Lisas, the first as we know her, the second and third furtively insinuating a chocolate eclair down her inscrutable throat: 'Naughty. But Nice.'

> The Mona Lisas smile is a well-known mystique, famous, like Art, for its incomprehensibility. But here we have a perfectly ordinary homey explanation! She is thinking of a real dairy cream cake . . . although this is a joke, it is one with very deep-lying implications, about art, inferiority and the *relief* at being able to joke about something one feels is alien. And this relief is exactly like the pleasure of letting oneself go, and having a nice (but naughty) eclair . . . the caption recognizes both the transgression of tampering with 'art' (naughty) and, simultaneously, the comforting sense such transgression brings (nice).[26]

The painting is also frequently ransacked for its 'authenticity'.

5 Konica Business Machines advertisement, 1988

Consider the Konica photocopier ad. Not a brilliant ad by any means, but an interesting example of one of the main roles played by art in advertising. Here, Mona Lisa meets her double in a colour photocopy, the latest generation of the reproduction culture. The joke depends on our seeing Mona Lisa not as priceless art, but as the archetype of the *uncopyable*. The smile has a new hue, this time it is the smugness of the unique, quietly exulting in her status as *the* icon of 'being that which she is'. But here she comes alive, shocked at the sudden rape of her aura, animated in startled *doppelganger* fright. Admittedly the resonances are not very profound. There isn't a whole lot about art and life waiting to be read out of that expression, merely a rather silly sense of disbelief at the quality of the reproduction, a disbelief that pokes fun at the supposed uniqueness of art, but more saliently at the presumed shortcomings of photocopiers, previously restricted to bad black and white.

A quick look at the copy shows us that what is going on here has less to do with art than with *communication*. The first paragraph rather curiously subsumes Leonardo into the terms of the photocopier age, and not vice versa, recasting him as an example of slow, low-tech. Similarly, the blonde giving herself a personality scan (and emerging from the innards of the machine as a passable parody of a Botticelli figure!!) is involved in a quite different use of self-reproduction. Unlike that served by oil paintings, this is to do with making an impact with communication, selling yourself, for which visible 'presence' becomes an invaluable asset. This is photocopying as glasnost; self-promoting openness, as advertising, not art.

This then is what has displaced art and junk as reference points in the ascription of value. It is the brand, or commodity, which has pride of place at the heart of culture, mediating between the erstwhile zenith and nadir of human creativity. And reading brands has left art void of value, and rubbish potentially full of it. The advertiser sees art as either an unimpeachable 'way of seeing' (made literal in products) or as the language of consumer kudos. To the student of culture, on the other hand, this has meant regarding art in one of two ways, as commodity or as ideology. What, in the light of John Berger, we have lost, is the capacity to read art metaphorically, or junk as literally that, worthless detritus, surplus to requirement. In its place we remain shackled to a new, and specious orthodoxy in which art has assimilated the ethos of advertising in a smart-money move of stunning vapidity.

The relationship between art and advertising remains more vexed than ever. With advertising now free of its inferiority complex, there is scarcely a traditional property of 'fine' art that it isn't appropriating to itself.

For those in the arts concerned by this, there are a number of responses. Either out-camp advertising-inspired art (Jeff Koons's vacuum cleaners, Jenny Holzer's flashing neon slogans); intellectually subvert it (Hans Haacke's addition of political polemic onto British Leyland ads) or wash one's hands of the whole thing and invoke Ruskin in your bid, once and for all to assert that art's *raison d'être* is spiritual nourishment, not trashy parody (the late Peter Fuller):

> For Gilbert and George, aesthetic judgment counts for nothing. They detest the idea of 'high art' and seem to believe that graffiti are of greater interest than the finest old master drawing . . . they do not produce art . . . they produce the advertiser's dream; a form of advertising that has nothing to sell but itself . . . and this, it might be said, is exactly the kind of contemporary art envisaged by *Ways of Seeing*.[27]

VOTE FOR CALIBAN

And Lannon's 'New ways of seeing' begs powerful questions too. It is all very well giving advertising a quasi-anthropological credibility as a sort of art, akin to those other systems of man-made formal in-excess, like agriculture or architecture. But it is not advertising *per se* which transforms nature into the forms that epitomise culture, but *consumerism*, the outward expression of industrialism, itself the 'engine' of capitalism. Only in a very limited way then, can it be seen to be an end in itself – by those, for instance, who are looking for evidence of creative panache or technical skill. Otherwise, advertising is utterly committed to its commercial objectives.

It is not that Judie Lannon is wrong exactly. The thing is that advertising is not the same as consumerism. Advertising is a way of seeing that provides consumerism with its context and with its acceptability, and, arguably, then goes on to make consumerism the context and source of other social values. Nature does not just get turned into any old culture, but into specific cultural patterns, in this case consumer culture. Advertising has a role to play in this because it is one of the means we have for ensuring that our society remains a consumerist one. This is for us a political vision of what it means to be human; that as consumers, we are as close as we will ever realistically get, to being free-moving, social individuals. The anthropological view is a limited one therefore. All it does is recognise the way specific behaviours link individuals, artefacts and society in a characteristic of a specific culture. Anthropology is not an end in itself. Advertising is not human interaction writ large, except in a specific political way.

A brilliant reworking of the Lear/Crusoe theme is Adrian Mitchell's 'The castaways or vote for Caliban', a comic paean to human resourcefulness. Society plane-crashes into the Pacific and then reconstitutes itself on a desert island. Here, human creativity writ large is a depressing business, with the impulse to game, drama and text producing not cultural liberation but the same old sorry shibboleths of institutionalised community spirit, media heartiness and ersatz additions to nature:

> Next morning they held a committee meeting.
> Tom, Susan, Jim and Bill
> Voted to make the best of things.
> Mary, the eccentric widow, abstained.

> Tom the reporter killed several dozen wild pigs.
> He tanned their skins into parchment,
> And printed the *Island News* with the ink of squids.

> Susan the botanist developed new strains of banana
> Which tasted of chocolate, beefsteak, peanut butter,
> Chicken, and boot-polish.

> Jim the high-jump champion organized organized games
> Which he always won easily.[28]

Only Mary, the 'eccentric widow' remains outside this oppressive collective hysteria with which culture forces participation in its games and dramas. Like a quirky cross betwen Lear and Crusoe, she contents herself with her ellipses . . . her glazed silences across the desert-island-literary-themepark of commercial relevance. And she alone communes with the great cosmic odd-ball nobody has quite managed to brand as culture:

> But Mary the eccentric widow . . .
> Each evening she wandered down the island's main
>   street,
> Past the Stock Exchange, the Houses of Parliament
> The Prison and the Arsenal.
>
> Past the Prospero Souvenir Shop,
> Past the Robert Louis Stevenson Movie Studios,
> Past the Daniel Defoe Motel
> She nervously wandered and sat on the end of the pier of
>   lava,
> Breathing heavily,
> As if at a loss,
> As if at a lover,
> She opened her eyes wide
> To the usual incredible sunset.[29]

The joke here is the madness and unaccountability of the 'outsider', alienated from participation in 'organized organized games' and alone in tune to other forces. But within the poem, Mary is characterised as a complete solipsist, unable (and unwilling) to translate her perceptions into intelligible terms for the others. This is not done to undermine her, but to reinforce the contrast between conformity and vision. The poem as a whole, however, implies that it, as poem, is a more complicated example of its own subject matter than any mentioned within the poem, being, on the one hand, neither merely conformist rubric, nor, on the other, unintelligible private communion. The poem in which we locate this *inside* and this *outside* to culture is itself a socially organised insight of the individual poet's mind. The important thing is that it travesties the idea that anything can meaningfully survive outside the forms of culture. To stand outside culture is only a conceit, unless you literally stop communicating altogether. We are all condemned to an existence within the terms of our cultural organisations, but that in no way diminishes the need to investigate those cultures' characteristic forms. Judie Lannon's paradigm makes a virtue of this fact. But, just because there is no cultural outside does not give *carte blanche* to all that lies inside.

141

That is why that paradigm is so powerful in the way it mobi-lises strong currents in anthropology and cultural studies to a new, commercial end. And once in place, it is going to require a new way of reading, one that picks up on what Lannon misses – as Geertz puts it: 'If dramas, are, to adapt a phrase of Susanne Langer's, poems in the mode of action. something is being missed: *what exactly, socially, the poems say.*'[30] For which read ads. We need a new sense of how the formal properties within advertising really do reflect on our world, and this again is knowing 'how the said is rescued from the saying'. This is the new impunity of popular persuasion; in the methods lies the justification; in the 'how' lies buried the 'what'. And in the next chapter I will look at just how hermetically sealed from criticism the culture of advertising has become.

5

PAGE TRAFFIC
The language of advertising

Ads give us a taste of paradise, they are utopian. Their stories are of fullness of being, their conceits, of paradise consumed. Paradise is the logical *non plus ultra* of wishful thinking, but also, of course, of false consciousness. This is a strain of cultural pessimism as old as paradise itself.

That is why the question of language in advertising stretches from the puns it uses to the end of civilization as we know it. Language is in any case itself a polymath. It gets used to state, to beguile, and to lay down the law; usually, and somewhat problematically, at the same time. This has been evident since the Book of Genesis, whose pages of universal moment are, among other things, dramas of language, from the naming of creation by Adam to the catastrophe of persuasion that so shamefully sidestepped the divine commandment. Language, alongside work, was one of the mythic consequences of the Fall. That is why, especially since Milton, it has been a truism to see in the serpent a prime example of 'persuasive language', and to correlate it with the 'subtil wiles' of what we recognise today as advertising copy:

> What the serpent produces here is a sales pitch so transparent as to be almost risible. . . . Thus the scheme
>
> 1 The Teasing Question: 'Hath God said ye shall not eat of *every* tree?'
> 2 The robust Assurance: 'Ye shall surely not die'
> 3 The Authority: 'For God doth know . . . '
> 4 The Guarantee: 'Ye Shall be Gods'

Now is there not something not uneasily familiar about

143

these proceedings? They seem to embody a very durable programme of seduction, one that has everyday applications in the modern world of the adman and the punter.[1]

Satan is, in short, selling proto-humanity what looks like knowledge, but which ends up boiling down to sex and status – the self-conscious enjoyment of the ego and the senses, what was then the idiom of temptation, and what is today the idiom of aspiration.

Ever since Aldous Huxley's *Brave New World*, an ironic snippet from Shakespeare's most ambiguous heaven/hell (Prospero's island in *The Tempest*), consumerism-as-false-paradise has become a familiar topos. The social engineering, *ex utero*, of five strands of population, from alphas to epsilons (market segmentation gone ape), and the reduction of all stimuli to banal desire, pose what have since become major anxieties about the metaphysics of advertising culture. And following George Orwell, whose *1984* is the century's other great dystopia, the relationship between language and rationality has also taken on apocalyptic overtones (Newspeak was after all, a perverted return to a state of grace in which language was once again no longer needed).

Rhetorical and figurative language-use has a long tradition of being attacked and demonised. The grammarians of the seventeenth and eighteenth centuries were particularly stern in their castigation of language that deviated from the straight clear lines of unadorned literalness. It is little surprise that the most villainised genre of all should be advertising. Not only does it seek to persuade, but, even more invidiously, it persuades you to buy things.

The classic, liberal pedagogic critique of advertising (and mass-media in general) is Neil Postman's *Amusing Ourselves to Death*. Here TV commercials are the apogee of all that is wrong with saturation media-entertainment (shades of Huxley very strong here). Advertising represents a highly suspect epistemology, knowledge through image and emotion, rather than word and reason, infantilising the consumer and further limiting the scope for negotiating with the real world through rationality, and its mirror, plain language: '[during] the 1950s . . . the television commercial made linguistic discouse obsolete as the basis for product decisions. By substituting images for claims, the pictorial commercial made emotional appeal, not tests of truth, the basis of consumer decisions.'[2] But the idea that image-based communication strategies are somehow aberrations from a plainer, essentialist language-use has been one that philosophers have found extremely difficult to justify. It seems so obvious that such a spectrum should exist, with clear, no-nonsense language at one end and figurative indulgence at the other. But even the great linguistic philosopher Ludwig Wittgenstein ultimately came to 'deny that language has any abstractly essential nature, and argue[d] that it must be thought of instead as a diverse range of social games and practices'.[3] Even the sentence, 'the cat is on the mat', the standard first building block of all theories of reference, can also be regarded not just as a 'picture' of a state of affairs, but as a cliché with a life of its own, the sentence that philosophers *always* use in their pedagogic games. But even Neil Postman knows this, implicitly, because it is not too long before he is making clear what his real objection to advertising is; not its epistemological foundations, but its social agenda:

> What the advertiser needs to know is not what is right about the product but what is wrong with the buyer. And so, the balance of business expenditures shifts from *product* research to *market* research. The television commercial has oriented business away from making products of value and towards making consumers feel valuable.[4]

Just ask yourself the question, well, what *is* wrong with a business trying to make the consumer feel valuable, and you realise just how subjective Postman's hostility is, and indeed how rhetorically he disguises the fact. The other moralistic response to advertising rhetoric is to outgun it with some of your own:

> The purpose of human beings as represented in advertisements is not to be themselves; indeed it is scarcely to be human at all, for we are dealing with nothing less than a highly stylised iconography of transfiguration. . . . It is their role to point the way of salvation in a society whose profoundest meaning lies in the simple formulation 'I buy therefore I am'.[5]

Jeremy Seabrook is, of course, being ironic. He uses religious language because it's the idiom (sardonically used) of corrupt other-worldliness, and, paradoxically, the only idiom intense enough for his moral dismay. But that is all it remains, a liturgy of contempt, the mirror image of advertising rhetoric, but just as tendentious in its special pleading. Rhetoric can be sublime or ridiculous, but it can never, of itself, be cause for condemnation.

As one of modernity's dominant genres of creative writing, advertising has also spread much more ordinary dismay, particularly among the great and the good. They remain unimpressed by either the quality of ideas found in ads or their display of creative logic. Advertising is one symptom among many of a lamentable decline in the use of the English language: 'even among the highly educated, fluency is in decline. We even have bishops, doctors of divinity, who are as coherent and cogent as boxers or footballers.'[6]

More specifically, they hold advertising responsible for debasing the language. They point to the prevalence of empty verbiage ('Coke is it' – *is* what?); they accuse it of prostituting words ripe with medieval connotations (like 'luxury', 'prestige' and 'charisma'), and they hate it for its ugly, hyphenated neologisms – but above all, they deride the fact that advertising language 'becomes increasingly inflated in direct proportion to the inessentiality of the commodity being marketed'.[7] And we all know how fond advertising is of *vagueness*:

> Let's consider an example. 'Helps fight the symptoms of tooth-decay with regular use.' Does that mean 'stops tooth decay'? Come on now. Count the weasels: 'Helps' – goes an almost immeasurably small way towards, 'fight' – opposing but certainly not overcoming, 'the symptoms' – the symptoms, and that's all, of tooth decay, 'with regular use' – as long as you buy lots of it. That's four weasels in all, a real tribute to the copywriter concerned.[8]

It is of course, rather too easy to see in this the corruption of an erstwhile idyllic state, a time when 'tests of truth' were at one with demonstrative language. In Neil Postman's case, that golden age is of nineteenth-century print-culture, a premise that is both historically and epistemologically suspect. This type of criticism works by making advertising language seem the *opposite* of wholesome language-use.

The trouble with advertising is that whatever else it is, it is not formless, or without artistry:

The . . . advertisement has very little resemblance, in its method and in its socio-cultural presuppositions, to a speech of Cicero, a soliloquy in Shakespeare, a sermon by Donne, an essay by Dr Johnson, even a description by Dickens. And yet it *is* rhetoric. It reveals the rhetoricians ancient enthusiasms, for the latent aesthetics of language, and for the possiblity of exercising the power of design.[9]

For better or worse, the ad, rather than the essay, the sermon, the soliloquy, has become our cultural shibboleth: 'The ads are the masterpieces of the three-minute culture, and they are so clever we sometimes forget that all we can admire is their cleverness. . . . Cleverness is all.'[10]

This leaves us with the question, just what sort of language-use is advertising?

RELEVANCE

Advertising is, in substance, the language of vested interests, the best that it is *possible* to say, while teetering on the edge of what is *probable* (an inversion of the Aristotelian definition of metaphor). In form, however, its basis is not so much the deliberate falsehood as the exaggeration of a principle that underpins all communication, what linguists Deirdre Wilson and Dan Sperber call *relevance*.

> To succeed, an act of ostensive communication must attract the audience's attention. . . . Someone who asks you to behave in a certain way, either physically or cognitively, suggests that he has good reason to think it might be in your own interests, as well as his, to comply with his request . . . *the suggestion may be ill-founded or made in bad faith*, but it cannot be wholly cancelled . . . the host who asks his guests to eat automatically suggests that what he is offering them is edible, and indeed worth eating[11] [My italics].

Advertising is *par excellence* the 'act of ostensive communication', seeking to change how we behave both cognitively and physically. Success is made difficult by two, related problems – the enormous commercial pressure exerted by the client, and the frequent scarcity of something to say (has anyone really forgotten what sound milk makes when poured on Rice Krispies, or what champion breeders stuff their dogs with – it's obviously worth nearly £25m. to Kellogg and Pedigree Petfood that this remain the case).

In other words, the ad has to achieve *relevance* – indeed achieving it is only its starting-point. And this requires much more than just the judicious choice of words. Relevance is a linguistic and cognitive theory that stresses the importance to the communication process of context, inference and the disposition of the person being communicated with. All this is perfectly familiar to anyone working not just in advertising but anywhere in the media. Writing is only half the battle; knowing who you're writing for, and what the context is that it will be read in, are the real keys. It represents the sum total of what the advertising business purports to offer its clients. From the copywriters and art directors who devise the final campaign, to the market researchers and planners, the agency's real product is its understanding of consumer relevance; not only what consumers think of products, but, even more crucially, what they think of advertising.

The basic premise of advertising practice is that what you write isn't necessarily what people read. The advertiser who has expressed this the most elegantly is Jeremy Bullmore. In his article 'Getting explicit about the implicit', he outlines his version of relevance theory. He takes as his first example the advice given to the stock market by countless chancellors of the exchequer: 'Don't Panic!' and asks 'Does the pound stabilise or does it fall still further?'. Everyday life is full of these moments when what we infer radically differs from what was implied. The moral of the article is that communication is not a matter of a message conveyed intact between a sender and a receiver, via a medium, but a stimulus that prompts a response. 'So "Don't Panic" is not a Message: it's simply a stimulus. "I'll sell every pound I've got before the market closes," is one possible response.'[12] Advertising therefore has to make a virtue out of this fact. It has to accept that it can't bully people into doing what clients want, that it has to persuade the consumer. And if the receiver/consumer interprets the stimulus actively and not passively, then that process has to be made as enjoyable as possible. It makes sense to emphasise the consumer's participation in the ad, to cater for it with ads we enjoy decoding and relating to, rather than which annoy us as patronising or repetitive through not making room for our contributions.

The theory also embraces all those other minutiae of the communication process. Everything works as a stimulus, and not just the main body of copy or the main illustration:

> Stimuli can be – and are – not only verbal but visual . . . Many we may regard as tired: the Archers' accents, a Parisian accordion, the famed BBC seagull, Big Ben, a ship's siren. But they still excite a response; we know where we are. . . . The skill of the persuader is as old as rhetoric: first identify the responses you'd like; then, to conjure up the stimuli that should elicit them.[13]

But communication works as much by genre as by cognitive deduction. The *conditions of relevance* that advertisers have to recognise, and then exploit, are specific to advertising. This works both ways of course. The relevance of ads in general, is an indispensable part of how we read them in particular, just as what we think of evangelism will determine how we react to being door-stepped by Jehovah's Witnesses. It also determines how ads are written.

Copywriters are taught to assume the worst about those who will read and decode their ads, that they are writing for people cynical and apathetic about advertising, people, in other words, who have to be dissuaded from thinking ads 'ill-founded and made in bad faith'. The copywriter's big challenge is to over-come the boundless apathy and miniscule attention span of the average punter. We are a non-reponsive, fickle lot whose atten-tion needs to be wrought from us, stroked and gratified. Not only can the copywriter not take our response for granted, he or she can't even assume that there will be one.

That is why most copywriting advice boils down to (i) be singleminded, (ii) know exactly who you are talking to and (iii) have a big sustainable idea. Failing that, then resort to a battery of tried and tested formulas, all of which have, or once had, an approximation to precise and astonishing single-mindedness. What good ads all therefore have in common is their search for audience complicity and the presumption that the effort needed to decipher the ad had better be less than was used in writing it – or at least be more pleasurable.

The 80s, as we have seen, have been kinder to consumerism,

and have correspondingly taken a much more positive view of advertising, which in turn allows the creative greater leeway:

> In commercial response, advertising no longer merely offers merchandise, but suggests experience. The most successful television ads of recent years have been Bartle Bogle Hegarty's beautifully crafted campaigns for Levi's jeans and Audi's cars. These do not make an offer for sale, but rather seek to provide *ambience* and layers of imagery for the consumer to decode. In them texture is at least as important as message. Buy me and become me, they seem to be saying.[14]

Although there are shifts in what people allow advertising to mean to them, what remains constant is the fact that what people take out of an ad is more important than what went, *per se*, into it.

> Now what about the times when you have nothing to say? . . . Not only is there very rarely anything you can say about [the product] the public doesn't already know, but they are also products which command the largest appropriations. They spend a great deal of money, they often use a great many changes of copy, and yet there is nothing to say. The principle here is quite simple: *When you have nothing to say, use showmanship.*[15]

'Showmanship' is what in any case brings people into the business, and what makes the job of copywriting one of the most keenly sought-after. It is language-use at its most pleasurable and most hedonistically satisfying. It also goes beyond the lexicon of selling, the vocabulary of copy. Advertising communicates with every atom of its shallow being, with its production values, with its casting, its setting, its voice over, its props. Television commercials are still predominantly shot as though they were cinema features, in 35mm with all the post-production trimmings. This automatically sets them apart from the vast bulk of competing television, which rarely rises above 16mm film or, more usually, videotape. A lot of commercials go one step further and deliberately crop their pictures, top and bottom, to make them look as though they were shot in cinemascope. This represents the rise within the advertising business hierarchy of the art director, not only happy to see him or herself at the heart of a very lavish production process, but conscious that a visually literate audience will feel cheated with anything less.

But the main point of this extravagance is not just a technical preference for one form of stock over another, but the desire to stick out from the rest of the media and to endow brands with added values deriving from as many different sources as possible, from the production values as well as the creative idea. It also helps preserve commercials from the threat of bathos. A ravishingly well shot commercial lifts the advertising proposition away from the danger of less than flattering paraphrase.

The 1989 spate of lead-free petrol ads, from Shell and Vauxhall, all featured panoramic montages of countryside imagery, rabbits, deer and small children. The use of wildlife shots of cuddly rabbits in a commercial for unleaded petrol gains the benefit of the doubt only if it looks *so* cuddly that there seems no point laughing at the conceit 'bunny equals less dangerous hydrocarbon'. Production values allow you to link products to added values that on paper would seem risible.

Nothing in an ad is left to chance. The Clapham setting in an *Observer* commercial is, to a London audience, obvious indication of the right type of reader – people capable of paying six-figure amounts for Victorian terraced housing. To anyone elsewhere in the country, the effect falls flat – such a street looks merely ordinary. The ad is therefore shown only in the South-east.

> Everything has to be perfect. In a feature film you might have a scene of two men talking in a bar over a glass of beer. If you turn that glass of beer into a product the approach is different. What does the beer look like? Is it being shown to its best advantage? Is it the right colour and is there the right amount of head on it? Does it look fresh? It must be the perfectly pulled pint.[16]

It is this formal regard for what it is possible, though not always that probable, for a product to look like that motivates all those, probably apocryphal, tales of doctored products. Apparently, cars featured in press ads have rocks put in the boot to make them sit better on their suspension. Food is notoriously the subject of artful adulteration. And with the advances made in post-production graphics, with programmes like Paintbox and Harry there is unprecedented scope for polishing up the flaws of the everyday and reinforcing the ad's capacity to be a window on paradise.

'Showmanship' works because we have learned the selling power of ads that have become more and more oblique, ads that stretch what is manifest in communication, namely,

> that people will pay attention to a phenomenon only if it seems relevant to them . . . this amounts to saying that an ostensive communicator necessarily communicates that the stimulus she uses is relevant to the audience. In other words, an act of ostensive communication automatically communicates a *presumption of relevance*.[17]

This 'presumption of relevance' lies at the heart of both writing and reading ads. It informs the rhetoric with which a stimulus motivates the desired response and steers the reader/viewer from stated to intended meaning. Advertising is relevance mythopoeically expanded. The 'presumption of relevance' explains why when confronted by a waterfall next to a magnified packet of cigarettes, we work towards the interpretation intended, even when supremely and literally impossible (that we could smoke something so associated with running water) – freshness, coolness, naturalness. A waterfall might just as easily be a symbol for torrential forces of nature – a menacing reason to teach our children how to swim. Or why a bleak converted warehouse may be nirvana to a 23-year-old bond dealer, but empty hell to his 60-year-old retired great-uncle.

It's why we derive *stimulation* (or not) from word play and puns; *reassurance* from dulcet body-copy; *a sense of inclusion* from clipped syntax; *stimulation* from highly wrought production values; *ravishment* from a stunning visual; *inalienable confidence* from the fit between headline and image, etc. etc., all of which are not only common attributes of contemporary advertising, but precisely what we demand of our ads – that they give us pleasure. None of which would have these effects *outside* the medium of advertising. Statements that are in content utterly banal, even when made hesitant, can, as soon as made the basis for an ad, take on resonance and gravitas – 'Probably the best lager in the world'.

It is also why most academic studies of advertising talk only minimally about the nuts and bolts of the industry. Much more interesting than how media departments work, or whether UK advertising is more creative than that of other countries, is how we interpret ads. The four seminal books in this tradition all have in their titles this preoccupation with advertising as a key to understanding how it is we understand; *Decoding Advertisements* by Judith Williamson[18] makes ads the vindication of late 70s avant-garde hermeneutics – feminist semiology and psychoanalytical deconstruction. Gillian Dyer's *Advertising as Communication*[19] also uses ads to break down how various theories of meaning work before using those theories to break down particular types of advertising. Vestegaard and Schroder's *The Language of Advertising*[20] overviews and analyses advertising's 'strategies of address', such as sex, class and ideology, in order to present a semiological anatomy of late capitalism.

The most exhaustive book in this tradition is Leiss, Kline and Jhally's *Social Communication in Advertising*[21] that appends its history of the growth of advertising on both sides of the Atlantic with a litany of reading methodologies, from semiology and content analysis to combined semiotics and content analysis, from structuralism to anthropology, from icons to social policy, in a piece of saturation semiotics that leaves not a methodological stone unturned but also makes you understand why no adman has ever lost a wink of sleep worrying about academic censure.

Implicit to all these books, and the scores of others like them, is the realisation that *meaning* is a complicated, messy concept, for which we have a battery of interpretive strategies, none of which alone is adequate. Linguists like Sperber and Wilson offer this notion of 'relevance' as a way of cutting through the morass of other competing theories. It can do this because it asserts a general principle inherent to all communication, namely things mean what they do because it makes no sense for them not to. With that axiom in place, all you need to do is unpick the pragmatics of how a particular piece of communication works – because it is inconceivable that it wasn't designed to work. Communication does not come out of a vacuum.

The cognitive psychologist Jerry Fodor says something similar in his book *Psychosemantics*. So much of what we say, and is said to/at us can be seen to conform to large, general patterns adequate to the task of making life 'make sense' – other things being equal:

> Commonsense psychology works so well it disappears. It's like those mythical Rolls Royce cars whose engines are sealed when they leave the factory; only it's better because it isn't mythical. . . . That's . . . how we infer people's intentions from the sounds that they make . . . and all this works not just with people whose psychology you know intimately . . . it works with *absolute strangers*.[22]

Understanding how meaning works is basically a pragmatic exercise. The relationship between a stimulus and its response may not be an automatic one, that much is conceded. But to allow that fact to suggest that neither philosophy nor psychology can ever really get to grips with objective reality is something that all three of these writers, Dan Sperber, Deidre Wilson and Jerry Fodor, set out to rebut. The adequacy of intention (the intention to be relevant, that is), is made axiomatic – on the grounds that basically, those 'other things' which snarl up absolutes will, to all intents and purposes, 'always be equal'.

MISREADING ADS

But will they? The closer you look at it the quicker you realise that 'the presumption of relevance' is often just that – the unwarranted taking of assent for granted. Politically, the gap that separates the two poles of communication has a very real and tangible analogy in the stratified structure of consumer society – and with it, in the enormous potential for *mis*-interpretation:

> The mass commmunication universe is full of discordant interpretations. . . . For a Milanese bank clerk a TV ad for a refrigerator represents a stimulus to buy, but for an unemployed peasant in Calabria the same image means a confirmation of a world of prosperity that doesn't belong to him and that he must conquer. That is why I believe TV advertising in depressed countries functions as a revolutionary message.[23]

So, while ads have the virtue of not only promoting particular products, but of providing society with 'a relentless propaganda on behalf of goods in general', they do so only by disguising just how *un*equal other things actually are:

> [The urban poor] are not spoken to or for: the three-

minute culture has nothing to say to them . . . the songs speak of a world of love which for them means teenage pregnancy in a council flat, of a world of consumption which means rummaging for discarded bell-bottoms in the Oxfam shop. . . . Mass culture talks the language of social inclusion: everyone drinks Coke, everyone can afford Levi's jeans. It is an agreeable fantasy but it is a fantasy whose effect is to make the facts of exclusion invisible.[24]

The relevance of ads is about *choice*, and choice has political significance in terms of what it means not to have it – on the one hand structural inequalities across society at a macrolevel denying whole classes of people access to opportunities (the socialist view), and on the other, a shackled market prohibiting consumer gratification and stifling the competitive urge, and the incentives of reward (the enterprise culture view). Because advertising symbolises 'choice' writ large, it is little wonder that those who take the latter view are basically pro-advertising ('to be successful consumer goods have to offer something more culturally seductive than mere efficiency. Customers demand what the advertisers call *shared values*'[25]); while those who take the former view tend to be much more scathing ('the sad fact is that many people, while recognizing the frustrations of their lives, are caught up in the fantasies offered by ads and are unable to see through them and their false utopias'[26]).

AUTHORITY AND ASPIRATION

Advertising will, of course, concern itself much more with those who don't have to do what the ads say than with those who couldn't even if they wanted to. The closer you get to your target audience, the harder your general proposition. I can't remotely afford a BMW, which makes the proposition that it is just about the best car there is entirely plausible. It's those on five times my salary who need to be persuaded not only that the BMW is about the best car there is, but also, that the Mercedes Benz isn't, or rather, the BMW's 'bestness' is more appealing, more relevant than is the Merc's.

Ads wriggle out of the true/false dichotomy by posing as games, things we participate in rather than interrogate. Carlsberg's use of the word 'probably' to qualify the utterance

'The best lager in the world', is a joke. It appears to admit that no ad can ever really use the formula it would most dearly like to 'X is the best in the world' because it is too subjective. But by making it a joke, they do more. The ads reveal that to all intents and purposes the question of Carlsberg being the best is meaningless, both literally and symbolically. Everybody knows lagers are indistinguishable, especially the ad agency. And everyone knows that saying its the best in the world is empty boasting.

Their latest poster campaign has taken this a stage further. The new posters feature objects with variations on the phrase 'Probably the best lager in the world' etched or branded on the side. On first appearance it is not at all clear what the thing in the image has to do with the beer – a bull, some pies, a boiled sweet, a red-tinted fish and a grilled pastry. Of course, they're jokes; bull, pork pies, humbugs, red herrings and waffles – they're visual puns enacting euphemisms and slang for lies, for the games we play with deceit, and using the ad's own stimulus and response to erode even further the *lie* at the bottom of this particular brand loyalty.

Any use of language that works by stimulus and response, rather than by factual assertion ('performative' rather than 'constative' to use the linguist's distinction) needs a pragmatic basis. In this case, it is one of *authority*. Utterances like 'I sentence you to five years in prison', or 'I hereby name this ship . . .', or 'I declare you man and wife' are all examples of strong performative language. They don't represent states of affairs, they cause them. They are meaningless, however, when given out of context, mere empty husks.

Weaker examples of performative language abound in everyday speech. Every time we beseech, recommend, guarantee, promise, nag, murmur sweet nothings, we use language as an expression of credibility – precisely the linguistic twists that ads are full of. One would promise to do something when merely stating an intention is not felt to be enough. They all *aspire* to the condition of strong performative utterance, while acknowledging that they fall short of it.

What gives these utterances their credibility, when absolute authority is missing, are various social codes. A promise is believable when made by someone who values being regarded as honourable; similarly, a guarantee carries weight when someone's reputation is at stake. Advertising is no exception. It lays its claim to be taken seriously on the fact that we want ads to be true – there is so much to be gained when they are, and when people believe them to be true. The discourse of advertising is that of *aspiration*.

Aspiration is activated, whipped into being, 'performed' through added values (basically sex and status). These are the things in the light of which we brand, market and position ourselves as desirable, lovable people, and against which products achieve their compulsive indispensibility. Advertising has to be struck in an idiom that maximises assent and minimises dissent. One of the problems, for advertisers, is not being able to legislate for how people read the ad; factors of class, gender, age, social and ethnic background will crucially influence the process by which stimulus becomes response. The terms of aspiration have the advantage of being hard to reject outright; beauty, longevity and success are all powerful things to bait your traps with. They also have the added advantage that should *you* feel rejected by *them* – spurned, ugly, awkward, average – this will be seen as your problem and not the advertiser's.

But the advertiser still faces two fundamental problems when encountering our interpretative unreliability. The first occurs when an ad tries to produce a response that *isn't* aspirational. And the second is that while obviously not intending to cause offence, advertisers neverthless want the responses to their ads to be as strong as possible. But motivating by sex and status depends on images that are of gender and class, the two categories, along with race, most likely to outrage.

Both of these problems erupt the moment we *choose* not to read ads 'properly'.

Between 1984 and 1986 the government sponsored a campaign of ads that addressed the problem of heroin addiction. On posters and TV we were offered bleak and haunting variations on a 'Heroin screws you up' theme. One particular poster featured the wasted and ravaged features of a junkie, under the strap-line 'Skin-care by heroin'. With sallow, blemished skin, lank, matted hair, hollow eyes and gaunt cheeks, the visual of the boy was clearly meant to reflect ironically on the copy, styled as it was in the idiom of a cosmetics ad. The campaign reinforced this theme witha plethora of 'before' and 'afters', sequences of gradual and inexorable personal decay and degradation at the hands of drugs.

The effectiveness of this approach, however, was soon to be questioned. It was discovered that in some parts of the country the posters were being pinched off their hoardings and turned into pin-ups; something had obviously gone far wrong when cautionary images turn out to be rather attractive. Even more worrying was the growing sense that the image of the drug user was actually being found attractive, even seductive. Perhaps the whole basis for the campaign had been misconceived:

> Alan Stevenson is not the only one to suspect discrepancies between the reality of the junkie's self-image and (ad agency) Yellowhammer's approach to the social problem of drug-taking in its current 'Screws you up' campaign. . . . Peter Laurie (a sociologist and himself an ex-junkie) in his book *Drugs*, was writing way back in 1967: 'The self-indulgent melancholy of the adolescent [junkie] is one of the sharpest pleasures . . . [to use] heroin is in the eyes of the world, to commit suicide; and the addict has the *pleasure* of being around to see the effect of finality. *He hugs the catastrophic image of the junkie . . .*'. Heroin may screw you up, but the junkie already knows this and may even revel in the fact.[27]

There is overwhelming evidence to support this view:

> Whereas earlier explanations were based on the view that addicts are in a sense compelled to addiction by some kind of individual pathology, research into drug-taking careers demonstrate that users exert substantial control over the progress of their drug taking. The research has focused on three main stages in an opioid using career; in initiation, continuation and cessation.[28]

Most disturbing of all, however, was the discovery that alongside the predictable desire to try drugs out of curiosity was the desire actually to savour the 'lifestyle' of the junkie:

> Some addicts reported that they began opioid use in order to become part of the world of addiction. To some users, the symbolic meaning attached to addiction was considered as or more important than the effects of the drugs themselves. Some addicts admitted that at the time of first opioid use they wanted to become addicted in order to

share the lifestyle of addicts: 'I was already addicted before I'd ever tried anything. I wanted to be a junkie. I had this romantic image of what it was like to be one.'[29]

This is why the campaign had such little effect. Far from countering the reasons people have for trying drugs, it actually mimed and reinforced them. The soberly alarmist and chic down-at-heel images illustrated in the classic advertising manner the intangible self-image/lifestyle end-benefits of a consumer product. The agency had actually managed to brand heroin! By appealing to what they thought a universal value of consumerism (surely no one could actually want to look so unsexy, and so sick) Yellowhammer succeeded in promoting the junkie's self-image.

To premise the campaign on the traditional notions of brand advertising proved pitifully inappropriate, borne out by the final irony that the *intended* irony had collapsed into lethal counter-productiveness. The campaign's cutting edge was its irony, its implication that orthodox vanity here addressed in an anti-cosmetics idiom, would prevail over whatever dark forces they presumed responsible for drug taking. In trying to be anti-aspirational, the chosen stimulus failed to produce the right response, and perversely, succeeded in seeming glamorous.

What proved sad about this was that drugs, far from being an exception to advertising's articles of faith, were, in fact, among some of the intended audience, its weird apotheosis. Yellowhammer chose to use irony for the one thing for which irony was (ironically) the worst possible idiom. In addition to the lifestyle-driven volition demonstrated by addicts is the fact that drugs monstrously exaggerate all normal consumerism; they transform the ordinary into the extraordinary, otherworldly bliss of fantasy and pleasure and express a whole lifestyle in so doing, all to the tune of complete price inelasticity. Supply and demand are linked in cruelly manipulated exponential ratios, in a way that mirrors the great object of advertising, which is to dampen price sensitivity and to bolster up what people are willing to spend on a brand as much as possible (price being as relative a part of branding as any other). Addiction is the ideology of advertising taken to its logical conclusion. Not only did Yellowhammer get it wrong by underestimating the perversity and self-destructiveness that the consumer impulse can reach,

but in so doing, they failed to take into account two important corollaries of the use of advertising in socially-loaded
contexts.

First, lifestyle brand advertising can only ever talk the language of consumerism; no other response is possible, not even
that of *not* consuming. Second, branding is itself an ideology,
with its own momentum and frames of reference, its own world-
view and prescriptive drives. In short, it was more than an
example of the contest between creativity and research in advertising method, it showed what happens when you forget that
consumerism by lifestyle and self-image is a language and value
system of its own, and cannot be turned, by irony, or good
intentions, to any other end.

SINDY, PLAYMATE OF THE MONTH

In 1984, a poster campaign for Sindy dolls appeared all over
London. It featured the doll, spreadeagled against a spoof
Caribbean setting, beneath the headline, 'Playmate of the
month'. The feminist wrath it incurred was the subject of an
acrimonious column in *Marketing Week*, in which Iain Murray
lashed out, once and for all, against such loony nonsense:

> We have all known for some time that women's groups are
> not too keen on dolls of any kind, mainly because such
> playthings encourage ideas of sexual stereotyping at an
> early age. Little girls who play with baby dolls may, if we
> are not careful, grow up with the idea that there is some-
> thing natural about the maternal instinct.[30]

His shrill and defensive sarcasm offers a fascinating vision of
adspeak tearing itself into dialectical pieces. His apoplectic bile
rapidly disintegrates into a pitched battle between advertising
and propaganda, nature and politics, terms he manically polar-
ises, but which become more and more rabidly confused until,
like man and pig at the end of *Animal Farm*, one can no longer
really distinguish them. This, then, is a contest between
common-sense literalness, and benighted political inference.
The natural and the literal are perverted by the political and the
interpreted; to make any political claim against an ad is, for him,
to corrupt the natural and literal innocence of the manufacturer's obvious intentions. 'Sindy's offence was to be seen

posing under the headline "Playmate of the Month". In the eyes
of the feminists that meant that she was being made to look like
the centrefold model of Playboy magazine.'[31] Propaganda, he
explains, vandalises natural instincts, rubbishing them as
oppressive myths. The doll, the martyred icon at the heart of
this tug-of-war is to the advertiser a surrogate for a baby, a
symbol of the maternal instinct; and therefore proof and guarantor that what it represents is as natural as rainwater.

So how does this explain his next piece of arch attudinising:

> Sindy, Barbie, and the rest are particularly objectionable
> because the fantasy world that they occupy is unashamedly
> glamorous. Sindy is extremely fashion-conscious – her
> wardrobe includes an elegant sequined evening gown – her
> hair is always styled, and of course, she wears make-up. In
> short, she is clearly a sucker for all the meaningless trap-
> pings of bourgeois society.[32]

First, how can *this* doll embody a maternal instinct when it is
marketed not as an infant but as a mini-adult? How can Sindy be
innocently neutral when part of the fantasy world of girly sexual
glamour? Sindy is the child consumer mawkishly role-playing
her entry into what for advertising at least, is the most important
instinct of all, the one that says personality is what you make of
it, and sexuality the central pivot to lifestyle as glamour. How
also, can it make sense to accuse the ad's critics of *both* reading
too much into an image (porn where none was intended) *and*
implying that society comprises 'meaningless trappings'?

Against this emerges Murray's own parody of what feminist/
agitprop dolls would be like, fully bearing out that it is *his*
assumption every bit as much as theirs that a brand/icon is
inevitably packaged in terms of the values of the market/culture
of its origins, and can never be a beacon for the natural, the
innocent and the untainted:

> One can only speculate on the kind of dolls the protest
> industry would favour. The Greenham doll, perhaps
> dressed in a boiler suit with billy can and galvanised
> chamber pot accessories. Or the Flying Picket doll, which
> comes complete with a Police Brutality doll for hours of
> stimulating play. And instead of a doll's house, how about a
> tight-knit community soup kitchen?[33]

A whole social agenda gets pilloried by Murray, with odious self-satisfaction, and finally, with gross disingenuousness. In this manichean world in which he vents his dull paranoia the feminist project gets contrasted to the one he is defending, by amazing sleight of hand. A corollary of the natural is the literal, and here the responsibility for all the fuss is put squarely down to warped response 'in the eyes of the feminists' where should have been merely literal take-out: 'the little girls *would* interpret the headline in its literal sense. . . . As for the parents . . . the headline . . . *would not* have been found offensive.'

It is surely incredible that anyone would have wanted to defend this ad, let alone use it as the flaming torch in a crusade against the truism that advertising deals in stereotypes, and that stereotypes are often suspect. The ad was repulsive (unwittingly one would imagine) with its ghostly paedophilia, its equation of doll and toy-girl, sexuality presented as something to be ogled and fondled, undressed and posed.

What really emerges from this is the nature of stereotyping as much in the ad as in the mud-slinging that surrounded it. The episode demonstrated the way the branding process embraces the 'target' consumer. To 'respond' to an ad is necessarily to respond *as* a stereotype. The logic of branding includes the consumer who brands him or herself in the act of 'consuming' the ad. It is another consequence of branding that if the only things that are capable of significance are the non-functional aspects of what we buy, then everything else becomes, literally, *in*significant.

Such classifying of people works to both *include* and *exclude* people (and their characteristic responses) from the world of social relations from which advertisers draw their stimuli. If a 'yuppie' is someone who cannot live outside the 'I aspire therefore I am' ethos of advertising, then his or her opposite is the 'lesbian' or 'animal liberationist', or anyone who lives beyond its pale. Research may vindicate stereotypes, but it does not justify how they are used.

But more interesting still was the letter and the editorial comment that letter caused in the subsequent issue.

The letter shows that against the poisonous polarising stereotypes of Murray's brand ideology, there exists only one sort of genuine response. What is displayed in the letter is language used in a way diametrically opposed to the way the advertiser uses it. At the heart of what Tamara Palshi is saying lie two things: a declaration of being the person she is and an assertion of certain principles, both offended by the ad:

> I am neither an ardent feminst, nor gay, nor lesbian, not black, nor coloured, nor an under-estimated housewife, nor an animal liberationist, etc. On the contrary I am a professional woman, working with children. I found the aforementioned poster distasteful; without being influenced by any pressure group I felt that rather than 'Play-mate of the Month' being intended literally for young children, it was I, the adult, who understood a broader connotation . . . (neither am I a sexually inadequate/frigid/inhibited woman).[34]

Her strategy for escaping the logic of branding which in Murray's hands invidiously stereotypes *all* opinion-holders, is to cordon off her sense of self, and her principles, and to rewrite the relationship that exists between them. She thereby locates the responsibility for the effect an ad has in the idiom/image chosen, and not in her own sexual/social identity. This has the effect of making explicit the role played by notions of perverse sexuality and extremist partisanship in Iain Murray's defence of advertising common-sense psychology. And by doing this, she severs the corrosive equation of opinion and stereotype that is at the heart of the branding process, and challenges its odd view of itself as an art free of ulterior purposes, somehow innocent, natural and candid.

Her rhetoric is *under*-motivated, to avoid being dismissed as special pleading (which begs the question, what if she *had* been one of the things she claimed not to be). Murray's, on the other hand, is as over-motivated as the rhetoric he defends, that of brand advertising. His is a fury common to all advertisers challenged by a deviant reading, and stems from their largest frustration of all – that they can't *make* us read their ads 'properly'.

6

KNOCKING COPY
Advertising and its critics

ADVERTISING IN THE MOVIES

Advertising has never been short of enemies, usually though, people secure in their sense of superior self-worth; academics, artists, tax accountants. But the most relentless, systematic and vitriolic scourge of Madison Avenue has been Hollywood, a case of Sodom cocking a snook at Gomorrah. This is a doubly wounding blow to the advertiser's vanity, not just because nobody likes to have their spotted soul explored in cinemascope, but because adland is besotted with movies.

> Cinema despises advertising. It treats the industry and its practitioners with derision, it holds them up as objects of mockery and satire, it lambasts them for the sins of cynicism, deception, greed and contempt for the public (sins which quite justifiably could be laid on the doorstep of its own foyer).[1]

Perhaps there is a hint of displacement going on here, the transferral to another medium of Hollywood's own self-loathing? More likely an explanation for the short shrift that adland has consistently got from the movie-makers is that by attacking commercials and those who made them, Hollywood was in fact attacking the new competition from television. Attack being the best form of defence it clearly made sense to see off the new rival by rubbing our noses in the banality and duplicity of the commercials that were television's *sine qua non*. This also explains, perhaps, why advertising has been much more kindly treated on American television, from the ingenuous charm of Samantha's copywriter husband, Darren, in the 60s comedy series *Bewitched*, to the sophisticated moral dilemmas of

Thirtysomething, both series which reflected and explored key moments in the rise of the consumerist society, the boom years of the 60s and the late 80s.

But whatever the explanation, cinema's attack has lasted nearly fifty years, and has been remarkably consistent, on both sides of the Atlantic. From films like *The Hucksters* (1947) to *Crazy People* (1990), the advertiser and his fatuous, hollow job have been endlessly lampooned. These films are so numerous they almost constitute a genre; they certainly share a handful of identical themes and plot structures. Ad-films' central characters are invariably at the mercy of bosses who are irredeemably wed to the profit motive; Sidney Greenstreet expectorating on the conference room table ('You have just seen me do a disgusting thing, but you will always remember it') set the mould in *The Hucksters*. Against these implacable tyrants, the central character inevitably comes face to face with the great vices of the advertising business; its manipulation of a gullible public, transient celebrity and undeserved success, and nose-dives into black disillusion, emerging either questing for dignity and idealism (Clark Gable in *The Hucksters*, Cary Grant in *Mr Blandings Builds His Dreamhouse*, Tony Randall in *Will Success Spoil Rock Hunter?* (1957), Jack Lemmon in *Good Neighbour Sam* (1964) and Albert Brooks in *Lost in America* (1984)); or else even more satanic than before he met his Mephistopheles (Oliver Reed in *I'll Never Forget Whatshisname* (1967) or Richard E. Grant in *How To Get Ahead in Advertising* (1989)).

Even more telling are the cameo roles and background details. The best of these are the classic films *Twelve Angry Men* (1957) and *North by Northwest* (1959). The former stars Henry Fonda as an architect who is part of a jury considering what looks an open and shut case of murder. The other eleven jurors, picked to represent a cross-section of American white male citizens, include an adman played by Robert Webber. Fonda's penetrating moral integrity forces his more volatile and prejudiced colleagues to reconsider the case and its anomalies, and gradually, after ferocious argument, the accused's guilt becomes untenable. In the meantime, it is Webber's asinine fatuousness that makes it inconceivable that he could be anything other than an adman. 'Um, if no-one else has an idea, I may have a cutie here. I mean, I haven't put much though into it. Anyway lemme throw it out on the stoop and see if the cat licks it up.'

Altogether more suave (admen are, after all, charmers as well as buffoons), is the character played by Cary Grant in the Hitchcock classic, *North by Northwest*, Roger O. Thornhill (the 'O' stands for 'nothing', in order to make the name a wry acronym: 'ROT, it's my trademark'). Luckily for adland, his professional duplicities ('In the world of advertising there's no such thing as a lie, only expedient exaggeration', he quips to his secretary) become forgiveably pale when compared to those of international assassins.

Nor has it been any great surprise that advertising should have been used in 80s Britain as the vehicle for much more ambitious political and cultural satire – *The Ploughman's Lunch* (1983), *Honest, Decent and True* (1986) and *How to Get Ahead in Advertising* (1989) are the three key examples. Written by Ian McEwan, Les Blair and Bruce Robinson respectively, they form three of the angriest diatribes against Thatcherite Britain. Slightly less vitriolically, the BBC series *Notes from the Margin* had six writers 'review' the 80s (it was transmitted at the end of 1989). What was curious was how four of them based their avowedly critical pictures of what had happened to Britain in the 80s on advertising conceits; the myth of the 'new man'; the transformation of Britain into a history theme park; the arrival of new age, post-consumer values and the advertising's use of ethnic diversity as a new, global, added value.

Similarly, *The Ploughman's Lunch* had as its central metaphor for all that was rotten in the state of early 80s Britain, the kitsch nostalgia of an Ovaltine commercial being shot by the cynical (but sagelike) Frank Finlay. He explains that the 'ploughman's lunch' was a marketing fabrication designed to flog pickle. Against the background of the Tory Party conference, media toadies and loathsome publishing sycophants, the film warns us against allowing history to be tampered with.

Les Blair's television play was previewed in the *Listener* thus:

Satirised in the sixties, semiotically worked over in the seventies, advertising in the eighties has had a disturbingly easy ride. Now ubiquitous, it's also, for some reason, prestigious. Even many of its left-wing critics have lost their ideological confidence: instead of challenging the ground rules, old opponents now rush to join what seems to be the only game in time. Which is one reason to welcome Les

Blair's often sharp and cynical *Screen Two* send-up 'Honest, Decent and True' (BBC 2).[2]

His pincer-movement on his target are not surprisingly, aimed at both the style and artistic pretensions of the business:

> the film's location . . . is a perfect contemporary advertising microcosm of style, stupidity, sex and self-loathing. . . . Blair's target here is perhaps not only the advertising industry but the state of our imagination, as creativity and commerce converge. 'The pun' remarks a copywriter, 'has taken over from the epic novel as the cultural focal point of our society'.[3]

But it is *How to Get Ahead in Advertising* that tried to take the advertising game the furthest as a satire on the thick-skinned underbelly of 80s consumer complacency. The central character has writer's block thinking up a campaign for an anti-boil cream. His consequent frustration becomes rapidly darker and more unhinged, until finally a pimple growing on his neck becomes a fully-fledged carbuncle, a grotesque *alter ego* that argues with him. Motivated from the outset as an explicitly political piece 'about my perception of where the country is going', Robinson's attack on advertising quickly becomes clumsy, overdone and tiresome. Perhaps too it was the film that showed up all too obviously the contradictions in the critique that uses advertising as a universal condemnation of society.

What these movies remind us, however, is just how widespread and how overfamiliar the criticisms of advertising are. Not many of the films that have advertising as their subject are much good as films, and even fewer work as effective indictments of advertising. For that we need to turn to a medium that in many ways parrots the views found in these films, but with much more portent – the academic.

AD BATING

Venting ideological spleen at advertising has itself become something of a critical industry these last two decades or so. A mixture of high moral dudgeon and sonorous jargon is an irresistible one. It's a rhetoric that has at its disposal whole tracts of vulgar Marxism, unwieldy communication theories and a lexicon of theory-speak, reinvigorated recently by semiology and feminism with which to lambast the icon market-place. These, combined with the fact that ads, glamorous bijoux of all our most obvious social vices, are the (crudely) realised artefacts of specific prior intentions, ensure an enviable point and weight for the project.

A typical example of what I mean is a book called *The Language of Advertising*, by Vestegaard and Schroder,[4] two Danish professors of English, which is prey to the most common vices of academic social comment, that is, jargon, self-righteousness and fundamental flaws of logic. In the words of one reviewer:

> [this] is a painstakingly earnest work, strongly influenced by structuralism and written in the sort of pseudo-intellectual patois affected by Barthesian critics: e.g. 'the text is a structured unit – it has texture', 'the metalinguistic function focuses on the code', and 'the concept of deictic anchorage'.[5]

But, even more crippling than this, is, ironically, the same confusion between qualities seen as 'natural' and those qualities of social origin that infect the more pretentious advertisers themselves:

> the moment you pause to think, the discourse loses its coherence. This is particularly so in the last chapter, *The Ideology of Advertising*, where the authors . . . tell us that it is a fact that a mother's love for her child is not natural, but a socially and historically determined option (pp. 145–46) yet urge on us the desirability of spontaneous human relationships and feelings (p. 172) and think we should leave our eyebrows 'as nature created them' (p. 157). In short, they will have Nature when it suits them, and Culture when it does not.[6]

As an intriguing final note, the reviewer places this book and his critique of it right at the heart of that ambivalence to culture that I have tried to show as characteristic of Roland Barthes:

> When Dennis Potter reviewed the English translation of Barthes's 'Mythologies', he suggested that Barthes would be perfectly at home as an ad man. I remember finding the

suggestion irritating and implausible. Unfortunately for me, it turns out that Barthes did once do work for an advertising agency, Publicis, and wrote a study for them *L'Image publicitaire de l'Automobile. Analyse Semiologique (1966)*.[7]

It is revealing that for Pateman the thought should be so intriguing, even galling, that Barthes should have been found fraternising with the enemy. But it does allow us one final irony:

> PHILADELPHIA, NOVEMBER 22, 1985. Torben Vestegaard and Kim Schroder, coauthors of 'The Language of Advertising', are the winners of the 1985 Orwell award, given by the Committee on Public Doublespeak of the National Council of Teachers of English. . . . The award, named for [sic] George Orwell, author of the novel '1984' and 'Politics and the English Language', recognises individuals for distinguished contributions to honesty and clarity in public language . . . this is the eleventh year of the Orwell award, established in 1975 to enhance public awareness of the need for critical reading and critical listening and viewing the messages of public spokespersons.[8]

Obfuscatory prolix, crassly shifting ideological parameters – it is hard to see how these things would have endeared themselves to George Orwell!

THE COMMODITY FETISH

The problem with culture is that it is both a literal and a metaphorical concept. Its objects work as both material entity and communicative icon. Indictments of advertising work by making a simple separation between the two, advocating a benchmark of rationality for judging consumerism and a criterion of functional worth for evaluating production. But it should by now be clear that images and symbolic meanings are not foolish adjuncts to a product, but central to it. It should also be clear that consumer behaviour cannot be neatly categorised as logical or cognitive, but must be seen as emotional and affective in equal measure. Values as central to consumer behaviour as liking or disliking things should make it obvious that rationality *per se* is not the prized bottom-line for behaviour as we are taught to think.

Critiques of advertising, and they are numerous, are exaggerated critiques of capitalism. The advertisement is doubly culpable, a highly suspect thing in its own right (an image), and an image of something even more suspect, the commodity. This represents false consciousness at both the material and the symbolic level. This rhetoric goes back to Marx, and in particular, to his notion of the 'commodity fetish' outlined in *Das Kapital*.

For Marx, the 'commodity' is not, as it might seem now, just a reductive tag, because although 'at first a very trivial thing, and easily understood', it nevertheless epitomises, rather numinously even, the central mysteries of capitalism:

> A commodity is therefore a mysterious thing, simply because in it the social character of men's labour appears to them as an objective character stamped upon the product of that labour. . . . This is the reason why the products of labour become commodities, social things whose qualities are at the same time perceptible and imperceptible to the senses.[9]

But commodities do not merely act as the vehicles for the 'social character' of the labours that produce them. They dissimulate those origins: 'the existence of things *qua* commodities, and the value-relation between the products of labour which *stamps* them as commodities, have absolutely no connexion with their physical properties and with the material relations arising therefrom.'[10] And they do this precisely to substitute those material values with more seductive values, ones that have all the allure and persuasion of religious magic:

> In order, therefore, to find an analogy, we must have recourse to the mist-enveloped regions of the religious world. In that world the productions of the human brain appear as independent beings endowed with life, and entering into relation both with one another and the human race. So it is in the world of commodities with the products of men's hands. This I call the Fetishism which attracts itself to the products of labour, so soon as they are produced as commodities, and which is therefore inseparable from the production of commodities.[11]

The use of the word 'Fetish' is a powerful stroke; it consolidates the sense that this is a polemic being delivered from a position beyond the 'mist-enveloped regions of the religious world'. But it is a word with more connotations than this, not just a secular term of abuse for the religious; it is a much stronger word than 'idol', which is an image or symbol that is highly venerated by a particular community.

> This distinction (between 'idol' and 'fetish') clarifies some of the specific force in Marx's choice of 'fetishism' as his concrete concept for commodities. Part of this is rhetorical: the figure of 'commodity fetishism' (*der Fetischcharacter der Waren*) is a kind of catachresis, a violent yoking of the most primitive, exotic, irrational, degraded objects of human value with the most modern, ordinary, rational and civilized.[12]

The word 'fetish' was therefore a highly-charged value-judgement, particularly at a time when patterns of industrialisation and conumption ('modernity') were first establishing themselves, and when their supporting ideologies of progress and rationality were in such contrast to how 'primitive' cultures of the Empire were viewed: 'In calling commodities fetishes, Marx is telling the nineteenth-century reader that the material basis of modern, civilized, rational political economy is structurally equivalent to that which is most inimical to modern consciousness.'[13]

This line of argument really catches light, however, when applied not just to the early forms of industrial capitalism, but to the later forms of mass consumerism and, naturally, advertising. Just consider these sub-titles from chapter 2 of W.F. Haug's seminal book *Critique of Commodity Aesthetics: Appearance, Sexuality and Advertising in Capitalist Society*:

1 The technocracy of sensuality – in general
2 The high status of mere illusion in capitalism
3 Aesthetic abstraction, philosophical foreplay
4 Aesthetic abstraction of the commodity; surface-packaging-advertising-image
5 The mirror-image of desire as deceptive illusion
6 Corrupting use-values; their feedback to the structure of needs

7 The ambiguity of commodity aesthetics exemplified by the use of sexual illusion[14]

This critique of capitalism's use and abuse of appearance, and sensuality to gull the masses is saturated with the concept of the 'fetish' as false consciousness, false needs and false values, writ large. It was analyses like these that made us familiar with a cynical interpretation of how consumer demand would be sustained and kept profitable; deliberate obsolescence; deceptive packaging; endless redesigns; aesthetic innovation continually done for the benefit of the entrepreneur rather than the consumer; the subordination of use-value to exchange-value.

Mass-media conspiracy theories like this, are all too often prey to extraordinarily paranoid hyperbole. This is Haug complaining about the invention of the brand name 'Hush Puppies', accusing it of symbolising a type of consumer lobotomy in which shoe-wearers are literally turned into 'hushed puppies', lapdogs to a treacherous corporate cynicism:

> In 1958, somewhere in the American Deep South, the sales director is said to have come across a group of people eating popcorn, and throwing some to their barking dogs with the words, 'Hush puppies!'. Watching this scene, a good idea came to him. It might profit his firm to offer something to pacify another kind of noisy 'dog'. This, of course, was the public – the world of buyers.[15]

And to make this even more cynical, the public weren't even asked if they liked the new brand name, they were simply treated to it as a *fait accompli*, after all, the whole point was to mute the consumer: 'The point is, that the "user" came last in the sales department's calculations, and success has proved them right: the user's judgement could easily be remoulded, and bought off by the dog-symbol.'[16] This not only seems remarkably unlikely given the enormous lengths companies go to in researching these things with consumers, but it is contradicted by Haug's next assertion, his contempt for the fact that the fawning German consumer actually came to quite like the name:

> The trademark's success is reflected in the approval of *Frankfurter Allgemeine Zeitung*'s business section. 'This endearing little chap . . . who seems a bit of a clumsy fellow but lovable from the moment you set eyes on him, with his

long brown ears and white nose, now has friends in over 46 countries.' Without this disguise, the greed for profit which pacifies people like barking dogs would never have so many friends from all over the world. The animal suggests a quality of shambling loyalty intended to buy off and silence the buyer's reasonable mistrust.[17]

'Reasonable mistrust' of what? That the shoes weren't really made out of basset-hound? This is the sort of remark that gives ideological pique a bad name. The success of the brand-name reflects the associations it triggers off in the consumer about the shoe, and not on the name's abilities to neutralise consumer vigilance. 'Hush Puppies' conjure up, in my mind at least, the positive qualities of favourite suede shoes, of their texture, and of the way that shoes make you conscious of your own movements. If you didn't have a vision of advertising as a sort of social opiate, numbing our critical faculties, then you couldn't write polemic that sees its mission as being the opposite of this, mobilising popular wrath.

But Haug was doing more than merely cataloguing the cynical tricks of capitalist economies, he was being an iconoclast, disrupting a whole view of the world. Like Marx before him, his critique is a sustained assault not just on a political practice, but on a way of knowing the world, in just the same way that postreformation protestants accused catholics not just of doctrinal error, but of idolatry.

> Indeed to a devout Puritan, the difference between heathen fetishism and Catholic idolatry was not terribly significant . . . there is a similarity, not just among different sorts of of image worship, but among different kinds of hostility towards image worship. . . . The typical features of iconoclasm . . . involve a twofold accusation of folly and vice, epistemological error and moral depravity. The idolater is naive and deluded, the victim of false religion. But the illusion is never simply innocent or harmless . . . it is always a dangerous, vicious mistake that not only destroys the idolater and his tribe, but threatens to destroy the iconoclast as well.[18]

But the use of the term 'fetish' only works if we all agree that objects endowed with non-functional meanings are a bad thing.

To tell a West African worshiper of fetishes that his talis-
mans and amulets are, to him, magical objects that contain
a supernatural presence is only to tell him what he already
believes. To tell a capitalist that gold is his 'holy grail' by
contrast, is to utter a slander that he will deny with all his
heart.[19]

The African tribesman has no problem with his magic-objects,
because he has no problem with being an African tribesman. It is
only if the accusation of being no 'better' than an 'African
primitive' cuts you to the quick that being accused of having
fetishes will constitute slander. If, on the other hand, you con-
duct an anthropological study of a culture's mores that doesn't
aim to inferiorise its subject, then the mechanisms of cultural
process start to seem much less threatening. Sociologists, and
advertisers, have been busy trying to do just this, by keeping the
question of consumer value separate from the question of
ideology.

HIDDEN VALUES

In his survey of where, post-Barthes, we now stand in terms of
interpretation, Christopher Butler tackles the question of
ideology:

The notion of ideology is a complex one. It can have a
descriptive sense which presupposes a neutral observer: as
when the anthropologist describes a 'cultural system' – its
kinship-relations, its scientific and religious beliefs, its legal
institutions, and so on, and their interaction.[20]

'Ideology' is both a way of describing what makes a particular
society tick, and, more positively, what allows us 'to participate in
frameworks of belief that make life "meaningful" for us and
help us to feel that we are part of a culture'.[21] And on both these
counts, advertising, as accounted for by the cool anthropology of
advertising gurus like Judie Lannon,[22] smells of roses.

But there is another use of the term ideology, an oppositional
one, pledged to the analysis of underlying, and often covert
ways of thinking. To investigate hidden values represents a
quest for irony, for a sense of gap or hiatus between intended
and unintended meanings, and is particularly appropriate 'in

media like advertising and television, where there may well be strong motives for disguising them (or at least in advertising, for working by indirection)'.[23]

This involves the shedding of critical light on the implicit assumptions stereotypically present in an ad, and on the nature of the artifice used to create the illusion of the natural. An example of the former is quoted from Barthes: 'the advertiser's phrase "Secretaire, je veux être impeccable" reflects a whole series of assumptions concerning the subordination of women: 'a whole ethos of acceptance of masculine prerogatives.'[24] Butler goes on to cite Catherine Belsey's analysis of perfume branding as a further example of that ideological critique of the 'indirection' of advertising method:

> Here different smells, which are not all that easily discriminated in fact, have to be artificially differentiated by the advertiser. He does this by associating them in his advertisement with a 'social meaning', so that 'the product becomes a signifier of specific cultural or ideological values'. This is seen by the way in which different perfumes are aimed at different types of women, from the daydreamer to the 'liberated' woman.[25]

But by now it is clear that far from blowing the lid off the whole business, all that she has done is reiterate utter marketing truisms – that functionally indistinguishable products have to be 'positioned' in a relative, but not, for all that, an arbitrary, way. Apart from perhaps making the business look a little cynical, what we see here is that critic and advertiser are locked into endlessly reworking each other's methods in complementary idioms. The critic succeeds in being censorious by tone of voice alone; as Butler himself concedes, the task of indictment is a second, and different project: 'What advertisements thus reveal in fact are the norms for their own interpretation, and it is a separate question whether our oppositional model can show that such norms are objectionable.'[26] This breaking of consumerist butterflies on dialectical wheels was beautifully lampooned in a Private Eye skit on Ben Elton, a radical London comedian who regularly rubbishes the assumptions of ads with a (brilliant) *reductio ad absurdum* translation into literalness of their added values. What the 'Great bores of today' column did was satirise the cliquey self-evidentness behind this type of political humour, its chic repertoire of coded cues for ideological contempt:

> . . . good evening . . . all right . . . .OK . . . yeah . . . well . . . Mrs Thatcher! . . . right know what I mean . . . seen that advert on the telly . . . nuclear family buys washing up liquid . . . sexist . . . all-right . . . seen that other ad on telly . . . where the bloke wakes up to find a bloody helicopter overhead? . . . OK, know the one? . . . Yeah, that'll happen in Thatcher's Britain all right . . .[27]

In other words, what a social scientist has to do is acknowledge the profoundly socio-cultural significance of commodities and avoid evaluating them in strictly economic terms: 'commodities have importance as signs or symbols and not merely for the intrinsic satisfaction which they might bring . . . the ultimate problem in understanding industrial societies is not how goods come to be made, but how they take on meaning.'[28] But, according to Colin Campbell, it requires a hands-off tolerance that few social scientists can long sustain, especially when it is their own society's practices that are being explored: 'the discussion of consumption by social scientists is singularly marked by a tendency to substitute moralizing for careful analysis, thereby causing existing theorizing to be marred by intrusive observations of an ideological nature.'[29] The target for this style of academic critique is usually the consumer, whose credulity and greed, manipulated by the dark forces of advertisers, so raise the hackles of the thesis-writers:

> These two factors operate, when combined, to generate a view of modern consumer behaviour as a form of conduct which is both 'irrational and reprehensible'. Irrational in the sense that such endless wanting is 'meaningless' from the point of view of the individual consumer, who is impelled to behave in this fashion by forces beyond his control; and 'reprehensible' insofar as the image of human nature appealed to in explaining this conduct presents individuals in an unfavourable light.[30]

It is very hard, then, to make ideology a central concern without falling prey to easy (and patronising) scorn. The whole business of getting some kind of critical handle on the belief, now rampant in advertising circles – that advertising genuinely mirrors the world as it is socially and psychologically structured – is much harder than it looks.

NEW TIMES

The impasse reached by these attempts at complete ideological indictments of advertising made some kind of re-evaluation inevitable – if only because Britain in the 80s was in the middle of one of the most transformative periods in its recent history. The irrelevance of the old moral antipathy to consumerism was not only becoming apparent in principle, but in practice, as three successive elections saw a Tory government committed to 'enterprise culture' returned to power, by a constituency of voters who could in no way be written off as either a privileged elite or a duped proletariat. It was becoming obvious that the old models used to condemn advertising were not 'oppositional', but denigratory.

With the explosion in consumption during the 80s, it became politically inevitable that the left would have to reconsider its superiority complex about shopping. In condemning advertising, the left was in effect, condemning the people who used it, with misleading and obsolete assumptions. This has produced a corrective tendency in left thinking designed to take better account of how advertising works, what the process has to offer a left determined to catch up on lost ground. Advertising was, as usual, merely part of a larger problem, that of the increasingly inescapable sense that the left was becoming alienated from the rapidly changing face of 80s British culture.

Such thinking took three main forms. It involved a recognition of the limitations and inadequacies of the traditionally hostile view of advertising, and above all, the recognition that critiques of advertising had lost their oppositional force. The second strategy was to analyse advertising and shopping as forms of popular culture in their own right, alongside pop music and fashion. And thirdly, the left explored the extent to which advertising could be used for *its* ends, as liberating and counter-cultural.

The disillusionment with the old left anti-consumer moralism was intellectually spurred on by two forces coming out of various media and communication departments in the polytechnics and universities – the study of popular culture and the rise of postmodernism. Each challenged the political and aesthetic certainties that underwrote the old view of cultural processes. Even more than fashion or pop music, advertising was *the* test-case, because, more than the others, it embodied the most damaging contradictions that left-wing theory has to deal with, speaking as advertising purports to do to people entirely in terms of what they 'want', and in a language purposely honed to pleasurable comprehension, to effective relevance.

NEW TIMES

By the mid-80s it was as obvious to the left as to anyone how things had changed in our culture, and that the advertising process was central to large parts of that change. Indeed, the speed and enthusiasm shown by the Labour Party in its embracing of public relations, image consultancy and media sophistication may have looked like a braver breaking with the past than it in fact was. It is easier, after all, to write off your troubles as merely a problem with image management. So far anyway, the use of Tory presentation techniques has had little effect; perhaps Britain in the 80s rejected more than just the Labour Party's image.

Things had become more relative, but increasingly in a way underwritten by consumerism, especially by the notion of identity – corporate, gender, ethnic, national, even individual. Advertising was the industry quickest to exploit the extent to which identity is something constructed, something invented and controlled.

The marketing process straddled the cultural and the material, the public and the private spheres with increasing confidence. Our world was splintering into the fragmented analogies of the advertising proposition – the tone of the ad, its production values, the media used to broadcast it, the picture of the target group, the product itself, its packaging, name, even its price, the retail environment it is stocked in, the lifestyle it becomes a prop for. The identity of the consumer is tied up with the identity not only of the brand, but of the company that produces it. Lifestyle becomes the nexus between corporate identity on the one hand and our personal lives on the other.

It was, in short, making a nonsense of the assumptions on which the old view rested. The traditional equation between advertising and false needs was simply too clumsy – and also patronising; shopping is what people actually *do*, and enjoy doing. Despising this fact was something guaranteed to keep you deeply alienated from a large part of everyday life.

Furthermore, the social value and meaning of objects far outstrips in range and subtlety the crude Marxist distinction between 'use' and 'exchange' value. Third, the role played by desire and pleasure cannot be ignored, or written off as mindless hedonism. And fourth, patterns of consumption offered more fertile insight into how class groups intersect than could be gleaned from the nineteenth-century categories of traditional political thought. You may not like advertising, but it pays to understand it.

As long ago as 1986, Kathy Myers was admonishing the left for their theoretical naivety about advertising, and its role as a potent form of popular culture:

> consumption – why and how people consume goods – has never been treated as an important part of economic theory. This is because consumption is thought to be a 'reactive' process, quite crudely reacting to the fruits of industry – that which has already been produced . . . this theory that consumption is 'outside' economics also affects the way in which the left sees and understands the role of commodities in our lives. It links up inextricably with the idea that the world is divided into socially useful and useless goods and that advertising is responsible for the stage management of the latter.[31]

And urging them to take seriously not only the advertising process, but its pivotal position in British culture:

> Advertising is a metaphor for the age . . . it still provides the most sophisticated economic and ideological analysis of the desires, aims and ambitions of that strife-torn plunder pit called Britain . . . it provides an analysis which is, by definition, political. The left ignores that at its peril.[32]

This dismissive reappraisal of why the left had such a problem with consumption became one of a host of major themes explored between 1987 and 1989 in a project rather bravely named *New Times*, the intellectual left's boldest bid for late 80s relevance, sponsored by the magazine *Marxism Today* and championed by Stuart Hall and Martin Jacques. *New Times* addressed a changing British culture by paying especial attention to the new alliances between class and the economy, the new patterns of work and leisure, social formation, the new urban geography, and most crucially, the new politics of identity. Implicit in this approach was the recognition that ten years of Thatcherism had put paid to some of the older sacred cows of left thinking, and that older orthodoxies were ill-equipped (and ill-disposed) to understanding the diversity of consumer lifestyles that were coming more and more to determine social and political life.

But above all, this attempted rehabilitation of the importance of advertising as a social index was part of an attempt to make left theory more democratic, less patronising and more alive to the political possibilities in those areas of people's lives that the left had abandoned to Thatcherism. In his essay 'The politics of consumption', Frank Mort redresses the dismissive disdain usually vouched the subject:

> Consuming, as opposed to producing, was at best handled as secondary and trivial, confined to the private, feminised sphere of household duties, and personal life. At worst, consumption was cast as a moral evil, buying off working people with an orgy of goodies – or so the argument often went.[33]

It is one of the key contentions of popular culture that the advertising process is not necessarily a Thatcherite phenomenon, it is merely that it was the right who most successfully co-opted the mid-80s consumer boom. Frank Mort's point is that if you call to mind how *branding* works, then it becomes clear why understanding consumption is so important, and so open: (i) advertising works on the back of a *dialogue* between manufacturer and consumer and it recognises that (ii) objects *mean* by virtue of how they are *used*, and that neither of these terms is ever *fixed*, (iii) those meanings take on emotional as well as rational forms, (iv) meanings are expressed through intangibles as well as concrete things, (v) consumers create those meanings not just as individuals, but also on the basis of ever-changing group affiliations and (vi) that consumption is one of the most potent crossing points between the market (the public sphere) and the individual (the private sphere) – and that values can go between *both* those spheres.

Advertising could, at the very least, be credited with an inter-esting *empirical* grasp of social attitudes. As cultural studies became more preoccupied with a materialist view of society, then the brand-led research conducted by ad agencies, and their corollary views of social groups, were not to be ignored:

> marketing has produced pervasive classifications of 'social types' in the 1980s (the yuppie is the most obvious example). We use these categories as a kind of social shorthand even if we are reluctant to find ourselves re-flected in them. We live in a world and in bodies which are deeply scored by the power relations of race and class, sexuality and gender but we also live – whether or not we know it consciously – in a world of style-setters, innovators, sloanes, preppies, empty nesters . . . dinkies . . . casuals, sensibles, the constrained majority, and todays's prime tar-gets, the pre-teens and woofies (well-off-older-people). . . . We may find such forms of knowledge immoral, objection-able or sinister . . . but the fact is they do actively create and sustain one *version* of the social.[34]

The fact that this type of research produced results that trans-gressed the established ideas of class attitude, *and* that they involved coming to terms with what people wanted to become, gave it a relevance to cultural politics that it had not traditionally been credited with: 'Such a mix of traditional social/academic work and commercial/marketing knowledge functions would take the Left beyond the ghetto of "miserabilism" to which it is regularly consigned by the loony Right.'[35] Advertising was sophisticated enough to be taken seriously, but also crude enough to be readily comprehensible; it therefore offered a valuable 'half-way' house between 'old' and 'new' times, a power-ful symbol of the transition that political thinking needed to make. Things like 'niche marketing' and 'lifestyle segmentation' not only tell you a lot about 80s thinking, but contain within them assumptions dear to the political postmodernist – not least a radical notion of 'identity': 'as in the marketplace, so in the political meeting, postmodern structures of identity are less centred around (sic) the certainty of the fixed self.'[36] Advertising recognises that people's sense of who they are is expressed and acted upon in complex and shifting ways. Most suggestive of all was advertising's emphasis not on the fixed human nature of the individual, but on the extent to which identity is culturally constructed. This chimed in, after all, with the cultural theorist's own project, which was to gain recognition for the importance of such categories as race, gender, class and sexuality at the expense of the more traditional Western faith in the transcendental subject.

And furthermore, people were credited with a more flexible ability to deal with the 'subjectivities' constructed in the ads. Just as we are getting better at understanding the extent to which our identity is socially constructed, the less of a problem this is becoming as a critical truism. We know that the 'you' posited by the ad will always necessarily be a social construct, in the case of advertising that of the 'aspirational consumer'. But we are also perfectly capable of holding onto the fact that there are a plethora of other 'you's that can be constructed by other media. We don't necessarily have a problem with this; after all we know that it would make no sense for an ad not to posit its 'you' as an aspirational consumer, and we wouldn't thank them for it if they didn't.

After all, the subject-position 'aspirational consumer' is actually rather an important one. It takes us into one of the most vexed political criteria, that of choice, because the 'aspirational consumer' is doubly built around the notion of being able to choose. As I said earlier, choice is important in terms of what it means to be denied it. Anyone can *choose* to live in decent housing; but that choice only means something if you can then afford to buy that housing – or have a local authority able and willing to supply it to you on terms that you can afford. *Both* of these things can be denied, because choice isn't just a monopoly of the market.

The great lesson in public housing, for instance, has been what happens when you stop treating people as though they had a choice, as though they were aspirational consumers, rather than powerless clients, as any apostle of community architecture will tell you. Just because you don't purchase the property doesn't mean you shouldn't be treated as though you had. This is an entirely different argument from the privatisation one, which is not about choice at all, but about paying for choice. Not being an 'aspirational consumer' is, on one level, to be stripped of the capacity to make choices likely to improve or safeguard a desired quality of life, and it is just as easy to deprive someone of this by setting up a price threshold as by being bureaucratic and authoritarian. We may not always admire the types of communication that do address us this way, much of which is sycophantic and insincere (the patois of American fast-food outlets, for example, or the spuriously personalised address on junk-mail envelopes), but a world in which no one ever feels it necessary to cast you in the role of 'aspirational consumer' is a grim prospect, just ask the East Europeans.

DEVIANT CONSUMERISM

But if the study of popular culture was motivating this reappraisal of the *content* of the consumer society, then postmodernism was also making certain critics reconsider its *forms*. Interest in shopping as a social activity had become inevitable (as it began to replace more traditional popular activities, like sport, and as it began to be catered for by larger scale changes to architecture and urban topography, as well shifting patterns in the economy, the rise of credit and the increase in disposable income).

But alongside this, far greater interest than ever before was also being invested in taking interpretation out of the literary, and applying it to other cultural forms. Theory gave us the opportunity to *read* ads with more bravura and insight than ever before, and as post-structuralisms's baroque obscurities became the friendlier, party-clothed paradoxes of postmodernism (the non-fixedness of meaning, the constitutiveness of discourse, the relativism of 'difference'), so consumption looked the place where you could both have fun and be intellectually hip. Traditional literary comprehension and traditional economics both gave way to newer ways of understanding culture, culminating in an unprecedented interest in advertising, the place the two met.

> Recent years have seen an explosion of interest in a whole range of cultural texts and practices which had previously been scorned by, or remained invisible to, academic criticism. Contemporary cultural critics . . . take as their subjects sport, fashion, hairstyles, shopping games and social rituals, and unabashedly bring to bear on these areas the same degree of theoretical sophistication as they would to any high cultural artefact. In a sense this is a postmodern phenomenon, for it is the mark of that levelling of hierarchies and blurring of boundaries which is an effect of the

explosion of the field of culture described by [Fredric] Jameson in which the cultural and the social and the economic are no longer easily distinguishable from one another.[37]

Having swept aside many of the left's old assumptions, the space was cleared for the left's most daring attempt to reclaim consumption for its ends – deviant consumerism. A common complaint about the sort of rhetoric or text that is the opposite not just of advertising, but advertising's media neighbours, fashion and the style press, is one about their language: 'In the pagan, postmodern world in which some of my students live . . . *Ten 8* (a pedagogic arts magazine) is the profane text – its subject matter dull, verbose and prolix; its tone earnest and teacherly.'[38] Or, like feminists who have a problem with fashion:

> The 'eighties girl' . . . associates Feminism's proscriptive attitudes with 'bossy' welfarism of the Labour years which was dismissed in the political climate of the 1980s as totally obsolete. So it is not feminism *per se* they reject, but this morally authoritarian, feminist hegemony and the lifestyle associated with it.[39]

Both examples find a type of political liberation in consumption, in the pages of *The Face*, and *Elle* respectively. Both reject not politics *per se* but politics-that-is-the-opposite-of-consumption. Boring and didactic, boring because didactic, because obsessed with the notion that you can define value with reference to some notion of the *authentic*.

> An unresolved tension between 'authenticity' and 'modernism' haunts contemporary feminism. The recurring theme of women's relationship to nature, of women's utopias, and of the vision of a wholly other world in which 'women's values' hold sway suggests a longing for a more 'authentic' world, closely bound to 'nature', in which we will find our true selves. Engagement in the political battle, the use of avant-garde art, the appropriation of jazz and rock by women's bands and of an anarchic tradition of humour by women comics, and the belief in the social construction of the gendered self represent the 'modernist' approach.[40]

It suggests a major reappraisal in what we mean by the *com-*

modity. As a term, commodity has, since the time of Walter Benjamin, betokened something essentially false, inauthentic, politically suspect:

> Walter Benjamin noted how in the film industry mechanical reproduction preserves 'not the unique aura of personal truth but the "spell of the personality", the phony spell of the commodity'. . . . So the aura of traditional culture – as natural, expressing fundamental truths, proceeding from the individual genius author – is set aside.[41]

The result of this separation has been a dual view of cultural products, a 'hedonistic' versus a 'moralistic' one: 'either doing your own thing is okay, or else it convicts you of false consciousness. Either the products of popular culture are the supports of monolithic male ideology, or they are there to be enjoyed and justified.'[42]

But the process initiated by 'the film industry mechanical reproduction' has carried on unabated, and reached the critical mass necessary to inscribe a whole world-view around it – namely postmodernism. The problem for cultural politics was therefore how to deal with the commodity, how to valorise pleasure, the trivial, the short attention span. Postmodernism was about releasing different energies, emancipated from bondage to an 'authentic' that has the power to shame the category of the 'phony'. The commodity fared rather well from this, it became the object of these new energies – like the language of the new era, the 'commodity' lost its proscriptive and judgemental inauthenticity; witness the changing status of fashion in feminism, a politics with more grounds than most to despise merchandising:

> In the early years of the Women's Liberation Movement, the entire package of fashion was condemned by feminists. Liberation meant breaking out of the straitjacket of controlled feminity. Dress, fashion and cosmetics were considered to be trivialities which functioned ideologically to construct a false feminity. . . . The Women's Liberation Movement rejected fashion with anger, an anger informed by its recognition of fashion as an essential articulation of the ideology of feminity, a manipulative discourse about what women are, should be, or might become.[43]

185

Fashion could only be reclaimed after women had reclaimed for themselves what fashion meant. By the mid-80s, a complete reorientation had been achieved, and fashion 'meant' glamour, pleasure, desire, disguise – but this time, of a sort controlled by those who consumed it, rather than by those who produced it – i.e. by women rather than by men. As late as June 1990, a radical feminist could write:

> it is *Elle* magazine which has most accurately reflected the postmodern [as] *zeitgeist* – *Elle* in the 1980s was truly a sign of the times . . . it was both radical and instinctively in tune with those times, in its recognition of how key issues like pleasure, consumerism and most importantly the exploration of cultural diversity, had transformed what it was to be modern, to be liberated, to be the New Woman.[44]

Again, the pattern is a consistent one; what rescued these things for those in opposition to dominant cultural patterns, from the impasse of oppositional politics, was postmodernism – a force that most tangibly exists as consumerism:

> While Feminism was worrying about concepts like 'fragmentation' and 'identity' *Elle* . . . was playing with them. . . . For *Elle*, the image was all, or almost all; words came a definite second. In a world where the only certainty was uncertainty *Elle's* faith was in the surface alone . . . the Elle reader could reinvent herself being a little bit of this, and a little bit of that . . . models were androgynous or parodies of feminity, racially varied and sexually amorphous. Our unpleasant confusions about our identities . . . melted into a pleasurable seductive ambiguity.[45]

And with the shifting self so skilfully exploitable by advertising and by style/glamour mags, 'the idea that we can be manipulated in any straightforward way seems less and less credible':

> Fashion, far from being a source of oppression and manipulation of women, has become increasinglly associated with strategies of resistance to fixed images of feminity . . . women have always had a complex relationship to consumption. Potentially both subversive and repressive, it has been represented as an opiate that kept the downtrodden Stepford wives in their fur-lined domestic prisons, but it

has also been one of the few opportunities for the same women to express power and self-assertion. . . . It is no surprise that the 80s girl is more attracted by the rhetoric of *laissez-faire* freedom that is so seductively presented by the right.[46]

But for those no longer so plagued by hatred for the profit motive, the compromises of fahion-consumerism are very seductive. They lead the cultural critic to locate the key distinction *within* the market, and not outside it – for 'niche market', read 'subculture':

Consumerism, however, is not the same as consumption, or for that matter, use. . . . Mass culture as re-usable and disposable consumption as other than dictated by the billboards, is one of the reasons why sociologists fell in love with sub-cultures. Their very existence testified to the fact that rampant consumerism could be challenged. Culture, sodden with symbolism, could be consumed in a powerful and political way.[47]

'Deviant' consumerism allows the radical critic to have his/her cake and eat it, to be hip about pleasure, frivolity and self-expressiveness, while at the same time not capitulating to the advertisers. This consumer outdoes the advertising process, taking its added values and recasting them for their own purposes. After all, the branding process contains the seeds of its own dissolution; if it is true that objects have no fixed meaning, that consumption is active, that you consume images as well as things, then it is true that you cannot rely on the added values fostered by the ad having authority over others; the ad and the commodity were starting-points, not end-points. . . . This is the great white hope of oppositional culture that wants to *buy into* consumerism without *selling out* to it, that wants to make consumption, rather than non-consumption, the opposite of consumerism. It's the idea that after advertising had stolen 'culture', then postmodern 'culture' could steal it back again. No one was pretending that this was going to spell the death of consumerism, but we could live with that.

Postmodernism and popular culture have given intellectual respectability to the incursions made by commerce on culture. They have made it seem not only inevitable, but pretty desirable to boot. Together, they arguably represent advertising's final triumph over its cultural critics. Advertising's most conspicuous cultural success has been in the way it has taken over the concept of *value*. Both intellectually, and in the market place, value has been made contingent, ideologically elusive and subjective. Advertising has brilliantly used the youth-market commodity pop music to transform *value* from something that used to be seen as the opposite of hype to something completely compatible with it, while at the same time being able to sell pop's opposite, rock (and more recently, classical) as music with inherent value:

> hype will always be a highly charged issue in pop and rock because it raises the question of the music's value: is this value intrinsic or is it determined purely by the market-place? If it does have intrinsic value (the rock belief) then hype is the market's attempt to distort our perceptions for commercial gain – to manipulate the public's responses, persuading them to accept what is flashy and meretricious rather than what is serious and good. However, if you think the value of music is determined by what people get from it (the pop belief) – i.e. it is entirely subjective and only as valuable as the audience feels it to be – then hype is simply part of what we enjoy in pop. If it sells, it's good; if not, not. . . . Much of the tension and excitement in popular music comes from the way it shifts between these two modes, so that the question of truth and significance and lasting value is always up for grabs.[48]

If value is a case of what you get out of something rather than a specific thing you invest into a product, then the emphasis is necessarily on the consumer, and the consumer's ability, or willingness, to create those values. This seems an emancipatory ethic, both in terms of what it allows us to be interested in (i.e. anything we like) and in terms of allowing us to be more important than the commodity. It empowers the individual aspirational consumer, and to an extent therefore offers the dissenting voice some scope for expressing itself, albeit in a partial and inauthentic way:

> One way for 'deviants' to disturb the dominant is by developing its recommended values (conspicuous consumption, material aspirations, masculine aggression) with an un-

acceptable excess. Rock music is consumer capitalism writ too large, and some performers, expecially since punk, cultivate artificiality rather than authenticity. . . . As there is no essential meaning or value to the artwork, so with popular music; it is not essentially either subversive or conformist. Rather there is a contest between diverse and shifting strategies of subversion and containment.[49]

Advertising can add both types of value with equal ease, but it is the pop definition of value that suits it the best, because it allows the advertising to be closer in kind to the product, and thereby more closely in control of how both are consumed. And it is pop-value that has grown most during the 80s. Again and again products and institutions have had to sell themselves in terms of what people get out of them and not in terms of their intrinsic ability to confer cultural prestige. Not that it really matters, because either way, the advertiser can co-opt culture at will.

This has had the effect, however, of giving other cultural forms the *appearance* of being more counter-cultural than they really are. Magazines like *The Face*, for instance, were always good at undercutting the old idea that being anti-consumerist was somehow to be counter-cultural in an interesting way: '[*The Face*] rejects the role of the media as a brainwashing device, and argues that through resistance, people use commodities to their own advantage, to create their own style, not to "live out" the world purveyed by advertising'[50] . . . but only if you take *The Face* literally (and rather naively) at face value. The style magazine was not about counter-culture; it was about hip consumerism, which is to say, subversive of any overt commitment, left or right. The added values that had greatest currency in this type of magazine were those that juggled style and disaffection, giving ballast to the 'look' with shards of attitude, but always treating commitment as empty posturing. Believing and buying were the two poles of the magazine's world, each rescuing the other from their inevitable descent into pretension on the one hand and mindlessness on the other.

Its values may be pop or postmodern, but they were still *added values*. *The Face* was a brand, just more self-conscious than most others, but with a readership profile as slavish to it as possessed by any successful publication. To read into it any genuinely radical project, as Kathy Myers seems on the verge of doing, is to overstate the subversiveness of postmodernism, and, also perhaps, the ideological bad faith of consumerism. Manufacturers are just as able to sell us free-floating hedonistic signifiers as they are patriarchal straitjackets; their loyalty to the profit-motive comes before any other cultural project, and as long as that is being catered for, then they're hardly likely to feel the victims of consumer sedition.

And Dick Hebdige knows this too, and only too well.

> Do you remember John Berger speaking from the heart of the First World in the television version of *Ways of Seeing* in 1974 as he flicked though a copy of the *Sunday Times* Colour Supplement, moving from portraits of starving Bangla Deshi refugees to an advertisement for Badedas Bath Salts? 'Between these images', he said . . . 'there is such a gap , such a fissure that we can only say the culture that produced these images is insane.' *The Face* is composed precisely on this fissure. It is the place of the nutty conjuncture.[51]

The difference between Berger's 1974 *Sunday Times* Colour Supplement, and Hebdige's 1986 *The Face* does suggest a considerable shift in cultural/media values. But in one sense Berger is wrong, it was not by virtue of *producing* those images that 'the culture' proved itself insane; it was by virtue of their unthinking juxtaposition. It's an important slip, because it was precisely the recognition of the wide spectrum that exists between 'images'; the gulfs that exist between different agendas, different points of view, different ways of commodifying those agendas and points of view, that produced the obsession with relativism that underwrites both *The Face* and Hebdige's own critique of *The Face*.

Both Hebdige and *The Face* inhabit a world-view in which Berger's outrage has no point of purchase. Berger's disgust depends on the status of the advertising image, and it is valid only if advertising and photojournalism exist in our culture as moral opposites; this in turn can happen only if you believe that the relationship between self and world mediated and realised by an image is a moral one; and it can only be moral if you believe that images yield up truth, and truth's opposite, fraudulence. It is a judgement based on the content of the photos, and the content of their discrepancy, it is an outrage founded on a faith in the authentic.

Hebdige describes the erosion of these premises in post-modernism, and how little they apply to the aesthetic promiscuity of *The Face*'s world-view, a view that has chosen to collapse the idea (i) that images derive from a moral hierarchy of subject matter and intention, (ii) that we engage with the world directly through image and (iii) that this engagement necessitates ethical choice.

For Hebdige this isn't, prime facie, a bad or immoral thing, it's merely an inevitable one: 'As the related strands of social and aesthetic utopianism in Art are unravelled and revealed as untenable and obsolescent, advertising takes over where the avant-garde left off and the picture of the Post is complete.'[52] The person who wants to put advertising *back* in its place without harping back to a pre-postmodern world-view, who wants to reinvent utopianism, (or even just the possibility of a counter-culture), has a real problem. How does Dick Hebdige separate *his* postmodernism from that of *The Face*? How do you distinguish a utopianism that is beyond the compromises of consumerism from the spurious 'universalism' of the unreconstructed leisure/elite snob?

In short, what do you do with the fact that culture and commerce are now fully intertwined, that there no longer exists any point in culture safely outside the terms of commodity relations, neither in the concept of the fine arts, nor in the 'authenticity' of subcultural self-affirmation.

Where are the limits of consumerism to come from? Energised and made respectable by pop culture, postmodernism and the politics of individual gratification, the market place has never looked so impregnable to the usual shibboleths of enlightened culture. Art has long ceased to have anything to say about the poverty of commodity relations; ideological admonishments fall on deaf ears and a genuinely radical counter-culture petered out years ago. It is arguably consumerism's greatest achievement, making resistance to it appear so drab, boring and wrong.

And the apologists and apostles of marketing are only too aware of this. They are now transforming the concept of the future, once so tainted with the totalitarian and the anti-individual, into commodity propaganda of enormous confidence. The apparent collapse of centrally planned socialism in

Eastern Europe has presented the consumer lobby with concrete and theoretical vindication. Little wonder that some extraordinary claims are now being made: 'We are now entering a second Reformation. Just as the nation-state took over from the Church, so now the market is about to take over from the nation-state.'[53] This fantastic hubris does however beg the question that the limiting factors on consumer capitalism will be material (things like nationalism, fundamentalism, the ecology); the other value-systems *not* based on market hegemony will look even punier. Leaving aside the imponderable questions of nationalism, religion or the environment, what, in the meantime can be done to salvage something of culture from the claims of the market? For those unhappy about consumer dominance of culture, there is little to do but bang on the old drum:

> The elision between cultural and commercial values . . . marks the transformation of culture into style. The manipulation of style turns thoughts, feeling and associations into commodities for circulation by the information industry. Control of a product's appearance and associational context – eroticism, class status, power – is a means of controlling the thoughts and feelings of their purchasers. The critic Rosemary Betterton points out that the possibilities held out to women by the fashion industry, of changing identity by adopting a new style, in fact channel and limit their potential identities, 'by substituting a series of products for a truly different self-image. Women are sold their own images in the form of commodities.' . . . Creativity is no longer what we make, or what we think, but what we buy.[54]

Culture is prostituted by *commerce*; just as personal identity is prostituted by *style*. Rhetoric like this argues that there is a difference between potential identity and bought identity, between making, thinking and buying, but again, rhetoric is all that it remains. Advertising has proved just how problematic popular culture and postmodernism are. These theories have become victims of their own success, incapacitated by the same materialist relativism that had challenged those traditional cultural criteria posturing as universals. If consumerism is now something that is impossible to evict from the cultural, then the point should no longer be escaping it, but working out your relationship with it – a question as pressing for the pop-starlet out to mint a formula, as for the critic still committed to a culture not completely annexed to the market.

Perhaps there will never be a clear-cut answer. Commerce and culture have interpenetrated each other too thoroughly and too quixotically for that. Just as commercial criteria have risen up the cultural ladder, so cultural ones have descended it. What is extraordinary about any cultural form is that no matter how populist it is, it is still subject to the same concern – is it any good? We watch soap operas – but not just any soap opera; we listen to pop, but somehow distinguish Stock Waterman and Aitken from Jazzie B, while dimly aware that actually, they are different in degree rather than kind; we can listen to Nigel Kennedy perfectly able to see (i) yes, he's challenging the elitist stereotypes of classical music, (ii) his image is an annoying affectation. Endlessly we ask these questions; it happened in political theatre, yes it was relevant, but was its demise during the 80s actually that bad a thing? No, *The Face* doesn't harbour genuine sentimentality, no love, or despair, for that you go elsewhere. Why was it *Woman's Own* that criticised the latest James Bond film for its sexism, and not *Marxism Today*? Why is it that criticising political t-shirts is as politically useless as actually wearing them?

The notion of quality control is actually not that far removed from cultural value. It is contingent, subjective, ideologically uncommitted – and proof that we are pretty robust in our negotiations with the contradictions and the promises of consumer/culture. But for those still baying for advertising's blood, this is never going to be enough.

NOTES IN THE MARGIN

How do you reclaim all those values that used to seem beyond price, but which marketing and research brought to heel?

In May 1988, BBC2 screened a series of personal polemics exploring the 80s called *Notes in the Margin*. The series invited some key writers to pick, and then analyse, key themes of the past decade. These covered the 'new man', theme-park Britain, ethnic diversity, new age naturalism and the literary marketplace.

None was explicitly about advertising and yet each was saturated with it. The great advances of 80s culture, new sexual politics, national identity, global cultures, green politics and packaging the aesthetic – all drew their expression from the market place.

Wherever you turned it seemed that it was in the ads that you found not just your evidence, but your agenda. Advertisers had spent the 80s becoming less and less inhibited about marketing social and global trends, and selling themselves as the answer to greater numbers of social problems. And because advertising cannot afford the luxury of half-measures, these wishful interventions into the largest themes of Western angst became more and more defining and less and less reflective.

What each of the *Notes in the Margin* did, in varying degrees, was to see advertising as the best place from which to *begin* the critique, rather than merely as the place where you ended it. Programme one took us into a Saatchis' board room, and used one of the agency's own senior planners as proof that the 'new man' was an image in contradiction of the facts, a new, sellable fantasy that flattered male consumers embarrassed by machismo. Programme two had Philip Norman squirming at any evidence of the adman's art in the packaging and marketing of 'Britain', and its 'heritage'. Programme three gave Ros Coward the chance to wax lyrical about our new inwardness and respect for the spiritual that is in nature, by not only celebrating people who worship rocks, but crediting the people who sold us Aqua Libra with visionary insight. (Naivety as boundless in the cynic as in the romantic.) While Stephen Heath was worried that global images in advertising were camouflaging the real nature of ethnic diversity.

Even when caustic and sceptical, these documentaries bore witness to one great ad truth, you can only understand *why* people are thinking what they are when you understand how that idea is being *consumed* – in other words, who's selling it, and who's buying into it. And unless it is being visibly consumed, it probably isn't that significant. The pattern of consumption is not the whole story. But to ignore it is tantamount to getting the story completely wrong.

7

LOST IN THE POST
Advertising and the future

No one would claim, not even Charles Saatchi, that advertising has all the answers. As a form it is more capable than most of being misleading, deceitful, exploitative, demeaning, irritating and wasteful. There is also something deeply suspect about its characteristic tones of voice, its oscillation between arrogance and servility, especially when pretending to be in some sense genuinely participatory. As an industry it produces loathing – and self-loathing – in abundance. But it has also managed to shrug these things off, to make them look like the sour grapes of an anti-entrepreneurial elite no one is listening to any more.

At one level, the battle against advertising has been lost. It is no longer possible to knock it out with one iconoclastic generalisation. Consumerism has kept one step ahead of deconstruction, outmanoeuvring the siege-machinery of interpretation, in energy, wilfulness, and chutzpah that make 'having a problem' with it seem intellectually top heavy. We all know the drawbacks and contradictions in consumerism, but mix and match our way round them. It is just no longer clear what consumer dissent is in opposition *to*. It used to be obvious, because Marxism, psychoanalysis and feminism told us what. They were all about coming to terms with the various hegemonies at work in the world – capitalism, imperialism and patriarchy. These things are all highly problematic, not just in themselves, but in so far as all hegemonies are about the deployment of power. How does power work, and how should its workings be understood and contained? Various theories have arisen; most started out paying special attention to economics and the use economics made of images to disguise itself.

Clearly consumerism, especially as represented in advertising, is implicated in those hegemonies. But all that such critical analysis has done in developing ever more sophisticated notions for how images transmit power, is supply the creators of those images with more sophisticated blue-prints – and supply the rest of us with an arsenal of concepts with which to unpick those blue-prints. Elizabeth Wilson's book *Adorned in Dreams: Fashion and Modernity* defends fashion from its ideological detractors because (at least according to the blurb) 'it goes beyond the politics of gender and class to reflect the complexity, vitality and allure of fashion itself'.[1]

'Hegemonies' only work as oppositional polemics when there genuinely is some kind of discrepancy between the stated meanings of a cultural practice and its intended meanings, when there is something to be gained by moving from the 'complexity' of the thing itself to some underlying ideological politics. But when the terms of those underlying politics become overfamiliar they lose their interpretive edge. As we become more clued-up as consumers (of both theory and products), the problem becomes less one of recognising ideology in itself, than one of knowing how much of a problem something *really* is, as well as knowing where the problem really lies – in the material world? In the world as created by the media? In the interface between the two? In the way the images are produced? Or in the way they are consumed?

The story of advertising has been one of endlessly using the forces levelled against it for its own purposes. It used to be enough to condemn advertising as irrational and exotic, until that became the science of branding. The trouble is that *cultural materialism* – the redefinition of 'culture' as political – has been too successful a move; it has not only armed a generation of critics with new tools, but it has also given the advertisers intellectual *carte blanche*. The 90s have two key issues to learn how to live with – consumerism and relativism – the legacies if you like, of an 80s dominated by popular culture, postmodernism and the politics of individual gratification.

It is no longer enough to pin all your disdain on the fact that lurking behind the image is profit motive – witness the art world, in which nothing is so commodified as the anti-commodity. Styles follow the markets, which follow the money, and money got into intangibles in a big way during the 80s. It's a situation we understand, one that we've got used to. It is what happens when culture becomes more interesting than politics, and shopping more interesting than culture.

Advertising no longer stands culpable for being what it is – *not* high art, wedded to the profit motive, committed to consumption, to selling and to pleasure and the irrational. These categories relied for their judgemental efficacy on ideologies that guaranteed a distance between commerce and culture and between culture and politics. The institutions designed to guarantee those ideologies are in a state of crisis – museums, the academy, the politics of use-value rationality, 'culture' in its old, autonomous sense. These are, in other words, postmodern times. The battle has stopped being a strategic one played out on the broadest front; it has become tactical and pragmatic.

POSTMODERNISM

Postmodernism is a variety of different things. It is both an aesthetic and a theory explaining that aesthetic. It is used as a term that radicalises the contemporary, providing an explanation for cultural products as diverse as the films of Ridley Scott and the architecture of Piers Gough. Postmodernism is also a discourse that cares to excess about the conditions of its own possibility, and for making the best, combative use of those conditions. At its laziest and most promiscuous, it makes a great virtue out of diversity, of periods, styles, places. As a pose, it allows you to be everywhere and nowhere (rather than merely somewhere); everyone and no one; anytime and no time. It is faster, giddier and cleverer in its attitude than the modernism it supersedes. It is big on not meaning what it says (irony), on not originating its own materials (pastiche) and on not being as naively legible as its rivals (parody). Above all it makes a virtue out of the fact that the old distinctions between commerce and culture no longer obtain.

Its critics therefore see it as the aesthetic of contemporary capitalism, as reducible to economic factors as modernism and romanticism were in their turn. This is the third distinctive phase of capitalist development:

> [Fredric] Jameson distinguishes three epochs of capitalist
> expansion: market capitalism, characterised by the growth
> of industrial capital in largely national markets . . . mono-
> poly capitalism, which is identical to the growth of imperia-

lism, during which markets grew into world markets, organised around nation-states, but depending on the fundamental exploitative asymmetry of the colonizing nations and the colonized who provide both raw materials and cheap labour; and, most recently, the postmodern phase of multinational capitalism, which is marked by the exponential growth of international corporations and the consequent transcending of national boundaries. Far from contradicting Marx's analysis of the operations of capitalism, multinational or consumer capitalism is 'the purest form of capital yet to have emerged, a prodigious expansion of capital into hitherto uncommodified areas'.[2]

The most alarmist prophet of all this is Jean Baudrillard, who:

> assumed the role of Andy Warhol, and went on to write about seduction in which there appears a whole rhetoric of demolition, inversion and provocation. In the ad-filled, media-created contemporary mindscape all is flat and thinned out; surfaces without depth. No 'reality' other than appearances. What you see is what you get. . . . Once seduced we are in the postmodern world of pure floating images – hyperreality. . . . First, he says, the image reflected reality, and now, in its final phase, the image bears no relation to any reality, and nowhere is more 'hyperreal' than America: 'Disneyland is there to conceal the fact that it is the "real" country, all of "real" America, which is Disneyland (just as prisons are there to conceal the fact that it is the social in its entirety, in its banal omnipresence, which is carceral).'[3]

In a similar vein, Baudrillard denounces the mass-media that are so compromised by the 'hyperreal' order that they have given rise to, that 'genuine' communication is completely impossible: 'It is not as vehicles of content, but in their very form and very operation, that media induce a social relation. . . . The media are not co-efficients, but *effectors* of ideology . . . the mass-media are anti-mediatory and intransitive. They fabricate non-communication.'[4] But as Alan Sinfield points out, this sort of nihilistic bravura doesn't so much challenge the collapse of culture into commerce as perversely speed it on its way:

> Another response to the collapse of cultural value is to call

it Post-modernism. . . . Post-modernism proclaims the end of both [art and politics]; that there are now no effective hierarchies in cultures, no depths beneath surfaces, no totalities through which to organize fragments; and no political theories adequate to the dispersion of significance in the postmodern world . . . [it] depoliticizes culture by imagining it as flowing, necessarily with the stream of consumer capitalism. No position is envisaged from which to speak that is in advance, or even outside of the general position.[5]

So, how can the cultural critic respond? Either he or she can try to privilege those forms and discourses that are ignored, or repressed by the 'dominant' and pin his/her hopes on diversity to provide a position outside the culture/commerce nexus. Or, like Stephen Bayley, he or she can celebrate the equation of commerce and culture by stylishly and opportunistically speaking up for enlightened, bourgeois consumerism's power to shape the world agreeably. Or, like Robert Hewison, he or she can try to see what a post-consumer view of the arts might look like.

What both the advertiser and the cultural critic agree on is that this is a problem for a culture that has, by and large, freed many of its citizens from basic material wants. The question now is who is going to inherit that culture? Those who invest products with the social values that go beyond need and use; or those who invest those values in non-commodity forms? Has the question of 'the quality of life' moved on from consumerism, or has consumerism, finally, moved beyond all its political and cultural opponents? This is above all a postmodern question, because it is in postmodernism that advertising and consumerism have achieved their strongest hold over culture.

It's not difficult to see why advertising should so welcome what postmodern times have to offer. Not least in creative terms, the new stress on pastiche, irony, baroque gratification and fast-cutting have been a gift to the art director's ego. Ads really are 'state of the art'. And at a more strategic level, postmodern phenomena have equipped the advertiser with new languages and new added values, trawled from what used to be of only marginal interest to the big multi-nationals.

Paradoxically, capital has fallen in love with difference;

advertising thrives on selling us things that will enhance our uniqueness and individuality. . . . From World Music to exotic holidays in Third-World locations, ethnic TV dinners to Peruvian knitted hats, cultural difference *sells*.[6]

Difference here implies more than just variety, it is a crucial and contentious concept. With it comes the full range of ideological and historical divisions with which individuals, communities, countries and continents, are riven. People who are 'different' are 'other', and this is as often as not the source of conflict rather than harmony (think of the Rushdie affair). In other words, 'difference' brings with it an inflammatory and controversial baggage, of little interest to companies seeking marketing opportunities. Therefore, 'difference' has to be turned into something more manageable – 'diversity', the pseudo-ecumenical piety of Coca-Cola, or the Moonies:

In the commodification of language and culture, objects and meanings are torn free of their original referents and their meanings become a spectacle open to almost infinite translation. . . . Otherness is sought after for its exchange value, its exoticism and the pleasures, thrills and adventures it can offer. The power relation is closer to tourism than imperialism, an expropriation of meaning rather than materials.[7]

And within 'diversity' as such, there is the new commercial appeal for marketing things that start off life on the peripheries, or underground. In pop and fashion especially, there is huge commercial interest in subcultures, and in packaging the music and dress codes of precisely those groups who use music and dress to counter their social subordination. In an age of niche marketing, these are the sources for added values that command the highest margins. And while some critics see both these forces as something to be welcomed, it is pretty clear that they don't in themselves represent anything more than shopping getting cosmopolitan – this is not about lending a voice to the globe's dispossessed. Those who hold out hope that the importing of marginal voices is somehow going to disrupt the dominant heart of multinational capitalism forget that the 'dominant' and the 'marginal' are by no means diametrically opposed forces, forever at war:

For, after all, what is dominant in contemporary culture is the projection of a universe of multiple differences. If it is the case that the rock music industry requires a stable and reproducible product, it is equally the case that this industry depends upon the periodic invasion of difference and innovation. Indeed, the rock music industry is probably the best example of the process by which contemporary capitalist culture promotes or multiplies difference in the interests of maintaining its profit-structure. If there is a dominant in contemporary rock music, it is the dominance of multiple marginality.[8]

Or, in the case of fashion:

Codifying, simplifying, and sometimes even diversifying subcultural styles for the market-place (the appearance in the fashion houses of a sedate form of punk is one example), the fashion industry simultaneously stimulates its own markets and drains the energy from its subcultural prey.[9]

THE LANGUAGES OF POST-CONSUMERISM

Consumerism is therefore invulnerable to the grand gesture either within it, or from without. It has become this powerful because it is so good at taking aspects of the world and making a virtue out of them. The world is a place riddled with cultural difference; so advertising gives us diversity. The world is full of people only recently getting used to the idea that their opinions desires and aspirations are important; so advertising makes anything that doesn't speak this language appear irrelevant and ineffectual. Our culture is full of potential and contested meaning; so advertising co-opts the ones it wants and makes anything offering you meaning without consumer gratification seem redundant and boring. Advertising's power comes from both its ubiquity and its partiality. It can go everywhere because it only has one job to do – add value.

As a way of understanding the world, advertising is therefore fantastically limited, but fantastically pervasive. It is the shibboleth idiom of a consumer culture. But it is also more than this – better than almost any other language, advertising signifies by default, it sheds light on an enormous array of contemporary world concerns, but always with the same partiality and limitation. Learning to decode that partiality has become a major cultural exercise.

Advertising is demotic rather than democratic; it reflects diversity, but not difference; it addresses the socially constructed individual, but only as consumer; it continually researches the social, but only to work out by how much it can be safely altered; it is, in short, deeply compromised (of course, it's got a job to do).

The post-consumerist manifesto has to either transcend advertising, or undercut it. There are two directions it can take. Characteristically, the critique of consumerism will either preach the importance of values that lie beyond buying things, or else it will preach the importance of objects that fall short of the promise of advertising. We will be urged to reject consumerism either in favour of values that you can't merely buy; or in favour of a lifestyle that isn't glamorous, instantly gratifying, obsessed with bigger, better and more. It would be a world where we would have to make *less* use of things, and in which we would have to sustain better interpersonal values. Life needs to be simpler and more meaningful; ecology for example, demands the first, while forces like feminism demand the latter (with considerable overlap).

But any such critique soon finds that it has been left very little cultural space on which to find a point of purchase. The middle ground, the material/symbolic nexus at the heart of any culture, has become stronger, because so much wider, and it is dominated by advertising. The importance of objects on the one hand, and the priorities in our lives that they cater to, are things that advertising has invested billions in moulding; advertising has a stranglehold on that bridgehead between the private and the public spheres. Trying to outflank it is very difficult.

After a period of unprecedented expansion, not only in size, but in cultural influence, advertising has challenged, and in many cases, suspended the old hostilities towards it. Having reached some sort of zenith, there are few people who can deny the importance of understanding consumerism – as Michael Grade put it, market discipline is a good servant, but a dangerous master. Consumerism is a powerful way of thinking once unleashed, and not easily checked, least of all by merely denigrating it.

Advertising has, as I have tried to show, colonised the populist core of what we mean by language, art, culture and politics. It has seen off the hierarchical distinctions used in each of these categories to subordinate it. Consumption is now the basic mode for all activity in our society, not reading, not using, not appreciating, not participating, not producing but *consuming*. It is now how we appropriate the world around us. And built into this is the demand that the world accommodate us better, that we consume it more not less; in other words, we consume *aspirationally*. Our world-view is now dominated by reflecting and catering for this fact. It consequently depicts the people who inhabit it primarily as *aspirational consumers*, that is the subject-position our culture articulates the most often, and with most conviction.

All the things that used to stand over and above consumerism, those activities we regard as more valuable than consumption, that use of language that goes beyond ad copy, that sense of the self less determined by what we own, or want to own – have been roughly shoved aside, their self-evident worthiness subjected to scrutiny and challenge. At one level this is cause for real concern; but on another, consumerism has given the highest basic position from which to *begin* advocacy for other things. It makes the prophets of value work much harder to demonstrate that their visions of post-consumer cultural values are as coherent and relevant as they think. It makes the usual sources of cultural apocalypse justify themselves too – the art gallery, the political theatre, the polemical soap-box.

Never has it been *more* important to investigate the limitations of this consumer hegemony, never more important to explore the possibilities that lie beyond it. This is particularly so as consumerism becomes increasingly the dominant model for all political and social action; when the question of AIDS is for so long seen merely as an issue of *not* consuming drugs intravenously, or sex promiscuously, rather than being about providing an adequate infrastructure. The structures of collective action have collapsed, and been replaced by a system that pretends not to be a collective (far less a coercive) thing. The limitations of these collective ideologies have become irreversible, now it's the turn of capitalism and consumerism (already subject to enormous internal strains after ten years of apparent global triumphalism).

But never has it been so difficult to locate the starting point from which to do it. The spirit of consumerism is too powerful and too pervasive now to be vulnerable to a critique that isn't equal to it. The job is therefore not one of trying to demolish consumerism for the sake of it, or of endlessly yearning for a position in culture vouchsafed immunity from the market. Instead, the job is twofold.

On the one hand, we have to remember that an inevitable corollary of brand advertising is that its commercial viability utterly depends on our liking it, even more so when there is precious little else with which to disinguish one product from another. Advertising that does not successfully talk to its consumers will have failed. The power of the consumer to determine what 'successful' advertising is, is enormous.

And second, the power and influence of advertising will be kept in check only if the cultural 'product' that the rest of the media produces succeeds in being more complex, accessible and interesting than the marketing strategies designed to promote them. This of course will depend on exactly how our 'culture industries' are allowed to evolve; with market disciplines pressing but not oppressive, it seems possible that the conceits of marketing will remain a strong cultural starting-point, and not its inevitable conclusion.

Advertising's cultural triumph was a double one; it exposed as hopelessly naive two strains of cultural thinking, the idealist and the oppositional. If the language of values and dissent is ever going to become relevant again, it will have to do so without merely cocking a snook at consumerism. Both art and politics will have to rethink their relationship to the structures that support them, and develop a way that neither just capitulates wholesale to them, nor simply wishes they didn't exist. The challenge is there, if the 90s are up to it.

NOTES

INTRODUCTION

1 James Webb Young, *How to Become an Advertising Man*, API, New York, 1963, p. 7.
2 David Ogilvy, *Confessions of An Advertising Man*, Longman, London, 1964.
3 See in particular the series called *Advertising Works*, published by Cassell, London, which comprise those case-studies awarded prizes by the IPA in their biannual competition. The latest volume is *Advertising Works 5*, 1988.
4 Vance Packard, *The Hidden Persuaders*, Penguin Books, London, 1960, p. 11.
5 *Campaign*, August 1984.
6 *Campaign*, February 1985.
7 BMW advertisement.
8 Michael Wood, *In Search of the Dark Ages*, BBC Books, London, 1981, p. 13.
9 ibid., p. 14.
10 ibid., p. 13.
11 ibid., p. 13.
12 ibid., p. 14.

1 OBJECTS OF DESIRE

1 Stephen King, *Developing New Brands*, J. Walter Thompson, London, 1984, p. 8.
2 J. Walter Thompson agency memo, July 1985.
3 Chris Williams, *Campaign*, December 1985.
4 J. Walter Thompson agency memo, July 1985.
5 Stephen King, op. cit., p. 16.
6 *Campaign*
7 Raymond Williams, quoted in Gillian Dyer, *Advertising as Communication*, Methuen, London, 1984, p. 7.
8 Stephen King, op. cit., p. 34.
9 Jeremy Bullmore, *Campaign*, February 1986.

10 Barry Day, in Torin Douglas, *Complete Guide to Advertising*, Macmillan, London, 1983, p. 7.
11 Judie Lannon, *Advertising to the New Europeans*, J. Walter Thompson agency memo, July 1990.
12 ibid.
13 ibid.
14 Eric Clark, *The Want Makers*, Hodder & Stoughton, London, 1988, p. 67.
15 ibid., p. 169.
16 Stephen King, op. cit., p. 36.
17 ibid., p. 38.
18 Eric Clark, op. cit., p. 163.
19 McCann Erickson agency report, London, 1985, quoted in *Campaign*, 22 November 1985.
20 ibid.
21 ibid.
22 Eric Clark, op. cit., p. 168.
23 Judie Lannon and Peter Cooper, 'Humanistic advertising: a holistic perspective', *International Journal of Advertising*, vol. 2, 1983.
24 ibid.
25 ibid.
26 J. Walter Thompson creative pitch document, Summer 1985.
27 ibid.
28 ibid.
29 Stan Rapp, 'Beyond the niche', *Independent*, 11 December 1990.

2 DESIGNER DECADES

1 *iDeas*, Penguin Books, London, 1988, p. 12.
2 Gilbert Adair, *Myths and Memories*, Fontana, London, 1986, p. 8.
3 Judith Williamson, *New Statesman*, 15 January 1988.
4 ibid.
5 Sean French, 'As I please', *New Society*, 15 January 1988.
6 *Marxism Today*, April 1988.
7 Peter York, *Campaign*, July 1986.
8 ibid.
9 Yvonne Roberts, *New Society*, August 1987.
10 Ian Jack, 'The repackaging of Glasgow', in *Before the Oil Ran Out*, Secker & Warburg, London, 1989, p. 201.
11 ibid., p. 205.
12 ibid., p. 216.
13 *The Late Show*, BBC Television, 13 September 1989.
14 Susan Scott-Parker, *They're Not in the Brief*, King's Fund Report, London, 1989.
15 *The Dawn of Us'ism*, K.H.B.B. agency report, London, 1988.
16 *A Map of Greenland*, J. Walter Thompson agency memo, Summer 1989.
17 Frank Mort, 'The politics of consumption', in Hall and Jacques (eds) *New Times*, Lawrence & Wishart, London, 1989.

3 MARTIAN POSTCARDS

1 Craig Raine, *A Martian Sends a Postcard Home*, Oxford University Press, Oxford, 1979.
2 Paula A. Treichler, 'Aids, homophobia and biomedical discourse', in *Cultural Studies*, vol. 1, no. 3, pp. 264–5.
3 Brain Sutton-Smith, *Toys as Culture*, Garland Press, New York, 1986, p. 12.
4 ibid., p. 264.
5 T. S. Eliot *Notes Towards the Definition of Culture*, Faber & Faber, London, 1948, p. 31.
6 Neal Ascherson, *Observer*, 30 August 1987.
7 ibid.
8 MacDonald Daly, 'How to win friends and influence people', *Word International*, May 1988.
9 Roger Scruton, quoted in Tom Nairn, *The Enchanted Glass*, Radius, London, 1988, pp. 94–5.
10 ibid., p. 96.
11 Beatrix Campbell and Wendy Wheeler, 'Filofaxions', *Marxism Today*, December 1988.
12 ibid.
13 Roland Barthes, 'The kitchen of meaning', in *The Semiotic Challenge*, tr. Richard Howard, Basil Blackwell, Oxford, 1988, p. 173.
14 Roland Barthes, *Mythologies*, tr. Annette Lavers, Granada, London, 1973, p. 36.
15 ibid., p. 75.
16 Zygmunt Bauman, 'Unstately pleasure dome', *New Statesman*, 23 October 1987.
17 Graham McCann, *Marilyn Monroe*, Polity, Oxford, 1988.
18 Garry Wills, *Reagan's America*, William Heinemann, London, 1988.
19 Peter Conrad, *Observer*, 31 January 1988.
20 Clifford Geertz, 'Blurred genres', in Adams and Searle (eds), *Critical Theory Since 1985*, Florida State University Press, Tallahassee, 1987, p. 519.
21 Jerome Bruner, *Actual Minds, Possible Worlds*, Harvard University Press, London, 1986, p. 122.
22 ibid., p. 64.
23 W. J. T. Mitchell, 'The golden age of criticism', *London Review of Books*, 25 June 1987.
24 Alan Sinfield, *Literature, Politics and Culture in Postwar Britain*, Basil Blackwell, Oxford, 1989, pp. 23–4.
25 ibid., p. 25.
26 ibid., p. 24.
27 Paul Fussell, *Class, Style and Status in the U.S.A.*, Arrow, London, 1984, p. 47.
28 Jonathan Dollimore, *Radical Tragedy*, Harvester, Brighton, 1983, p. 15.
29 Gloria Steinem, 'If men could menstruate', in *Outrageous Acts and Everyday Rebellions*, Fontana, London, 1985, p. 338.

30 Michel Foucault, quoted in Philip Corrigan and Derek Sayer, *The Great Arch*, Basil Blackwell, Oxford, 1987, p. 4.
31 Chris Weedon, *Feminist Practice and Post-Structuralist Theory*, Basil Blackwell, Oxford, 1987, p. 338.
32 ibid., p. 17.
33 Philip Corrigan and Derek Sayer, op. cit., pp. 15–16.
34 ibid., p. 5.
35 Gill Seidel, 'Culture, nation and race in the British and French new right', in Ruth Levitas, ed. *The Ideology of the New Right*, Polity, Oxford, 1986, p. 110.
36 Brian Sutton-Smith, op. cit., p. 265.

4 REASONING THE NEED

1 William Shakespeare, *King Lear* act II scene iv.
2 Daniel Defoe, *Robinson Crusoe*.
3 Colin Campbell, *The Romantic Ethic and the Spirit of Modern Consumerism*, Basil Blackwell, Oxford, 1987, p. 1.
4 Northrop Frye, *The Anatomy of Criticism*, Yale University Press, Princeton, 1957, p. 105.
5 John Treasure, Advertising Association paper, 1974.
6 ibid.
7 Judie Lannon, 'Advertising research: new ways of seeing', in *Admap*, October 1985, pp. 520–7.
8 ibid.
9 ibid.
10 ibid.
11 ibid.
12 ibid.
13 ibid.
14 Mary Douglas, 'Goods as a system of communication', in Mary Douglas, *The Active Voice*, Routledge & Kegan Paul, London, 1982, p. 24.
15 Jonathan Culler, *Framing the Sign*, Basil Blackwell, Oxford, 1988, p. 168.
16 ibid., p. 171.
17 Robert Hughes, *The Shock of the New*, BBC Books, London, 1980, p. 344.
18 Alan Sinfield, *Literature, Politics, and Culture in Postwar Britain*, Basil Blackwell, Oxford, 1989, p. 235.
19 John Berger, *Ways of Seeing*, Penguin Books, London, 1972.
20 W. J. T. Mitchell, *Iconology*, University of Chicago Press, London, 1986, p. 202.
21 Kenneth Clark, *Civilisation*, BBC Books, London, 1969.
22 John Berger, op. cit., p. 135.
23 Colin Campbell, op. cit., p. 205.
24 Judith Williamson, *Consuming Passions*, Marion Boyars, London, 1986, p. 69.
25 Robert Hughes, op. cit., p. 348.

26 Judith Williamson, op. cit., p. 73.
27 Peter Fuller, 'The value of art', *New Society*, 29 January 1986.
28 Adrian Mitchell, 'The castaways or vote for Caliban', from *The Apeman Cometh*, Jonathan Cape, London, 1975.
29 ibid.
30 Clifford Geertz, 'Blurred genres', from Adams and Searle (eds) *Critical Theory Since 1985*, Florida State University Press, Tallahassee, 1987, p. 520.

5 PAGE TRAFFIC

1 Walter Nash, *Rhetoric*, Basil Blackwell, Oxford 1989, p. 1.
2 Neil Postman, *Amusing Ourselves to Death*, William Heinemann, London, 1986, p. 127.
3 Steven Connor, *Postmodernist Culture*, Basil Blackwell, Oxford, 1989, p. 203.
4 Neil Postman, op. cit., p. 128.
5 Jeremy Seabrook, 'Stereotypes in advertising', *New Society*, 18 March 1988.
6 Peregrine Worsthorne, *Spectator*, 4 March 1988.
7 Geoffrey Hughes, *Words in Time*, Basil Blackwell, Oxford, 1987, p. 160.
8 Martyn Forrester, *Everything You Ever Suspected About Advertising*, Roger Houghton, London, 1987, p. 31.
9 Walter Nash, op. cit., p. 27.
10 Michael Ignatieff, '3 minute culture', *The Independent*, 6 January 1989.
11 Dan Sperber and Deirdre Wilson, *Relevance*, Basil Blackwell, Oxford, 1984, p. 153.
12 Jeremy Bullmore, 'Getting explicit about the implicit', *Admap*, October 1984, pp. 499–501.
13 ibid.
14 Stephen Bayley, *Commerce and Culture*, Design Museum, London, 1989, p. 12.
15 Alastair Crompton, *The Craft of Copywriting*, Hutchinson, London, 1987, p. 36.
16 ibid., p. 110.
17 Sperber and Wilson, op. cit., p. 155.
18 Judith Williamson, *Decoding Advertisements*, Marion Boyars, London, 1978.
19 Gillian Dyer, *Advertising as Communication*, Methuen, London, 1984.
20 Torben Vestegaard and Kim Shroder, *The Language of Advertising*, Basil Blackwell, Oxford, 1985.
21 William Leiss, Stephen Kline and Sut Jhally, *Social Communication in Advertising*, Methuen, London, 1986.
22 Jerry Fodor, *Psychosemantics*, MIT Press, Cambridge, Mass., 1978, p. 3.
23 Umberto Eco, 'Towards a semiological guerilla warfare', in Umberto Eco, *Faith in Fakes*, Secker & Warburg, London, 1986, p. 141.

24 Michael Ignatieff, op. cit.
25 Stephen Bayley, op. cit., p. 11.
26 Gillian Dyer, op. cit., p. 78.
27 *Creative Review*, February 1986.
28 *The Howard Journal*, February 1986.
29 ibid.
30 *Marketing Week*, 15 February 1985.
31 ibid.
32 ibid.
33 ibid.
34 *Marketing Week*, 22 February 1985.

6 KNOCKING COPY

1 Tim Kirby, 'Adland's screen-tests', *Direction*, May 1989.
2 TV Briefing column, *Listener*, October 1987.
3 ibid.
4 Torben Vestegaard and Kim Schroder, *The Language of Advertising*, Basil Blackwell, Oxford, 1985.
5 John Mellors, book review, *London Magazine*, June 1985.
6 Trevor Pateman, book review, *The Sociological Review*, November 1985, vol. 33, no. 4.
7 ibid.
8 National Committee of Teachers of English Press Release, November 1985.
9 quoted in W. J. T. Mitchell, *Iconology*, University of Chicago Press, London, 1986, p. 189.
10 ibid., p. 189.
11 ibid., p. 189.
12 ibid., p. 191.
13 ibid., p. 192.
14 W. F. Haug, *Critique of Commodity Aesthetics*, Polity, Oxford, 1986, pp. 45–56.
15 ibid., p. 95.
16 ibid., p. 96.
17 ibid., p. 96
18 W. J. T. Mitchell, op. cit., p. 191.
19 ibid., pp. 192–3.
20 Christopher Butler, *Interpretation, Deconstruction, and Ideology*, Clarendon Press, Oxford, 1984, p. 103.
21 ibid., p. 104.
22 Judie Lannon, 'Advertising research: new ways of seeing', in *Admap*, October 1985, pp. 522–7.
23 Christopher Butler, op. cit., p. 104.
24 ibid., p. 104.
25 ibid., p. 104.
26 ibid., p. 104.
27 'Great bores of today', *Private Eye*, 11 July 1986.
28 Mary Douglas, 'Goods as a system of communication', in Mary

Douglas, *The Active Voice*, Routledge & Kegan Paul, London, 1982, p. 22.

29 Colin Campbell, *The Romantic Ethic and the Spirit of Modern Consumerism*, Basil Blackwell, Oxford, 1987, p. 00.

30 ibid., p. 00.

31 Kathy Myers, *Understains*, Routledge, London, 1986, p. 130.

32 ibid., p. 131.

33 Frank Mort, 'The politics of consumption', in Hall and Jacques (eds), *New Times*, Lawrence & Wishart, London, 1989, p. 165.

34 Dick Hebdige, 'After the masses', in Hall and Jacques, op. cit., p. 89.

35 ibid., p. 90.

36 Frank Mort, op. cit., p. 169.

37 Steven Connor, *Postmodernist Culture*, Basil Blackwell, Oxford, 1989, p. 184.

38 Dick Hebdige, *Hiding in the Light*, Routledge, London, 1988, p. 156.

39 Andrea Stuart, *Feminism: Dead or Alive?* in Jonathan Rutherford (ed.), *Identity: Community, Culture, Difference*, Lawrence & Wishart, London 1990, p. 34.

40 Elizabeth Wilson, *Adorned in Dreams*, Virago, London, 1985, p. 231.

41 ibid., p. 232.

42 ibid., p. 232.

43 Caroline Evans and Minna Thornton, *Women and Fashion*, Quartet, London, 1989, p. 1.

44 Andrea Stuart, op. cit., p. 31.

45 ibid., p. 31.

46 ibid., p. 32.

47 Kathy Myers, op. cit., pp. 141–3.

48 Mary Harron, *Pop as a Commodity*, Pantheon, New York, 1989, p. 219.

49 Alan Sinfield, *Literature, Politics, and Culture in Postwar Britain*, Basil Blackwell, 1989, p. 277.

50 Kathy Myers, op. cit., p. 143.

51 Dick Hebdige, *Hiding in the Light*, Routledge, London, 1988, p. 169.

52 ibid., p. 166.

53 *The Late Show*, BBC Television, 14 June 1990.

54 Robert Hewison, *Future Shock: A New Art for the Nineties*, Methuen, London, 1990, p. 59.

7 LOST IN THE POST

1 Elizabeth Wilson, *Adorned in Dreams: Fashion and Modernity*, Virago, London, 1985.

2 Steven Connor, *Postmodernist Culture*, Basil Blackwell, Oxford, 1989, p. 45.

3 Brian Rotman, 'Who is Jean Baudrillard?', *Guardian*, 21 October 1988.

4 ibid.

5 Alan Sinfield, *Literature, Politics, and Culture in Postwar Britain*, Basil Blackwell, Oxford, 1989, p. 291.

6 Jonathan Rutherford, 'A place called home', in Jonathan Rutherford (ed.), *Identity: Community, Culture, Difference*, Lawrence & Wishart, London, 1990, p. 11.
7 ibid., p. 11.
8 Steven Connor, op. cit., p. 189.
9 ibid., p. 193.

INDEX

213